Through
the Custom-House

JOHN CARLOS ROWE is professor and chairman, Department of English and Comparative Literature, University of California, Irvine. He is the author of *Henry Adams and Henry James: The Emergence of a Modern Consciousness*.

Through
the Custom-House

*Nineteenth-Century
American Fiction
and Modern Theory*

John Carlos Rowe

The Johns Hopkins University Press
Baltimore and London

Copyright © 1982 by The Johns Hopkins University Press
All rights reserved
Printed in the United States of America

The Johns Hopkins University Press, Baltimore, Maryland 21218
The Johns Hopkins Press Ltd., London

Library of Congress Cataloging in Publication Data

Rowe, John Carlos.
    Through the custom-house.

    1. American fiction — 19th century — History and criticism. I. Title.
PS377 .R64   813' .3'09   81-20866
ISBN 0-8018-2677-2   AACR2

For Kristin,
Kevin, Sean,
and Mark

In his room stood an American writing-desk of superior construction, such as his father had coveted for years and tried to pick up cheaply at all kinds of auction sales without ever succeeding, his resources being much too small. This desk, of course, was beyond all comparison with the so-called American writing-desks which turned up at auction sales in Europe. For example, it had a hundred compartments of different sizes, in which the President of the Union himself could have found a fitting place for each of his state documents; there was also a regulator at one side and by turning a handle you could produce the most complicated combinations and permutations of the compartments to please yourself and suit your requirements. Thin panels sank slowly and formed the bottom of a new series or the top of existing drawers promoted from below; even after one turn of the handle the disposition of the whole was quite changed and the transformation took place slowly or at delirious speed according to the rate at which you wound the thing round. It was a very modern invention.

— Kafka, *Amerika*

Contents

Preface   **xi**

1. Introduction: The Modernity of Nineteenth-Century American Fiction   **1**

2. "The Being of Language: The Language of Being" in Thoreau's *A Week on the Concord and Merrimack Rivers*   **28**

3. The Metaphysics of Imagination: Narrative Consciousness in Hawthorne's *The Blithedale Romance*   **52**

4. Writing and Truth in Poe's *The Narrative of Arthur Gordon Pym*   **91**

5. Ecliptic Voyaging: Orbits of the Sign in Melville's "Bartleby the Scrivener"   **111**

6. Trumping the Trick of the Truth: The Extra-Moral Sense of Twain's *Pudd'nhead Wilson*   **139**

7. The Authority of the Sign in James's *The Sacred Fount*   **168**

Postscript: Through the Custom-House   **190**

Notes   **196**
Index   **215**

Preface

This work is an experiment in intertextual criticism that reads six nineteenth-century prose texts in relation to six critical problems that exemplify the modern debate concerning representation and signification. The literary texts are interpreted as marginal to the main tradition of nineteenth-century American literature insofar as that tradition has been shaped by such familiar critical mythologies as the American Adam, Paleface and Redskin, the Quest for Nationality, and an American Renaissance. Generally considered secondary works in relation to established classics, such works as Thoreau's *A Week on the Concord and Merrimack Rivers* and Twain's *Pudd'nhead Wilson* have proven especially resistant to critical efforts to account for their anomalies within either the literary tradition or the order of the individual author's *oeuvre*. The inconsistencies, discontinuities, and even contradictions in the themes and forms of these works have caused critics to conclude either that they are insufficiently developed or that their apparent difficulties might be reconciled as deeper and profounder unities. As different as these two approaches might seem, they share many of the same presuppositions about artistic coherence, literary realization, and poetic value. This study is an effort to investigate those critical assumptions by means of a strategic *intertextuality* that is used to defamiliarize the critical conventions that continue to govern even the most avowedly revisionary interpretations of American literature.

In the first chapter, I analyze the theoretical reasons for this artificial method and clarify my conception of literary "modernity" as it applies to these nineteenth-century works. In the subsequent chapters, I use Heidegger's late essays to read Thoreau's *A Week,* Sartre's work on the imagination to analyze Hawthorne's *Blithedale Romance,* Freud's critique of unified consciousness to interpret Poe's *Narrative of A. Gordon Pym,* Derrida's revision of Freud's dynamic model of the psyche to interpret Melville's "Bartleby the Scrivener," Nietzsche's subversion of the subject to read Twain's *Pudd'nhead Wilson,* and the structural linguistics of Saussure and Benveniste to explore problems of narrative authority in James's *Sacred Fount.*

In view of this general organization, my reader might naturally assume that this study attempts to establish certain nineteenth-century backgrounds for twentieth-century modernism. Although it would be impossible and even undesirable for me to eliminate thoroughly such historicism from this work, the main purpose of these intertextual relations is to explore an idea of modernity that is fundamental to the literary function of language. Each of these anomalous works is viewed as a metaliterary reflection on the possibility of artistic representation that involves its author in an extended reflection on his own theory of literature. Much of the ambiguity and discontinuity in these works may be related to the authors' systematic critiques of their own poetic values. These works are efforts to reinvigorate their authors' imaginative powers, struggles not only to achieve some limited freedom from the conventions of the literary tradition and cultural code but also from the writer's tendency to be determined by his own prior production.

Each of these works attempts to go beyond certain impasses in nineteenth-century thought that are reflected both in the general cultural climate and in the author's own canon. In this regard, they share structural similarities with the modern philosophical writings employed as pretexts in this study. In their own efforts to revise, transform, or deconstruct a humanist heritage that finds its fullest expression in eighteenth- and nineteenth-century thought, these modern philosophers and linguists inevitably confront many of the same problems that beset nineteenth-century American writers concerned with the renewal of their creative powers. These conceptual homologies are explored in relation to a generally literary structure of modernity, which may be said to have relevance for every effort to signify, every struggle of an author to speak to the otherness of the world. As my subsequent critique of the structuralists' methods of transcoding and metacommentary ought to suggest, however, such a "structure of modernity" has relevance only as a *descriptive generality* for problems that signify only in the actual practice of interpretation. Indeed, the term *modernity* relates to a structure of language like Derrida's *différance,* which should be understood as neither a "word nor a concept" but as an "assemblage." [1] Such a general scheme suggests that modernity lurks as a possibility in every utterance, but that the degree to which it is repressed or exposed in the effort to signify ought to govern our understanding of whatever concept or message is involved. Short of the active interpretation of such repressions and revelations — itself a historical act of reading — our understanding of either literary modernity or linguistic *différance* must remain empty knowledge or self-evident tautology.

I am grateful to my friends and colleagues in the humanities at Irvine; they have helped teach me how fundamental comparatism and critical theory are for any understanding of language. The genealogy of any book is notoriously difficult to trace and perhaps impossible for its author to acknowledge, but my local influences have been powerful and are still familiar. Among these, I wish especially to thank Frank Lentricchia, who read the manuscript in several versions. His uncanny ability to detect contradictions or sophistries has helped improve this book in countless ways; his enthusiasm and support for the project were constant motivations. Eugenio Donato, Joseph Riddel, and Homer Brown have contributed directly to my thinking in this work; their patience and wit have sustained me on numerous occasions. I wish to thank the graduate students in my nineteenth-century American fiction seminar, where I first sketched out the argument of this book. I am also grateful for the support and useful criticism offered by Howard Babb, Alexander Gelley, Anton Kaes, Murray Krieger, Maria Ruegg, and Hayden White. The editors of The Johns Hopkins University Press, especially Ms. Carol Ehrlich, have helped me improve this book in many ways.

A summer research grant and funds for the preparation of the manuscript were provided by the School of Humanities at the University of California, Irvine. Ms. Jeanne Andrew typed the final manuscript with speed, good cheer, and interest. I thank the editors of *Criticism* and *Boundary 2,* for permission to reprint portions of this work that first appeared in their journals, and The Johns Hopkins University Press, publishers of *Glyph 2: Johns Hopkins Textual Studies.* I gratefully acknowledge permission to quote from unpublished manuscripts held in the Mark Twain Papers, Bancroft Library, University of California, Berkeley. I am especially grateful to the late Frederick Anderson, editor of the Mark Twain Papers from 1963 to 1979. Mr. Anderson not only opened the archives of the Twain Papers for me during my visits in 1977 and 1978; he also invited me to discuss my project with him. I learned a great deal about Twain and *Pudd'nhead Wilson* in our conversations. My thanks also to Mr. Robert Hirst, the current editor of the Twain Papers. I also acknowledge with thanks permission to quote from unpublished Mark Twain manuscripts owned by the Humanities Research Center at the University of Texas, Austin.

My wife, Kristin, has shared this book with me from its beginnings. I shall not calculate her contributions, but consecrate them with my dedication and love.

Through
the Custom-House

1.

Introduction: The Modernity of Nineteenth-Century American Fiction

Menard (perhaps without wanting to) has enriched, by means of a new technique, the halting and rudimentary art of reading: this new technique is that of the deliberate anachronism and the erroneous attribution. The technique, whose applications are infinite, prompts us to go through the *Odyssey* as if it were posterior to the *Aeneid* and the book *Le Jardin du Centaure* of Madame Henri Bachelier as if it were by Madame Henri Bachelier. This technique fills the most placid works with adventure. To attribute the *Imitatio Christi* to Louis Ferdinand Céline or to James Joyce, is this not a sufficient renovation of its tenuous spiritual indications?

— Borges, "Pierre Menard, Author of the Quixote"

For every image of the past that is not recognized by the present as one of its own concerns threatens to disappear irretrievably. . . .

To articulate the past historically does not mean to recognize it "the way it really was" (Ranke). It means to seize hold of a memory as it flashes up at a moment of danger.

— Benjamin, "Theses on the Philosophy of History"

This study follows a conceptual narrative that is reflected in the choice of particular intertextual relations for each of the following chapters. There are many other problem texts in this period that remain marginal to the dominant mythologies of the critical tradition; there is a great variety of modern philosophical writings that might be used profitably to broaden our understanding of nineteenth-century literature. My choices are neither arbitrary nor governed exclusively by the demands of individual chapters. The interplay of literary text and philosophical pretext is designed to explore an idea of modernity related to the literary function of language. Thus, the general movement of this work might be viewed as the gradual discovery of certain mutual concerns in literature and those modes of analytic thought (linguistics, psychoanalysis, historiography) that share the classical aims of philosophy. Each of the writers in the following chapters confronts directly the anguish of a thinker like Hegel, who struggled desperately to overcome the metaphorics of art in order to achieve the self-moving truth of philosophy.

In Chapter two, Thoreau's *A Week* is read in terms of Heidegger's effort in his late essays to reconceptualize the status of philosophic discourse, notably by relating poetry and thinking according to their mutual concern with the nature of language. This Heideggerian "conversation" between poetry and philosophy establishes one of the primary motifs in the remainder of this study, which regards the disciplinary boundaries that traditionally distinguish different humanistic discourses as indications of the necessary defenses employed by any determinate code to establish its claims to truth and meaning. What Heidegger terms "poetizing" (*Dichtung*) is a mode of thinking (*Denken*) that goes beyond mere poetic or lyrical expression, in order to reflect upon the poetic essence that makes such expression possible:

> Thinking of Being is the original mode of poetizing. In it language first of all comes to language, that is, into its essence. Thinking speaks what the truth of Being dictates; thinking is the original *dictare*. Thinking is original poetry, which precedes all poesy and poetics of art, insofar as poesy remains within the province of language in the work. All poetizing in this wider sense, and in the narrower sense of poetics, is fundamentally thinking. The poetizing mode of thinking maintains the governance of the truth of Being.[1]

Insofar as either poetry or philosophy remains analytically within its own rhetoric, then it belongs merely to poesy or poetics. Only the thinking that seeks to relate its discourse to language may be said to escape such defenses and limitations and thus approach the ontological categories traditionally associated with philosophic truth. As Heidegger's own style of thinking/ writing suggests, such a discourse would depend upon the interplay of expression and analysis and thus constitute the intertextuality of poetry and philosophy as they have been traditionally understood.

This general interrelation is illustrated practically in Chapter three, in which *The Blithedale Romance* is used as the focus for a comparative discussion of Hawthorne's poetic conception of the imagination and Sartre's phenomenological theory of the imagination as an autonomous mental function. Designed to help clarify the intentional process of consciousness, Sartre's theory raises questions about oneiric states, repression, and preconscious and unconscious forces that undermine the apodictic certainty that is the aim of Husserl's radical subjectivism. Husserl objected to the empirical naiveté of "psychologism," but the discussion in Chapter three attempts to demonstrate the limitations of an exclusively poetic or philosophic treatment of the imaginary.

In Chapter four, Freud's critique of consciousness as a unified process is introduced in relation to Poe's *Narrative of A. Gordon Pym,* in order to explore the limitations and possibilities of Freud's dynamic conception of the psyche as a system of differences. Derrida's attack on the conception of the Freudian unconscious as a distinct "reservoir" of psychic images (*Bildern*) may complicate the problem of analyzing psychic processes, but Derrida's understanding of the psyche as a writing machine that produces meaning only in the differential play of its own supplementarity promises a more general application of what Gayatri Spivak terms "the Freudian argument that the establishment of permanent traces in the psychic apparatus precludes the possibility of immediate perception." [2] In this way, Sartre's phenomenological critique of associationist theories of perception and imagination is challenged in turn by Derrida's reading of Freud, which might be said to begin with Derrida's infamous denial of perception itself:

> As to perception, I should say that once I recognized it as a necessary conservation. I was extremely conservative. Now I don't know what perception is and I don't believe that anything like perception exists. Perception is precisely a concept, a concept of an intuition or of a given originating from the thing itself, present itself in its meaning, independently from language, from the system of reference. And I believe that perception is interdependent with the concept of origin and of center and consequently whatever strikes at the metaphysics of which I have spoken strikes also at the very concept of perception. I don't believe that there is any perception. [3]

If the fifth chapter, Derrida's conception of a decentered, psychic "writing" (*écriture*) is used to read Melville's theory of representation in "Bartleby the Scrivener," a theory expressly antithetical to those traditional conceptions of representation that rely on a general metaphysics of presence to subordinate representation to an *arché* or *telos* beyond the play of its language. Relating what Derrida terms "ontotheology" to the social and political authorities undermined in Melville's tale, the chapter suggests that the consciousness criticized by Freud and the metaphysics attacked by Derrida are inextricably related to nineteenth-century concepts of law, property, propriety, and the general etiology of social authority. In this way, the discussion in Chapter five provides an introduction to Nietzsche's and Twain's respective genealogies of moral values in Western culture. Questioning naive distinctions between freedom and slavery in relation to the illusion of the self-sustaining individual, Nietzsche and Twain demonstrate people's bondage to their linguistic categories and sociohistorical situation.

Chapter six uses Twain's *Pudd'nhead Wilson* to explore the possibility of any viable "transvaluation" of cultural forces by one intimately aware of his own entanglement in the very rhetoric and values of that culture. Always already underwritten by others (history, tradition, education), the critic can never achieve a fully detached view of social injustice and thus must develop a form of expression that might internally question these habitual modes of perception and understanding. Working with fragments, parodies, aphorisms, and unpredictable stylistic juxtapositions, Twain and Nietzsche develop a verbal field in which they might intend the unintentional — that is, develop an artificial and often violently disjunctive means of exposing what has been repressed both in the culture and in their own perceptions of the world.

Reduced from omniscient authorities controlling their narratives to mere "puddingheaded clowns," whose fortuitous "mistakes" are often their most brilliant accomplishments, modern authors seem increasingly threatened by the determinants of language, culture, and psyche. In Chapter seven, James's beleaguered, maddened narrator in *The Sacred Fount* is used to explore the debate between structuralists and poststructuralists concerning the "subject" as a grammatical fiction. Frequently derived explicitly from Nietzsche's writings, this critique of the subject calls into question the very nature and possibility of a phenomenological concept of intentionality and traditional notions of causality. As Nietzsche writes in *The Will to Power:*

> We have interpreted the formulable character of events as the consequence of a necessity that rules over events. But from the fact that I do a certain thing, it by no means follows that I am compelled to do it. Compulsion in things certainly cannot be demonstrated: the rule proves only that one and the same event is not another event as well. Only because we have introduced subjects, "doers," into things does it appear that all events are the consequences of compulsion exerted upon subjects — exerted by whom? again by a "doer." Cause and effect — a dangerous concept so long as one thinks of something that causes and something upon which an effect is produced.
>   a. Necessity is not a fact but an interpretation.[4]

If the ontological subject is reduced to a mere grammatical shifter, then how is such extra-moral knowledge possible at all? By locating the subject as a "function" that reveals and represses the very linguistic conventions governing its field of circulation, we may begin to understand the limitations and possibilities inherent in this conception of the subject as a force in a signifying system.

These discussions of the metaphoricity of signification, the supplementarity of representation, the divided function of the authorial subject, and the psychic and sociopolitical repressions of metaphysical thinking generally describe the concepts of modern thought that are employed in this study.[5] These problems are familiar issues in contemporary theories of literature, language, and interpretation, but their relation to the idea of these representative nineteenth-century narratives as marginal to the main tradition of American literature still must be explained. In one sense, these literary works are marginal to the nineteenth-century tradition by virtue of their anticipation of certain dominant twentieth-century intellectual concerns. Yet, the reader will notice that no substantial argument is offered for the influence of these nineteenth-century works on the modern theories employed as interpretative devices. Even in those contexts where some case for specific influence might be made, I have carefully avoided such a historical argument. There is sufficient evidence to suggest that Twain was affected by his reading of Nietzsche.[6] Poe's influence on Baudelaire and the French *Symbolistes* is mentioned in Chapter four, but no substantive argument is offered for Poe as a source for the modern problems discussed in Freud's and Derrida's works. Melville's works were in part rediscovered by French existentialists and profoundly influenced the existential thinking of modern American writers as diverse as Charles Olson and Ralph Ellison. Yet, my reading of "Bartleby the Scrivener" is expressly designed to question a number of the basic assumptions governing the familiar existentialist interpretation of the tale. Had I wished to pursue an argument concerning the historical development of modernism, I would have served my purpose far better by studying the demonstrable impact of nineteenth-century literature on twentieth-century works. In order to deal with specific patterns of influence, however, I would have been forced to violate two essential strategies of this work.

First, this study attempts to break down the habitual disciplinary boundaries that tend to isolate common problems of interpretation confronting philosophers, literary critics, linguists, psychoanalysts, and historians. Studies of explicit influence tend to restrict themselves to particular disciplines; even broadly based approaches to the history of ideas or *Geistesgeschichte* generally employ a dominant discourse to control the metaphors and terms drawn from various other fields of inquiry.[7] In many cases, the interpreter concerned with historical movements is constrained by the very subjects of his or her study. Hegel was certainly influenced by Diderot, and Nietzsche by Emerson and Dostoevsky, but both philosophers wrote primarily for audiences trained in the technical problems of nineteenth-century philosophy. Poets and novelists have traditionally claimed a greater latitude in their use of sources and terminologies, often defending such eclecticism on the grounds that imaginative writers take the "world" and "life" as their subjects. In a certain perverse manner, I might suggest that the task of literary criticism has been defined too often in terms of disciplining such unbridled and irresponsible misreading by creative writers. Confining literature — or at least its study — within the limits of a definable discipline with a claim to scholarly integrity has motivated the production of the hermeneutic criteria associated with most schools of literary analysis and classification. The second essential strategy of this study is to violate deliberately those critical conventions that tend to dominate much of the practical interpretation of American literary works. The logic of this designed estrangement of the critical tradition is the subject of this introduction and the methodological basis on which the following readings of nineteenth-century American fiction must be evaluated.

Throughout this study, I discuss these exemplary literary texts as marginal to the main traditions of nineteenth-century American thought and literature.[8] These works are marginal in two significant and related ways: first, in relation to critical traditions that have canonized major or "classic" works in terms of certain mythologies that represent a particular historical and literary period; second, in relation to each author's own conception of his participation in a dominant intellectual movement and his subsequent effort to revise or revolutionize the basic concepts of such a movement. It is for these reasons that this study concentrates on those works by major nineteenth-century authors that have always proven to be the most resistant to coherent analysis and classification according to the requirements of the dominant literary tradition. Each of these texts continues to pose special problems for scholars interested in the work's genre, its place in the author's canon, its relation to certain psychobiographical concerns, and its relation to the school with which the author is most commonly associated.

As anomalous or marginal texts, these works have received an enormous amount of critical attention.[9] With the exception of Melville's "Bartleby," they have most frequently been judged to be internally flawed, inferior to an acknowledged classic, or thematically inconsistent with the rest of the author's *oeuvre*. "Bartleby" has, of course, been celebrated as a masterpiece of stylistic economy and ironic balance. Yet the very ambiguity and paradox that have contributed to this work's critical reputation are equally responsible for the notable disagreement among critics concerning its structure and significance. It is especially curious that the central subject of this acknowledged classic — the nature and practice of writing — has been virtually ignored by critics, except for a few interpretations of the story as an autobiographical allegory. There is unquestionably something uncanny about "Bartleby" for most literary critics, which makes it an appropriate center for this study of the protective defenses that govern the various schools of American studies.

Critical efforts to recuperate these marginal texts and integrate them into a dominant literary tradition are as interesting as those approaches that judge them as secondary. What is most remarkable is that many of the same presuppositions about artistic coherence, literary expression, poetic style, and narrative technique are shared by those critics who insist upon the originality of these works and those who judge these works to be derivative or insufficiently realized. In the following chapters, I discuss some of the common assumptions that support the most conflicting interpretations of these texts, but the most general and pervasive standards applied to them can be summarized briefly. The dominant formal criteria for evaluating these texts are generic consistency, narrative progress and development, organic characterization, and thematic and stylistic coherence. The fundamental criteria governing the historical study of these works are their relation to the development of basic literary movements, their contribution to the development of an authorial *oeuvre*, and their representation of contemporary sociopolitical features of the cultural period. Among a broad variety of formal and historical approaches, I find a persistent reliance on a familiar romantic paradigm of *Bildung* as the dialectical unfolding of oppositions that ultimately intends and is governed by a unifying *telos*.

This is an extraordinarily broad generalization that is by no means universally applicable, but it should not surprise anyone that it dominates the formal and historical study of American literature in the past half-century. In fact, as long as the critic maintains a certain attitude toward signification, then the practical consequences discussed above are inevitable. Quite simply, this assumption can be expressed in Jacques Derrida's terms as "the metaphysics of presence" or in Fredric Jameson's reading of Derrida as the "illusion of absolute transparency of meaning, or in other words absolute presence." [10] This apparently common-sense assumption about language depends upon the intentional reference of the verbal sign to that which motivates it or realizes it — a referentiality that in both cases points to that which ought to escape the linguistic chain of signifiers: perception, experience, meaning, truth, being.

Even those modes of interpretation that reject such a naive distinction between experience and its expression, knowledge and its representation, or truth and its imitation in favor of an apparently exclusive field of linguistic determination subtly reinstate the metaphysics of presence by maintaining a distinction between the *signifier* and the *signified*. Derrida's critique of structuralism is directed at precisely this analytic distinction within the sign itself: "The difference between signified and signifier belongs in a profound and implicit way to the totality of the great epoch covered by the history of metaphysics, and in a more explicit and systematically articulated way to the narrower epoch of Christian creationism and infinitism when these appropriate the resources of Greek conceptuality. . . . To these roots adheres . . . the distinction between the sensible and the intelligible — already a great deal — with all that it controls, namely, metaphysics in its totality. And this distinction is generally accepted as self-evident by the most careful linguists and semiologists, even by those who believe that the scientificity of their work begins where metaphysics ends." [11]

As Derrida demonstrates, this distinction is given scientific credence in Saussure's *Course in General Linguistics,* and yet it is in Saussure's problematic text itself that the crucial distinction between signifier and signified results in equivocation and even contradiction. Summarizing his own conception of the sign as an acoustic and conceptual complex, Saussure writes: "In language there are only differences *without positive terms*. Whether we take the signified or the signifier, language has neither ideas nor sounds that existed before the linguistic system, but only conceptual and phonic differences that have issued from the system. The idea or phonic substance that a sign contains is of less importance than the other signs that surround it. Proof of this is that the value of a term may be modified without either its meaning or its sound being affected, solely because a neighboring term has been modified." [12]

Saussure's own claim that neither ideas nor sounds exist prior to the linguistic system questions the very nature of the oppositions that he attempts to establish. If the idea is exclusively determined within the system of language, then it can be nothing other than a signifier — more properly, perhaps, an "economy" of signifiers. In similar terms, the simple characterization of the signifier as a mere phonic element establishes a false dichotomy between isolable elements of the sign that in practice and use (as Saussure himself recognized) can never be untangled. Thus, Derrida argues that the apparent difference of signifier and signified is in fact subordinate to the unity of the sign's conceptual reference, which produces a semantic mirage disguising the more fundamental difference that governs the order of every apparently unified sign. It is this difference in language that Derrida has expressed in terms of a chain of displacing figures for *écriture* (hymen, pharmakon, pli, spur, trace, etc.), each of which draws its appropriateness from the context of a particular deconstructive reading. In the neologism *différance*, Derrida establishes a general locus for these various supplementary terms:

> Différance is what makes the movement of signification possible only if each element that is said to be "present," appearing on the stage of presence, is related to something other than itself but retains the mark of its relation to a future element. This trace relates no less to what is called the future than what is called the past, and it constitutes what is called the present by this very relation to what it is not, to what it absolutely is not; that is, not even to a past or future considered as a modified present. . . . Constituting itself, dynamically dividing itself, this interval is what could be called *spacing;* time's becoming-spatial or space's becoming-temporal (*temporalizing*). And it is this constitution of the present as a "primordial" and irreducibly nonsimple, and therefore, in the strict sense, nonprimordial, synthesis of traces, retentions, and protentions (to reproduce here, analogically and provisionally, a phenomenological and transcendental language that will presently be revealed as inadequate) that I propose to call protowriting, prototrace, or différance. The latter (is) (both) spacing (and) temporalizing. [13]

In order to emphasize this characteristic of language, Derrida inverts the traditional privilege accorded to voice and utterance over the written and representational. The *différance* made explicit in writing, however, is equally at work in those speech-acts in which we assume the phonic and conceptual aspects of the sign to be unified in the message-sending process. As Derrida points out in his recent response to John Searle, writing merely indicates the *possibility* of communication with an absent receiver as well as the absence, or nonpresence, of an author/speaker. But it is just this possibility that continues to operate in all forms of communication, whether it is exploited and exposed or hidden and repressed: "If one admits that writing (and the mark in general) *must be able* to function in the absence of the sender, the receiver, the context of production etc., that implies that this power, this *being able*, this *possibility* is *always* inscribed, hence *necessarily* inscribed as *possibility* in the functioning or the functional structure of the mark. Once the mark *is able* to function, once it is possible for it to function, once it is possible for it to function in the case of an absence etc., it follows that this possibility is a *necessary* part of its structure, that the latter must *necessarily be such that* this functioning is possible; and hence, that this must be taken into account in any attempt to analyze or to describe, in terms of necessary laws, such a structure." [14]

This possibility of the waywardness of the signifier — the possibility that its message might be diverted — is precisely what motivates those enabling repressions governing all signifying systems intending truth, meaning, and understanding. Following implications in Nietzsche and Freud, Derrida insists that "writing is unthinkable without repression." [15] What is at stake in the Derridean project of deconstruction is not the impossible liberation of the signifying system (literary texts are less relevant here than the psyche itself as a writing machine) to an endless straying or anarchy of meaning, but the beginnings of a method of reading that would study the history-as-structure/structure-as-history of the various repressions at work in different cultural codes that promise a signified. [16] Thus, intertextuality is intimately related to the trace-structure of Derrida's sign; intertextuality does not indicate merely the strategy of reading one text with another but the fact that every text is itself always already an *intertextual event*. Despite his ostensible disagreement with Derrida, Harold Bloom clearly recognizes this fundamental intertextuality of writing: "A single text has only part of a meaning; it is itself a synecdoche for a larger whole including other texts. A text is a relational event, and not a substance to be analyzed." [17]

The general assumptions governing the practical criticism of the marginal texts studied in this work may be directly related to the paradigm of the sign that Derrida attempts to deconstruct. Few critics would claim to reveal the full transparency of a literary work's signified, but many practicing critics organize and execute their works in such a way as to imply quite clearly that their principal aim is to determine what E. D. Hirsch, Jr., calls the "relative probabilities" of the text's intention and context.[18] The difficulties of such a procedure have frequently been noted by critics of both "objective" phenomenologies like Hirsch's and more "subjective" phenomenologies associated with Poulet and the Geneva School. In both cases, the central difficulty involves the critic's process of reproducing "in himself the author's 'logic,' his attitudes, his cultural givens, in short his world."[19] The task is complicated not only by the difference in cultural contexts and historical rhetorics separating the critic from her or his presumed object of inquiry but also by what might be said to be the general intention governing the literary act itself.

The Russian Formalists argued that literature distinguishes itself from the automatized reflexes of ordinary verbal acts by virtue of its *estrangement* of the familiar and habitual.[20] The idea of literature as defamiliarization (Viktor Shklovsky's "*ostranenie*") has frequently been related to the ontological distinction between poetic and ordinary language that is a constitutive concept in much Anglo-American New Criticism. In part, this misleading comparison has resulted from the Formalists' own difficulties in developing a more comprehensive linguistic model, in which such "literary" disruptions would be related to the production of social and cultural codes.[21] Following Shklovsky's lead, Tynianov and others attempted to relate the basic literary paradigm to problems of historical evolution and development, but their writings rarely escape the boundaries of pure literary history and the formation of new schools of poetry. Both Roman Jakobson and the Prague Circle linguist, Jan Mukařovský, have attempted to situate normative and variant functions within a general linguistic model, but such approaches seem flawed by the analytic methods these theorists employ to study a linguistic process that by its very nature denies the possibility of taxonomic analysis.

Nevertheless, the general conception of literary language as the violation of the normative suggests that the primary artistic intention is to *locate* the illusion of the signified as it operates within a given culture. There is no presumed ontological difference between such modes of discourse; the literary work is decidedly *not* "lucid" and "self-conscious" in contrast with the "blindness" or "unconsciousness" presumed to characterize the everyday usage of cultural conventions. Wolfgang Iser summarizes clearly the dynamic relation of poetic deviation and social normalization that has been a general concern in many structuralists' efforts to describe a literary paradigm: "Put explicitly, it is that a violation of the standard possesses 'poetic quality' in so far as the standard is always evoked by the violation, so that it is not the violation as such, but the relation it establishes, which becomes a condition of 'poetic quality.'"[22]

Iser justifiably criticizes the limitations of the deviationist model, especially as it is used to catalog mechanically distinctive features of the "poetic" and the "standard." The deviationist model not only relies on the broadest and thus most rudimentary conception of literature, but its very formulation argues against the kinds of structural analysis that it has spawned. Iser quite properly points out that the theory itself describes a "virtuality" or "possibility" in the literary text, which is realized only in the actual interpretation of the work: "It is obvious that a violation of the standard and of the 'esthetic canon' can only have the function of producing the meaning potential of the text, and not of the way in which that potential is realized." [23] Thus, Iser considers the major limitation of this structuralist approach to be its disregard of the reader's function in determining the "poeticity" of the work as well as the "conventionality" of normative usage.

In my discussion of Derrida's critique of structuralism, I have suggested that the signified, or concept, is always an economy of signifiers enabled by repression (psychic or cultural) to function as the illusory unity of an idea or meaning that might be presented and thus said either to precede (originate or intend) or to realize (fulfill or complete) its verbal representation. If we assume that the disruption of the signified in the effort to overcome desiccated values and habitual meanings describes a general intention for literary production, then our critical effort to reproduce in ourselves the text's "intention" would require a subsequent violation of the text itself as a doubling of its literariness in our own efforts of interpretive understanding. If we were to concentrate on the semantic potential of the text as a measure of its literariness, then we would be compelled to disrupt by interpretation the text as a historical document or as an artifact to be reconstructed in terms of the context of its production. Our understanding of a text's "poeticality" is not served by cataloging distinctive features, but rather by *using* the text in our own efforts to pose questions about the development of accepted conventions in the literary and cultural traditions as well as in our own processes of understanding.

In fact, the majority of critical readings that attempt to make intelligible the work's intention and meaning actually seek to translate the work's estranged signifiers into concepts, or signifieds, that are more readily understandable. Thus, criticism often appropriates literature by conventionalizing it. Formal and historical critics committed to reconstructing the work's intention and historical context conventionalize the work by effectively reintegrating it into the dominant rhetoric of its cultural period, which is precisely what the text had attempted to violate in the first place. Of course, this consequence assumes that such an impossible task of contextual and historical reproduction is possible at all. Most critical conventionalizations of literature tend to translate the work either overtly or covertly into the rhetoric governing the critic's own culture. This seems to be the only possible mode of interpretation available to the formal or historical critic, who is always already determined by the rhetoric of his or her social environment. The poet, of course, is equally constrained by such historical and linguistic determinants, even though poets may define their own character in terms of a quixotic struggle for an impossible freedom of expression. In contrast, literary criticism and historicism appeal too often to the normative rhetoric of the culture as the only means of interpretative understanding. Such criticism reads in terms of a social rhetoric, whose very claims to literalness are designed to suppress and control the eccentric or the uncanny.

The idea of interpretation as the perpetually renewed act of historical translation has been viewed by many as a relativism that avoids the dangers implicit in more objective modes of interpretation. Yet, what Wesley Morris labels "'aesthetic' historicism" risks the same tendency to conventionalize the literary work that governs more scientific approaches to literary form and evolution.[24] Part of the problem is suggested in Roland Barthes's early effort to define the structuralists' conception of the critical activity:

> One can say that the critical task (and this is the sole guarantee of its universality) is purely formal: not to "discover" in the work or the author something "hidden," "profound," "secret" which hitherto passed unnoticed (by what miracle? Are we more perspicacious than our predecessors?), but only to adjust the language his period affords him (existentialism, Marxism, psychoanalysis) to the language, i.e., the formal system of logical constraints, elaborated by the author according to his own period. The "proof" of criticism is not of an "alethic" order (it does not proceed from truth), for critical discourse — like logical discourse, moreover — is never anything but tautological: it consists in saying, ultimately, though placing its whole being within that delay, what thereby is not insignificant: Racine is Racine, Proust is Proust.[25]

This quotation may be said to represent a particular structuralist attitude toward the reading of the past that seeks to avoid the naiveté of an "objective" or "positivist" historiography. Abandoning the alethic order, the semiotician apparently accepts the relativism of historical meaning and undertakes the task of "transcoding" the rhetoric governing the texts of the past into the available rhetoric of the present. Hayden White is one eloquent spokesman for the theory and practice of such transcoding; his study of the rhetorical models governing nineteenth-century historical thinking, *Metahistory*, testifies to the persuasiveness of such a method as an alternative to the intellectual no-exits of what White collectively tags "nomological" historiography. Yet, White himself succumbs to the dangers of this approach, especially in its application to actual texts, as the following passage from his introduction to *Tropics of Discourse* indicates:

> Understanding is a process of rendering the unfamiliar, or the "uncanny" in Freud's sense of that term, familiar; of removing it from the domain of things felt to be "exotic" and unclassified into one or another domain of experience

encoded adequately enough to be felt to be humanly useful, nonthreatening, or simply known by association. This process of understanding can only be tropological in nature, for what is involved in the rendering of the unfamiliar into the familiar is a troping that is generally figurative. It follows, I think, that this process of understanding proceeds by the exploitation of the principal modalities of figuration, identified in post-Renaissance rhetorical theory as the "master tropes" (Kenneth Burke's phrase) of metaphor, metonymy, synecdoche, and irony.[26]

Most of the criticism directed at White's rhetorical method has been concerned with the status of White's own discourse, which he claims to be "value neutral and purely formal."[27] It is no coincidence that both Barthes and White argue for a critical discourse that concentrates on "purely formal" relations. As Barthes explains: "The critic is not responsible for reconstructing the work's message but only its system, just as the linguist is not responsible for deciphering the sentence's meaning but for establishing the formal structure which permits this meaning to be transmitted."[28] Barthes and White merely shift their attention from the signified — always a "suspended meaning" for them — to the formal order of the signifier. The assumption that such transcoding can be undertaken on a purely formal level that avoids semantic determinations returns us once again to the binary structure of the sign, whose signifier and signified can be distinguished analytically. The structuralists' concentration on the linguistic system of the work inevitably involves the possibility of determining the infrastructure of language and thought that would ground the literary performance or historical event.

Such an approach depends to a large extent on White's conception of human understanding as a means of rendering the "unfamiliar" familiar, the "uncanny" homely. Although much understanding undoubtedly takes place in this general manner, the very idea of "literature" suggests the possibility of understanding the familiar in terms of the unfamiliar. Despite its limitations, the deviationist model still implies that one mode of human knowledge functions in terms of the disruption or dislocation of the apparently familiar and well-established. Unless we assume that literary defamiliarization is meaningless until it is reappropriated in terms of a conventional code by a critical act of translation, then we must grant this possibility of recognizing the power and locus of habitual values as a result of their estrangement. Not everything that we might consider humanly useful can be described as non-threatening or known by association.

In one sense, the aims of this study of the modernity of nineteenth-century American fiction would seem to find justification in the structuralists' commitment to the "intelligibility" of the present. Barthes writes at the end of "What Is Criticism?": "Thus begins, at the heart of the critical work, the dialogue of two histories and two subjectivities, the author's and the critic's. But this dialogue is egoistically shifted toward the present: criticism is not an 'homage' to the truth of the past or to the truth of 'others' — it is a construction of the intelligibility of our own time."[29] Yet, in the study of literary works, their historical interrelations, and their relevance for cultural meanings and values, the nature and function of such "intelligibility" still remains extraordinarily problematic.

White's conception of understanding does, of course, reflect the notable repressions that govern most acts of cognition, and it is the very presence of the "uncanny" literary work that reminds us that such repressions are operative in every signifying system. What should interest us about a literary text or historical event (itself a text of sorts) is not what has already been appropriated by the rhetoric and values of the present culture but what continues to agitate us or still threatens us with its own outwandering and eccentric character. The concentration by historians on periods of cultural revolution, disruption, and transformation is often less an exercise in periodization than an effort to restore to the historical process its rational and intentional meaning. The consequence of such study is most often the systematic repression of the forces governing such disruptive movements, and it is this sort of recognition that informs the work of a contemporary genealogist like Michel Foucault. Foucault clarifies the ways in which cultural historians have attempted to isolate contradictions and anomalies in order to master them by demonstrating their hidden principles of coherence: "The history of ideas usually credits the discourse that it analyzes with coherence. If it happens to notice an irregularity in the use of words, several incompatible propositions, a set of meanings that do not adjust to one another, concepts that cannot be systematized together, then it regards it as its duty to find, at a deeper level, a principle of cohesion that organizes the discourse and restores to it its hidden unity. . . . In order to reconstitute it, it must first be presupposed, and one will only be sure of finding it if one has pursued it far enough and for long enough. It appears as an optimum: the greatest possible number of contradictions resolved by the simplest means."[30]

Foucault argues further that a similar tendency operates in those approaches in which contradiction itself "is finally revealed as an organizing principle, as the founding, secret law that accounts for all minor contradictions and gives them a firm foundation: in short, a model for all other oppositions."[31] Both methods of interpretation presume structural distinctions between surface and depth, phenomenal appearance and deep-structure. In Foucault's own theoretical conception of "archaeological analysis," however, "contradictions are neither appearances to be overcome, nor secret principles to be uncovered."[32] Rather then treating either coherence or contradiction as governing principle, Foucault attempts to discover the relation of coherence and contradiction as the nexus in which an event takes place.[33]

Foucault's theory of interpretation in *The Archaeology of Knowledge* seems to go beyond some of the problems posed by his earlier works, especially *The*

Order of Things. In fact, *The Archaeology* often seems to undermine the basic assumptions of the earlier work. David Carroll suggests that Foucault attempts to counter objections to the discreteness of the various *epistemes* in *The Order of Things* by multiplying and dispersing these epistemological ruptures in *The Archaeology*. Carroll concludes that "Foucault cannot pluralize the *episteme* without questioning the concept itself: he cannot really argue for an open field without undermining the singular and determining nature of the context of any discursive act or *enoncé* — that is, without arguing against the basic premises and assertions of his own position." [34] Foucault's position seems especially problematic when one considers *The Order of Things* in relation to the theoretical discussion in *The Archaeology* and such essays as "Nietzsche, Genealogy, History" (1971). In this essay, Foucault adapts the method of Nietzschean genealogical analysis in a manner that seems difficult to distinguish from Jacques Derrida's own appropriation of Nietzschean hermeneutics: "Genealogical analysis shows that the concept of liberty is an 'invention of the ruling classes' and not fundamental to man's nature or at the root of his attachment to being and truth. What is found at the historical beginning of things is not the inviolable identity of their origin; it is the dissension of other things. It is disparity." [35] Such "disparity" seems a far cry from the play of presence and absence that Carroll criticizes in *The Order of Things* as a covert recuperation of the metaphysics of presence that Foucault attempts to supersede.

The appearance of Derrida in my reading of Foucault should help to make clear the sort of intertextual analysis proposed for this study. Edward Said's preference for Foucault's method of cultural analysis over Derrida's deconstructive strategies is governed in part by Said's conviction that what is valuable in Derrida's method of intertextual interpretation is preserved and broadened in Foucault's work. Thus, he opens his essay on Derrida and Foucault by comparing the "double writing" of both theorists: "This unbalanced and unbalancing (*décalée et décalante*) writing is intended by Derrida to mark the admittedly uneven and undecidable fold (*pli*) in his work between the description of the text, which he deconstructs, and the enactment of a new one, with which his reader must now reckon. Similarly in Foucault's case, there is a 'double writing' (which is not the name he gives it) intended first to describe (by representing) the text he studies, as discourse, archive, statements, and the rest, then later to present a new text, his own, doing and saying what those other 'invisible' texts have repressed, doing and saying what no one else will say and do." [36] Said thus suggests that the intertextuality involved has to do primarily with the confrontation of the "text studied" and the "text studying"; there seems little problem in "saying what no one else will say and do" in this analyzing text that has already freed itself from the repressions of the text studied. Said seems to recall the suspect claims of the structuralists to a purely formal level of analysis that has been achieved as the result of a systematic process of sifting textual disparities, unities, and repetitions.

For Derrida, however, intertextuality is not simply a new term for "transcoding" that maintains the distinction between the solitary and discrete text and the critical metalanguage in which its system is anatomized to reveal its pretensions to truth and meaning. Derrida's "trace" defines every text as always already an intertextual event, constructed of the retentions (in Derrida's postphenomenological terminology, the "economy" of motivating signifiers) and protentions (the necessity of supplementarity) that constitute the text as a "divided present." Eugenio Donato makes this same point even more cogently: "If, as Derrida puts it, linguistic signs refer themselves only to other linguistic signs, if the linguistic reference of words is words, if texts refer to nothing but other texts, then, in Foucault's words, 'If interpretation can never accomplish itself, it is simply because there is nothing to interpret.' There is nothing to interpret, for each sign is in itself not the thing that offers itself to interpretation but interpretation of other signs." [37]

Is it any wonder that most contemporary theoreticians linger on the verge of such a recognition, but invariably repress it? The problem of "reading" is so immensely complicated that the analyst is nearly willing to accept bad faith and slip unwittingly back into the old modes of analysis, refashioned and disguised but still betraying the same telling form beneath. Derrida's method of deconstruction, however, has the advantage of suggesting the ways in which an intertextual reading might be performed that would no longer accommodate the eccentricities of the literary to the normative rationality of cultural rhetoric and yet still avoid the danger of isolating the "literary" as a distinct cognitive and ontological category. Such a method of reading would have to follow the general intention of the literary work to expose the violence of all understanding and the supplementary displacements involved in every act of communication. A method of criticism that would preserve by violating the very force of literature itself to disrupt the normative and rational would contribute to the "intelligibility" of our own time, not merely by paraphrasing the texts of the past, but by allowing us to *use* the literary power of the text.

Derrida acknowledges in his own work that no act of interpretation escapes the will to power that is the resource and fear of language. To recognize the ways in which various interpreters have attempted to appropriate the past leads inevitably to a desire to escape either the naiveté or bad faith of one's predecessors. Yet, Derrida and the Foucault of "Nietzsche, Genealogy, History" recognize that such knowledge denies the possibility of a privileged vantage and that any effort to expose the legerdemain of cultural repression must involve itself in the very rhetoric that has motivated it (and for that very reason it seeks to unravel). As Derrida points out in his review of Foucault's *Madness and Civilization*: "There is no Trojan horse unrecognized by Reason (in general). The unsurpassable, unique, and imperial grandeur of the order of reason, that which makes it not just another actual order or structure (a determined historical structure, one structure among other possible ones), is that one cannot speak out against it except by being for it, that one can protest it only from within it; and within its domain, Reason leaves us only the resource of stratagems and strategies."[38] The "stratagems and strategies" of the deconstructive reading share the subversive impulse of literature in general. The aim of such agitation, however, is hardly the impotent irony of the decadent poet or the equivocal indeterminacy in some caricatures of poststructuralist interpretation, but instead the disruption of the normative and cultural signified (in Said's terms, the "place" of the signifier) for the purpose of revealing the power of that norm or convention — its power to suppress its own divided structure.

The historicism that conceives of literary history as a perpetually renewed translation of the past into the rhetoric of the present finally shares the conservatism that marks most criticism as the product of dominant cultural and institutional values. We need a more radical conception of the interpreter's imaginative powers, closer to the poetic sources they are used to study. As Walter Benjamin writes, "In every era the attempt must be made anew to wrest tradition away from a conformism that is about to overpower it."[39] To recognize that all interpretation functions by means of repressions and revelations that may be understood only in the powerful supplementary effort to appropriate their force — in a mode of analysis that in its own turn represses and exposes — this recognition is involved in the rhetoric of that metaphorics without origin or end that we term "literature." And it is only within this explicitly intertextual "play" that we might hope to make intelligible the force of the literary without taming it or rendering its provocations harmless.

Derrida's deconstruction, Foucault's archaeology, and Barthes's and White's structuralist approaches are not merely examples of a certain period in the history of ideas that we are accustomed to label as modern or postmodern. In Derrida's work in particular, one finds a structure of modernity that this study postulates as homologous with the structure of the literary in general. This modernity is the literary will to power that Paul de Man and Harold Bloom variously interpret as the differential impulse governing poetic utterance. Viewed in the context of Derrida's broader conception of the trace-structure of language, de Man's and Bloom's respective approaches to a more restricted literary discipline might be preserved as parts of a more general study of history as interpretation. Bloom's conception of the "anxiety of influence" as a literary "family romance" has a direct relation with the interpretative battles that Nietzsche considers fundamental to the appearances of sociohistorical values. What de Man views as the dialectic of temporality and atemporality in the poet's quest for an original voice is a restricted version of the more comprehensive historical transformations analyzed by Nietzsche, Foucault, and Derrida. In this way, Bloom and de Man can be used to develop a specific focus for the literary concerns of this study; I will stress their relation to the more general hermeneutic problems raised by Derrida and Foucault in order to preserve the necessary interrelation of literature and social reality.

Rejecting the traditional historical description of modernism, de Man insists that the term be considered first in opposition to the "traditional" or the "classical." The intention of modernity is motivated initially by the desire to escape or repress a past that would overwhelm the poet's own lust for originating power: "Modernity exists in the form of a desire to wipe out whatever came earlier, in the hope of reaching at last a point that could be called a true present, a point of origin that marks a new departure. This combined interplay of deliberate forgetting with an action that is also a new origin reaches the full power of the idea of modernity."[40] De Man's pretext in "Literary History and Literary Modernity" is Nietzsche's *Use and Abuse of History,* which prefigures the ways in which Nietzsche would subsequently transform man's "life-denying" impulses into ironic resources for his own life-affirming Will to Power. Both de Man and Bloom are fond of quoting Nietzsche's conclusion to *The Genealogy of Morals,* in which Nietzsche speaks of the "ascetic ideal" as "this longing to escape from illusion, change, becoming, death, and from longing itself."[41] Nietzsche's idea of such *ressentiment* shares the entropic tendency of de Man's conception of modernity as the freedom from time; both impulses anticipate their own inversion. Thus, Nietzsche writes that this asceticism "signifies, let us have the courage to face it, a will to nothingness, a revulsion from life, a rebellion against the principal conditions of living. And yet, despite everything, it is and remains a *will.* Let me repeat, now that I have reached the end, what I said at the beginning: man would sooner have the void for his purpose than be void of purpose."[42]

In de Man's terms, the very "antiliterary" impulse of modernity — its desire to escape the constraints of "re-presentation" — is ultimately responsible for transforming modernity into the very resource of literature: "Modernity invests its trust in the power of the present moment as an origin, but discovers that, in severing itself from the past, it has at the same time severed itself from the present."[43] The antiliterary impulse toward origination carries with it a demand for intense metapoetic self-consciousness. The more powerful the poet's effort to repress the burdensome tradition — to awaken from the nightmare of history — just so much more explicit will his or her metapoetic reflection need to be, because the work must claim impossibly to originate its own grammar. This very self-reflexivity — often considered the characteristic feature of literary modernism from Henry James to Wallace Stevens — is the moment in which modernity must relapse into history by acknowledging its desire to be the sign of its historical belatedness.

Such a process may seem exclusively "literary" in de Man's analysis, but it recalls a familiar Freudian pattern: the repetition-compulsion itself is proportionate to the strength of the repression. The "uncanny" — that "name for everything that ought to have remained hidden and secret and has become visible" — may be repressed again only with the promise of its repetition. As de Man writes: "As soon as modernism becomes conscious of its own strategies — and it cannot fail to do so if it is justified . . . in the name of a concern for the future — it discovers itself to be a generative power that not only engenders history, but is part of a generative scheme that extends far back into the past."[44]

A similar understanding of modernity informs Joseph Riddel's conception of the imbrication of historical modernism and so-called postmodernism: "The history of recent Modernism is the history of metapoetics, of a self-reflexive poetry which puts itself constantly in question as the only way of resisting the problematic of language. But in this very self-conscious, self-critical act, it throws itself beyond Modernism, beyond the fiction of recovered innocence, and into the freedom of a truly deconstructive adventure."[45] De Man undoubtedly would reject the implicit historicism of Riddel's view, preferring to stress this internal division of the literary as an "event" constituted only in terms of synchronic juxtaposition. Both writers, however, share the same general conception of this modern desire for an impossible *telos* — freedom from influence, history, re-presentation, language — that prompts a sort of rear-guard action, recognized only belatedly, that for this very reason returns the poet with even greater force to a historical situation:

> Modernity turns out to be indeed one of the concepts by means of which the distinctive nature of literature can be revealed in all its intricacy. No wonder it had to become a central issue in critical discussions and a source of torment to writers who have to confront it as a challenge to their vocation. They can neither accept nor reject it with good conscience. When they assert their own modernity, they are bound to discover their dependence on similar assertions made by their literary predecessors; their claim to being a new beginning turns out to be a repetition of a claim that has always already been made.[46]

In this way, de Man may offer a sort of ratio for the study of avant-garde literary works and movements which recalls the work of Tynianov and other Formalists on the problems of literary evolution: "The more radical the rejection of anything that came before, the greater dependence on the past."[47] This notion stems from de Man's own appropriation of a deconstructive conception of understanding, and it shares the general impulse behind Bloom's strong "misreading" as understanding that functions as a psychic will to power.

No national literature and no literary period better illustrate this "steady fluctuation" of the poetic "away from and toward its own mode of being" than nineteenth-century American literature.[48] Never in the history of Western literature has a tradition been established so fundamentally in terms of its own sense of belatedness and its own desire for independence and originality. For Harold Bloom, Emerson serves as the appropriate symbol of this yearning for release from the history, memory, and representation associated with Europe for the nineteenth-century American writer: "As the Emersonian, American sense of anteriority was greater, ours being the Evening Land, even so the Sublime was heightened, or repression augmented, if only because there was more unfulfilled desire to repress."[49] Yet, for Bloom it is the distinguishing mark of Emersonianism — and thus the American literary tradition that it paradoxically engenders — to expose through its own demonization of the Other that threatens poetic originality the inescapable historicity of the poet's situation. Adapting Nietzsche's Dionysian/Apollonian difference to his own theory, Bloom reads Emerson as the American poet who "believed that poetry came only from Dionysian influx [i.e., the 'poet's return to his subsuming precursors'], yet . . . preached an Apollonian Self-Reliance while fearing the very individuation that it would bring."[50]

For Bloom this is an informing American literary dialectic that shadows curiously a "dialectical" school of American criticism. The work of such Americanists as A. N. Kaul, Richard Poirier, Leo Marx, and Roy Harvey Pearce belongs to a tradition that originates in Richard Chase's concern with the paradoxical identity of the American writer. The psychic struggles of Bloom's poet reflect Chase's more formal treatment of the enabling confrontation of the "romance" and the "novel" in the American prose tradition. What Chase interprets generically as the idealistic impulse in the romance has certain affinities with Bloom's conception of the longing for the Sublime and the full realization of the Apollonian individuality of the poet. Similarly, it is Chase's "realistic novel" that might be said to betray the anxiety of influence as the pressure of history and the burden of the past: the inescapable rhetoric of temporality.

Unquestionably, Chase privileges those elements of romance in the American novel that contribute to its apparently distinctive capacity to "rest in contradictions and among extreme ranges of experience." Yet, it is clear that what Chase prizes in American prose is a certain "negative capability," which is facilitated by the unholy marriage of romance and realism: "The imagination that has produced much of the best and most characteristic American fiction has been shaped by contradictions and not by the unities and harmonies of our culture."[51] It is worth comparing this thesis in Chase's *American Novel and Its Tradition* with Bloom's revisionary criticism, which seems so antithetical to Chase's overt formalism:

Emerson's beautiful confusion *is* beautiful because the conflict is emotional, between equal impulses, and because it cannot be resolved. . . . He asks for a stance simultaneously Dionysiac and self-reliant, and he does not know how this is to be attained, nor do we. I suggest that the deeper cause for his impossible demand is his inner division on the burden of influx, at once altogether to be desired and yet altogether to be resisted, if it comes to us (as it must) from a precursor no more ultimately Central than ourselves, no less a text than we are.[52]

Chase knew quite well that he was speaking of literary forms only as a scholarly strategy to disguise his consideration of the metaphysical functions of the literary, which I have generally described as the internally divided struggle of de Man's modernity or Bloom's anxiety of influence. If Chase ends by privileging the romance (as his followers would end by privileging some form of social, literary, or historical reconcilation), then it is because he himself is a strong misreader who longed in his own way for the Critic's Sublime.

More important for us is the need to recognize the pervasiveness of this paradigm for modernity in the study of nineteenth-century American nationalism. The struggle for American literary independence is only secondarily a sociological study of the literary experiments and critical documents that constitute America's effort to escape "Europe." The true quest for nationality is primarily a study in the psychic defenses that constitute the very idea of literary modernity. And those psychic defenses are in themselves the motives for an inevitable epistemological and ontological questioning that compels the author or critic to repeat the basic moves of the metaphysician. Psychology may appear to replace metaphysics in the presumed historical development from the Renaissance to our own exhausted era, but such historical egotism merely exposes its own naiveté. Psychology and metaphysics are the twin functions of cognitive experience that found each other as "disciplines," as the deconstructive strategies of Derrida and the antithetical criticism of Bloom both suggest.

For Bloom, Emersonianism begets the American genealogy of the anxiety of influence with an intense awareness of its own internal divisions, its own double soul. Emerson recognized quite clearly that the precursor with whom the ephebe struggles is, in fact, the ephebe's own *Doppelgänger* and that the battle waged is a perpetually renewed conflict of the subject's own psychic powers and divisions: "This, I now assert, is the distinguishing mark of the specifically American Sublime, that it begins anew not with restoration or rebirth, in the radically displaced Protestant pattern of the Wordsworthian Sublime, but that it is truly past even such displacement, despite the line from Edwards to Emerson that scholarship accurately continues to trace. Not merely rebirth, but the even more hyperbolical trope of self-rebegetting, is the starting point of the last Western Sublime, the great sunset of selfhood in the Evening Land."[53]

Emersonianism represses not only the European tradition but the very element of the Emersonian self that internally threatens the possibility of originality and self-creation. Emerson is used to enact Bloom's own version of the American fall, in itself a sublime effort to forget the history that continues to agitate the "native strain" in American literature: *"In the beginning was the Lie.* All later lies are made against this giant Lie at the origin, and so all strong American poems whatsoever, being later lies, lie against time. But what was the Primal Lie, in an American imaginative context? Surely, it was the Emersonian denial of *Nachträglichkeit,* of being as a nation 'after the event.' This denial of our national revisionism, that made of all previous cultural history only a deferred action that prepared for our new stage of development."[54] Bloom's analysis of the American anxiety of influence reflects the characteristic move of the poet to recuperate the inevitable supplementarity not merely of the signifier but of one's own belated arrival, the poet inescapably a "trace" that is already expressive of a particular historical economy of "readings." Viewed in terms of de Man's modernity, Bloom's Emerson represents the general poetic effort to transform *Nachträglichkeit* — a Freudian notion that extends the range of literature and writing to include the function of the psyche — into the moment of origination, in which some "Amerika" is rediscovered.

Bloom attempts to argue that this Emersonian "lie against time" characterizes a logocentric impulse in American literature that he sets explicitly in opposition to Derrida's decentering, but the internal division of Bloom's Emerson is sufficient evidence that the presumed recentering of American metaphysics involves its own undoing. Bloom writes in *A Map of Misreading*: "In American poets, I surmise, the detachment must be more extreme, and the consequent resistance to decentering greater, for American poets are the most consciously belated in the history of Western poetry."[55] Bloom's judgment is limited here by his exclusive concern with American poets. Whitman may seem to rebeget the Emersonian self, confirming the master's own prophecies concerning his poetic transumption, but Whitman is a poor index to the nineteenth-century American anxiety of influence. Thoreau, Hawthorne, Melville, Twain, and James are only mentioned nominally in Bloom's writings, but in their prose works the explicit task of deconstructing the Emersonian denial of *Nachträglichkeit* is dramatized repeatedly.

Henry James understood this conception of America as modernity better than any of his predecessors. No literary *oeuvre* is more discordant or more expressive of the repeated effort to rebeget the self than James's voluminous production, as James himself indicates in the Prefaces to the New York Edition: "I saw therefore what I saw, and what these numerous pages record, I trust, with clearness; though one element of fascination tended all the while to rule the business — a fascination, at each stage of my journey, on the noted score of that so shifting and uneven character of the tracks of my original passage."[56] What James discovers everywhere in this process of imaginative re-vision is precisely the principle informing each of the individual works: the repeated desire to establish a structural center that is perpetually frustrated by the straying of the text. James endlessly worries what his works celebrate: the vagrancy of his writing, its inability to remain true to the original conception, which is the historical or imaginative *donnée:*

> The artist's energy fairly depends on his fallibility. . . . He places, after an earnest survey, the piers of his bridge — he has at least sounded deep enough, heaven knows, for their brave position; yet the bridge spans the stream, after the fact, in apparently complete independence of these properties, the principal grace of the original design. *They* were an illusion, for their necessary hour; but the span itself, whether of a single arch or of many, seems by the oddest chance in the world to be a reality; since, actually, the rueful builder, passing under it, sees figures and hears sounds above: he makes out with his heart in his throat, that it bears and is positively "used."[57]

Something besides the author or his original intention allows the architecture to cohere; for James, it is the exposure and even formal objectification of those unconscious forces of literary tradition and cultural convention that are always beyond but still operative within the authorial intention. In the effort to achieve his own particular voice, James's author is always entangled in the history that has motivated him. Self-rebegetting may be the endless project of the American Henry James, but the European James repeatedly writes of the impossibility of original self-expression.

Nineteenth-century American literature is characterized by this antiliterary impulse toward modernity as part of the very cultural situation in which it was written. Bloom clearly recognizes that the American writer suffers from a self-consuming hunger that is the very mark of his belatedness: "American poets, rather more than other Western poets, at least since the Enlightenment, are astonishing in their ambitions. Each wants to be the universe, to be the whole of which all other poets are only parts. American psychopoetics are dominated by an American difference from European patterns of the imagination's struggle with its own origins. Our poets' characteristic anxiety is not so much an expectation of being flooded by poetic ancestors, as already *having been* flooded before one could even begin."[58]

It is just the logic of such modernity that it turns against itself to become the most profound form of historicism. Only in this way may we begin to account for the notable generic confusion that maddens the critical cataloguer of the works in this period. What major work of nineteenth-century American literature belongs to any recognizable genre? The desire for nationalism in this period is expressed most directly in the marked ferment to produce new and original forms to express a distinctively American subject and theme. Admittedly, this quest for new forms is itself often explicitly antiformal; one need consider only the centrality of the journal and notebook in the writings of the American Transcendentalists. Yet, the very formlessness of American prose in this period is a strategy that evolves into a form in its own right. Thoreau's *A Week* and Melville's *Moby-Dick* are discursive and multigeneric in relation to those works whose forms they attempted to supersede. I am reminded all the more emphatically of the limitations inherent in the traditional romance by such mixed and bastard forms as Hawthorne's *Blithedale Romance* and Melville's *Confidence-Man*. *Blithedale* confuses and mixes elements of romance and realism in such a way that the ontological and epistemological contradictions governing both literary modes are revealed with particular force and clarity. The intertextuality of romance and realism is the distinguishing mark of Hawthorne's literary production, and it necessitates a perpetual renewal of the confrontation, which might be traced from the romantic synthesis of *The Scarlet Letter* to the clash of conflicting interests in *Blithedale*.

The very quest for new forms, which is such an essential part of the American's sense of belatedness, comes to govern the nineteenth-century writer's own conception of his career and *oeuvre*. American writers in this period seem especially dissatisfied with their own creative output; James's sense of the "deviations and differences" in his own work as in themselves the eccentric center for his own canon may be said to apply as well to the work of Emerson, Thoreau, Hawthorne, Melville, Whitman, and Twain. What governs these writings is what James terms "this infinitely interesting and amusing *act* of re-appropriation," which might serve as a description of the "historical" imagination of American writing in general. The marginal text in this study is considered to be an especially explicit expression of this dilemma; its central subject is most often the writer's own achievement and the desire for new and different modes of artistic representation. The notably mixed forms of these marginal texts, which contribute to those anomalies and contradictions that continue to baffle the critics, are expressive of these authors' efforts to rethink the entire question of literary language, its relation to normative discourse, its involvement in a historical tradition, and its own claim to "originality."[59]

With the exception of Thoreau's *A Week*, these texts are written at moments of creative and imaginative crisis, in which the author wanders dissatisfied with his prior production and yet still uncertain as to the direction his new work will take. In each case, the work performs an extended critique of the author's own literary intentions in his earlier work. Hawthorne's *Blithedale* thoroughly revises the conception of romance governing the structures of *The Scarlet Letter* and *The House of the Seven Gables*. Melville's "Bartleby" not only questions the possibility of Ishmael's "survival" in *Moby-Dick,* but prefigures the deconstruction of the "Central Man" that is performed in *The Confidence-Man*. In a similar sense, Poe's *Pym* revises the presumed "dualism" of the two realms at war in his early poetry and short fiction: the day and night, phenomenal appearance and supernatural reality oppositions that structure his early stories. Confusing these realms as the interrelated forces of the psyche, Poe prefigures that vision of unity in multiplicity that is worked out in the pseudoscience of *Eureka*.

In Twain's *Pudd'nhead Wilson,* the possibility of a detached and coherent "self" that is defeated but still promised in *Huckleberry Finn* is shattered by the rhetoric of a work that demonstrates the impossibility of any outside perspective on social corruptions. Slavery is no longer merely a sociological fact, but part of humanity's ontological nature. The deliberately disruptive and aphoristic style of *Pudd'nhead Wilson* thus anticipates the bleakness of Twain's final vision, which is less an apocalyptic nihilism than a recognition of the hermeneutic problems confronting the contemporary social critic. In a similar fashion, James's narrator in *The Sacred Fount* discovers his own bondage to the rhetoric of his culture and resigns any presumption of narrative "authority" for the sake of an inner critique of the cultural system of signification. By deliberately disrupting the normal circuits of the social code, James's narrator forces its members either to meet his challenge by exorcising him or by accepting a new awareness of their own social relations. In this way, James's narrator anticipates the narrative mode in the novels of the Major Phase, which is concerned with establishing a situation in which its characters will be compelled to rethink their own bondage to cultural values.

As his first major work, Thoreau's *A Week* cannot reflect on its author's literary history in the same fashion as these other works written in the midst of productive careers. For this reason, I have treated *A Week* as Thoreau's most extended effort to discover his own "original" version of Emersonian transcendentalism. The paradoxical nature of such a project is evident everywhere in Thoreau's appropriation of Emersonian values and his subsequent struggle to repress the presence of the master. The "failure" of *A Week* drove Thoreau back to a clearer and less problematic form of American romanticism — for that reason a less authentic appropriation of Emersonianism — that resulted in the more rationalized and formally coherent *Walden*.

In this way I attempt to situate these marginal works "historically" in relation to those retentions and protentions that may be said to operate in the literary tradition, the author's own *oeuvre,* and in the linguistic sign itself. These marginal texts tend to expose more fully the internal divisions that might be more adequately or thoroughly repressed in more coherent or consistent works. Nevertheless, the retentions and protentions given such free play in these anomalous works help make explicit the intertextuality that is implicit in every form of representation. It should be equally clear why it is necessary for this study of those texts to employ a supplementary pretext (in this case drawn primarily from twentieth-century modern thought) in order to emphasize the conflicting forces already operative in the literary text's economy of forces. The modernity of nineteenth-century American fiction is not presented as primarily a historical anticipation of twentieth-century thought, even though a convincing historical argument could be offered in terms of a more traditional approach. Instead, the divided structure of modernity as a characteristic of the literary function of language is studied by means of a critical appropriation that is required by the very intertextuality of modernity we have defined. In general terms, Derrida's deconstruction and Bloom's misprision both attempt to preserve the Nietzschean idea of interpretation as appropriation, of reading and writing as manifestations of an inevitable will to power. Bloom's conception of "misreading" is perhaps flawed by his insistence upon the orderly progression of the ephebe's transumption of the predecessor, thus reinstating a rhetorical deep-structure for poetry that is as untenable as Barthes's or White's structuralist projections. But the general conception of misreading as a method of interpretation attempts to preserve the force of the literary in the act of critical understanding. In Derrida's considerably broader context of language, such a method of literary interpretation might be extended to include the very methods of cognitive, psychic, and sociohistoric signification.

We ought neither to imitate nor translate the writings of our poets and philosophers; we ought to *use* those texts in the very interpretative spirit in which they were written to discover in a new sense the intelligibility of our own times. Such understanding can never take place outside the space of actual reading — in some impossible realm of hermeneutic abstraction — but only in the active effort to wrest the texts of the past and our knowledge of them away from habitual modes of behavior and unrecognized assumptions. As Bloom redefines the problem of literary history:

> The remedy for literary history then is to convert its concepts from the category of being into the category of happening. To see the history of poetry as an endless, defensive civil war, indeed a family war, is to see that every idea of history relevant to the history of poetry must be a *concept of happening*. That is, when you *know* the influence relation between two poets, your knowing is a conceptualization, and your conceptualization (or misreading) is itself an event in the literary history you are writing. Indeed your *knowledge* of the latter poet's misprision of his precursor is exactly as crucial a concept of happening or historical event as the poetic misprision was.[60]

In such moments, Bloom cannot be said to be speaking exclusively of poetry and literary history in their traditionally narrow definitions. Such psychic interplay is only nominally a battle waged within literature; in a much broader context it is the general effort of psychic writing that struggles for an impossible self-expression. Viewed in such a way, poetry and its history can no longer be restricted to familiar disciplinary boundaries, but must be seen as indications of a basic artistic impulse, analyzed by Nietzsche as the "fundamental will of the spirit":

> The power of the spirit to appropriate what is foreign to it is revealed in a strong inclination to assimilate the new to the old, to simplify the complex, to overlook or repel what is wholly contradictory: just as it arbitrarily emphasizes, extracts and falsifies to suit itself certain traits and lines in what is foreign to it, in every piece of the "external world." . . . This same will is served by an apparently antithetical drive of the spirit, a sudden decision for ignorance, for arbitrary shutting-out, a closing of the windows, an inner denial of this or that thing, a refusal to let it approach . . . an acceptance and approval of ignorance. . . . There also belongs the occasional will of the spirit to let itself be deceived . . . , a joy in uncertainty and ambiguity, . . . of the exaggerated, diminished, displaced, beautified, an enjoyment of the capriciousness of all these expressions of power. Finally there also belongs here that not altogether innocent readiness of the spirit to deceive other spirits and to dissemble before them, that continual pressing and pushing of a creative, formative, changeable force: in this the spirit enjoys the multiplicity and cunning of its masks.[61]

Nietzsche is writing about the "healthy man," whose multiple and protean powers (principles of growth and life) have been divided and thus corrupted in the course of a Western history dedicated to the denial of the interplay between expression and repression, memory and forgetfulness, dissimulation and truth. The very terms *writer* and *reader*, *poet* and *critic*, even *literature* and *language* designate a division of interpretative understanding into active and reactive forces that are already signs of cultural decadence, already an admission that criticism claims to be nothing but an empty repetition, a lifeless rememoration.

2.

"The Being of Language: The Language of Being" in Thoreau's *A Week on the Concord and Merrimack Rivers*

To learn means: to become knowing. In Latin, knowing is *qui vidit,* one who has seen, has caught sight of something, and who never again loses sight of what he has caught sight of. To learn means: to attain to such seeing. To this belongs our reaching it; namely, on the way, on a journey. To put oneself on a journey, to experience, means to learn.
— Heidegger, "Words," *On the Way to Language*

I have sought to re-name the things seen, now lost in chaos of borrowed titles, many of them inappropriate, under which the true character lies hid. In letters, in journals, in reports of happenings I have recognized new contours suggested by old words so that new names were constituted.
— William Carlos Williams, *In the American Grain*

Walden is Thoreau's perfect form; it has the mathematical precision of a musical composition. Thoreau certainly appears to demonstrate in this work the radically formalized truth he had foreseen in an earlier work: "The most distinct and beautiful statement of any truth must take at last the mathematical form."[1] *Walden* is "addressed to poor students," who love to play its verbal games and diagram its architectonic order in the place of healthier sport. Such economy and control are rare in the literature of the American Renaissance, which seems better represented by the outwanderings of Whitman or the divine rage of Melville. There is little voyaging here; this is a book of construction and possession: "In most books, the *I*, or first person, is omitted; in this it will be retained; that, in respect to egotism, is the main difference. We commonly do not remember that it is, after all, always the first person that is speaking."[2] All radiates concentrically from this artificial "I," whose insistent presence organizes and determines what we might see. Thoreau has much to say against ownership, but in this book he appropriates nature and brings it within his compass. The writing defines and encloses a transcendental fiefdom; *Walden* legalizes the everlasting wholeness of natural creation. All seasons speak the same truth in but varied manifestations, so that the poet need only lift the corners of his veils to disclose the divinity in things.

This is a book of discovery, but not of creation. Perhaps it is no accident that the most extended literary discussion concentrates on "Reading" rather than on writing. Of course, Thoreau emphasizes the intimate bond between the two activities: "Books must be read as deliberately and reservedly as they were written" (*Walden*, 68). Yet, *Walden* is primarily intended as a Baedeker to the order of nature, the primacy of which remains unquestioned. Writing is sacred and mystical in its universal appeal and endurance, but nonetheless secondary to the literal text of nature: "It is the work of art nearest to life itself" (69). "Reading" quickly gives way to "Sounds" more basic to "the language which all things and events speak without metaphor, which alone is copious and standard" (75). William Drake writes, "The step from 'Reading' to 'Sounds' is that from the language of men to the 'language' of things, from what can be said *about* nature, to nature itself."[3] The classics play an important role throughout *Walden*, but they must be put aside in the early stages of Thoreau's ritualized self-purification: "I did not read books the first summer; I hoed beans" (75).

Walden betrays the desire for an established metaphysical center to determine human behavior and organize knowledge. The metaphors of building and clothing appear to offer human beings the freedom of a creative imagination, but such activities are themselves merely techniques for discovering and obeying the dictates of an authoritative Being. Fishing, diving, and mining are basic to this work of reconnaissance: "My instinct tells me that my head is an organ for burrowing, as some creatures use their snout and fore-paws, and with it I would mine and burrow my way through these hills. I think that the richest vein is somewhere hereabouts; so by the divining rod and thin vapors I judge; and here I will begin to mine" (*Walden*, 66). Such deep diving intends to bring to light what is hidden, freeing what has been imprisoned in humans by their faulty methods of perception and cognition. *Awakening* is the avowed aim of *Walden*, and it means the *arising* of truth into consciousness by means of a systematic removal of barriers in order to open a path. For Thoreau, to awaken is to "come into being" rather than to "bring into being." Language facilitates such discovery only to the extent that it serves a prior perception and thus may be made "pertinent" to reality. Metaphor is employed ironically to reveal the "commonsensical" in everyday speech and thus to free us to receive the tangible, literal spirituality that only nature presents. As Drake remarks, "To say that nature has a language, is itself a metaphor. Metaphor as Thoreau speaks of it always defines human experience, *within human bounds.*"[4] Thus, in a work that is nothing but metaphor, Thoreau struggles to destroy the metaphorical in order to allow the presence of the indwelling god to emerge.[5]

The achievement of *Walden* is the result of this confidence that the natural origin of language escapes the symbolism of words and remains eternally and creatively present. In such a bookish work there is remarkably little reflection upon language itself, as if the natural facts were sufficient for the grammar of our lives. There is something disturbingly evasive in such passages as the following from "Higher Laws": "Every man is the builder of a temple, called his body, to the god he worships, after a style purely his own, nor can he get off by hammering marble instead. We are all sculptors and painters, and our material is our own flesh and blood and bones. Any nobleness begins at once to refine a man's features, any meanness or sensuality to imbrute them" (*Walden,* 147). Substituting the body for the materials of the sculptor, Thoreau disparages the symbolic mode of the traditional artist. True art speaks directly in and through natural existence, spontaneously manifesting itself in the life of the artist.

And yet, such sophistry is purchased only by means of an elaborate metaphoric structure yoking temple and body, style and behavior. Thoreau is able to elide the conventional distinctions between body and soul, substance and spirit, only by means of a language that operates by syntagmatic associations and paradigmatic substitutions essential to figurative language. Thoreau may employ language in *Walden* more cleverly than in any of his other works, but he scrupulously avoids the problematic of language itself. Emerson insists that "Nature is the symbol of spirit," thus suggesting a correspondence between the production of words as "signs of natural facts" and the recognition of "natural facts" as the "symbols of particular spiritual facts."[6] Emerson's view involves a rich and varied language coordinated with natural symbolism; Thoreau's insistence on the ultimate literality of natural facts reduces language to a secondary representation.

There are, of course, many ways in which *Walden* can be read as an extended meditation on the use and abuse of language. In *The Senses of "Walden,"* Stanley Cavell employs Wittgenstein to interpret *Walden* as the discovery of "what writing is and, in particular, what writing *Walden* is."[7] *Walden* certainly abounds with evidence that self-knowledge is as much a linguistic process as a purely natural one; in fact, the entire work turns on the doubling of the place of Walden in its textual realization. The awakening promised in the epigraph and the spring that concludes the work's seasonal cycles are metaphors for the composition of the text; the dwelling that Thoreau builds is ultimately a house of words. Yet, the aim of this "wording of the world" is a simplicity and clarity that result in the resolution of true self-knowledge.

The discipline of Thoreau's deliberation is equivalent to Wittgenstein's goal of learning how what we say is what we mean. Thoreau relies, however, on his confidence in a fundamental language of Nature from which human speech derives; Wittgenstein's problems are compounded by the fact that his investigations must remain totally within the domain of ordinary language. Wittgenstein must repeat the basic Kantian move of bracketing the thing-in-itself as unknowable, thus shifting the concern of understanding to the development of such internal linguistic distinctions as literal and figurative, grammatical and performative, conventional and original. In *Walden,* Thoreau decidedly does not bracket the thing-in-itself, even though he acknowledges the difficulty of expressing it. Cavell brilliantly suggests that Thoreau provides in *Walden* that "deduction of the thing-in-itself" that Kant "ought to have provided" as "an essential feature (category) of objectivity itself, viz., that of *a world apart from me in which* objects are met." [8] Transcendental deduction, however, can be performed only on a system of representation; Thoreau's ability to offer such a deduction of objectivity depends upon his confidence in the "language" of Nature, on the possibility of an "objective" language. Thus, Thoreau can assert in *Walden* what Kant in the three critiques only subjunctively "wished" for: that the order of the mind has a structural identity with the order of Nature.

The objectivity of Nature in *Walden* thus secretly governs the subjectivity of human language, which eternally symbolizes that literal origin. Cavell argues that "the externality of the world is articulated by Thoreau as its nextness to me." [9] This idea of the proximity of man and Nature determines Cavell's understanding of philosophical unity in Thoreau: "Unity between these aspects is viewed not as a mutual absorption, but as perpetual nextness, an act of neighboring or befriending." [10] I shall develop a similar notion of metaphysical difference in my Heideggerian reading of *A Week,* which draws, as Cavell's reading of *Walden* does, on Thoreau's paradoxical "friendship" (itself a metaphor for self-consciousness) as a complex of proximity and distance. However, I employ Heidegger's metaphor of the "between" (of earth and sky, of man and nature, of beings and Being), which differs crucially from "nextness."

The "neighborhood" of man and Nature is made possible by the authority of the language of Nature, whose objective and literal presence always exceeds human speech. When we say what we mean, when we speak deliberately, we approach the simplicity of such natural language, and words become facts. But the "between" of man and Nature describes a different space of human dwelling, because this between constitutes a relation that does not exist as a possibility prior to human language. In *Walden,* the language of Nature makes possible human speech, but the human language of *A Week* invents the idea of Nature as part of the measurement of our being. The grounding of human language in an inexpressible natural presence is symbolized in *Walden* in terms of building: a house, a self, a neighborhood with what *is*. The displacement of natural presence into the "difference" of human language in *A Week* is expressed in metaphors of voyaging, of traveling the between of beings and Being that is measured only by such movement. This "bridging" and "crossing" is the essential activity of metaphor. The text of *Walden* celebrates its departure from Walden as the realization of the natural experiment; the text of *A Week* celebrates the return to Concord as a "fall" into that language that has forever displaced the Nature it set out to discover.

In his description of the spring thaw flowing down the railroad cut, Thoreau offers one of the most extended and self-conscious verbal plays in *Walden*. The intricate blending of natural energies is a metaphor for the act of composition as an interpretation of specific phenomena in Nature: "As it flows it takes the forms of sappy leaves or vines, making heaps of pulpy sprays a foot or more in depth, and resembling, as you look down on them, the laciniated lobed and imbricated thalluses of some lichens; or you are reminded of coral, of leopards' paws or birds' feet, of brains or lungs or bowels, and excrements of all kinds" (*Walden*, 201). At such a moment language appears to call forth not only the intricate relations of the natural scene but also the pure metaphorics of such relations. Such poetry seems to constitute the truth of Nature by means of an integrated verbal display that challenges the self-sufficiency of natural phenomena. Everything observed seems to contribute to the production of signs that announce their metaphorical powers. Such technical descriptions as "laciniated lobed and imbricated thalluses of some lichens" signify through poetic complexes of alliteration, assonance, consonance, condensation, and syllabic rhythm. Yet, at such a critical moment Thoreau hesitates and then retreats, insisting that the true "artistry" remains external and divine: "I am affected as if in a peculiar sense I stood in the laboratory of the Artist who made the world and me, — had come to where he was still at work, sporting on this bank, and with an excess of energy strewing his fresh designs about" (202).

Metaphor has made such vision possible, but it is quickly rejected in favor of "such a foliaceous mass as the vitals of the animal body." And as if checking the dangerous excess implied in the verbal dance, Thoreau insists on dissecting words themselves to reveal their natural grounding, effectively emptying them of their autonomous powers:

> No wonder that the earth expresses itself outwardly in leaves, it so labors with the idea inwardly. The atoms have already learned this law, and are pregnant by it. The overhanging leaf sees here its prototype. *Internally*, whether in the globe or animal body, it is a moist thick *lobe*, a word especially applicable to the liver and lungs and the *leaves* of fat, (λείβω, labor, lapsus, to flow or flow or slip downward, a lapsing; λοβος, globus, lobe, globe; also lap, flap, and many other words,) *externally* a dry thin *leaf*, even as the *f* and *v* are a pressed and dried

b. The radicals of lobe are *lb,* the soft mass of the *b* (single lobed, or B, the double lobed,) with a liquid *l* behind it pressing it forward. In globe, *glb,* the gutteral *g* adds to the meaning the capacity of the throat. [*Walden,* 202]

Thoreau's phonemic, phonetic, and etymological analyses serve to restrain the flight of metaphor and situate the imagination within the "facts" of nature. Language is reduced to the physical associations of words and things that reveal a hidden natural form. *Walden* clearly argues for a natural principle of growth and unfolding that denies any sense of completion or closure, but language imitates that organic development only by means of a formal precision with respect to external facts that restricts imaginative play by narrowing the range of authentic (or pertinent) meanings. Emerson avoids some of these dangers by insisting that art is "a nature passed through the alembic of man. Thus in art does Nature work through the will of a man filled with the beauty of her first works." [11] For Emerson, both natural and linguistic symbolisms require a reciprocal interpretation, whereas Thoreau insists on the *presence* of unmediated truth in the earth's "living poetry."

Thus, in *Walden* every impulse to discuss poetics is quickly diverted back to the controlling meditation on the permanence and variety of natural forms. The mastery of this work relies largely on Thoreau's insistence that language and thought would be indistinguishable from natural phenomena if we fully understood our being. In his study of Thoreau, James McIntosh argues that the principal drama in *Walden* is the struggle of the "I" to sustain his integrity in the face of an encompassing natural order. Revisions made between 1847 and 1852 seem to indicate that in the process of composition Thoreau grew "less anxious to write of himself as a part of nature, more intent on asserting his intelligent separateness." [12] But the very diversity and activity that individualize the narrator and his style merely confirm the determining power of the underlying natural forms. The anxiety of alienation is neatly resolved as the *illusion* of separation that properly honed senses may see beyond. Every verbal strategy seems designed to measure and refine the a priori ground of being in nature.

A Week on the Concord and Merrimack Rivers (1849) is wilder and less "homely" than *Walden.* There is an authentic conflict between poetic expression and a determining natural order. Although *A Week* prefigures most of the basic tenets of the transcendentalism formalized by *Walden,* it leads Thoreau in certain directions that threaten to subvert his subsequent confidence in a metaphysics of natural presence. Appropriately, much of his doubt and equivocation concerns the relation of human discourse to natural form. *A Week* supplies the lack felt in *Walden* concerning the function and identity of the poet. As Robert Evans notes, "Thoreau left us no manifesto or defense of poetry — only the *Week,* in which he drew together most of his ideas concerning poetry and the function of the poet." [13] Thoreau may foreshadow the more rigorous naturalism of *Walden* when he writes that "the works of man are everywhere swallowed up in the immensity of nature" (*Week,* 416), but he introduces a more problematic conception of art when he suggests: "Art is not tame, and Nature is not wild, in the ordinary sense. A perfect work of man's art would also be wild or natural in a good sense. *Man tames Nature only that he may at last make her more free even than he found her, though he may never yet have succeeded"* (417; my italics). This reflection allows the possibility of a human poetry that would supplement the natural process, actively contributing to the unfolding of Being itself. Thoreau's modernity is best expressed in the notion that nature might be liberated and opened to its own being through human language. Thoreau's sentiment in this passage seems to combine two basic tenets of Emerson's radicalized version of romanticism: that the "poets are thus liberating gods" and by virtue of such imaginative freedom entreat us to "participate the invention of nature." [14]

A Week is a quest for the origins of poetry in both humanity and nature. The genetic critics are certainly correct in arguing that *Walden* refines the motley form of *A Week* by employing fewer literary digressions and quotations in order to center the subject of natural experience. Yet, the balance and control of *Walden* are achieved only by repressing basic questions about human discourse that surface in the discursive voyage of *A Week.* This distinction between the organization of these works affects other areas of concentration as well. *Walden* involves a withdrawal from social life designed to enable the "I" ultimately to achieve a higher form of communal existence. Although Thoreau writes repeatedly about the need to substitute more authentic communication for the conventional social "parlaver," there is less direct confrontation with the question of social intercourse than we might expect. "Life in the woods" remains a lonely experiment between two worlds. However, the entire narrative of *A Week* is controlled by the mutual voyage of the brothers, which figures variously as the relation between writer and reader as well as among individuals in society. Although the voyage is a departure from Concord, the brothers bear the essence of social intercourse with them. Simplified as a fraternal microcosm, social organization becomes a primary subject for continuing meditation. The extended essay on friendship that appears in "Wednesday" serves to organize Thoreau's related concerns with literary and interpersonal communication.

At first glance, *A Week* appears to be a cruder version of the same spiritual quest that organizes the form of *Walden.* Joyce Holland summarizes the accepted interpretation of the voyage motif: "Hence the upstream voyage becomes a voyage backwards through history to the pure and primal state, and the enduring moment of existence is shown by counterpointing the two symbolic motions 'up' and 'down.'" [15] Yet, the process of reducing "life to its lowest terms" in preparation for a new, spiritualized Concord spring is increasingly a literary task. The actual journey achieves greater naturalness as it is symbolized through a complex of poetical and historical references and allusions. As Robert Evans writes, "So often does he deal with poetry and poetics that these subjects become the major themes, or subject matter, of the book, while the journey down the Concord and Merrimack Rivers gently recedes from the reader's view until it is quite lost from focus." [16] Thoreau may argue in anticipation of *Walden* that the transcendentalist's "process of discovery is very simple. An unwearied and systematic application of known laws to nature causes the unknown to reveal themselves," but language in *A Week* is not merely a tool like "a plumb line, a level, a surveyor's compass, a thermometer, or a barometer!" (*Week,* 478–79). If language opens the path to universal knowledge, it also uncovers unconscious desires, dreams, fears, and passions. More directly than in *Walden,* Thoreau questions the adequacy of an immediate, sensuous communion with nature.

Every schoolchild knows that *Walden* is about innocence, the auroral Adam bathed in the primal light of nature. Writing that work is a formal attempt to preserve the meaning and truth discovered in the woods. In this sense, *Walden* displays a mode of writing that is fundamentally journalistic, not in the sense of recording events in linear sequence but in the close correlation of writing and experience. Although apparently but a short step from the formlessness of the *Journals, A Week* depends upon a fundamental difference between the experience of the voyage in 1839 and the writing of the text. [17] John's death (1842) figures pervasively in the work as the unspoken sign of an irrecoverable companionship. The more general dilemma of the historian reflects some of the personal anxiety Thoreau must have felt: "Critical acumen is exerted in vain to uncover the past; the *past* cannot be *presented;* we cannot know what we are not" (*Week,* 202). Thoreau may continue in this same passage to claim that "one veil hangs over past, present, and future, and it is the province of the historian to find out, not what was, but what is." However, such a conception of natural duration is complicated by the immediacy of the brother's absence, which continues to raise questions about the relation of experience and language, presence and representation. This anxiety concerning the dualities of transience and endurance governs Thoreau's discourse on friendship, thus extending the personal dilemma to the broader domain of social relations and human brotherhood.

A Week directly confronts our alienation from nature by attempting to reflect on the essence of language. The work is full of references to the Fall, all of which are closely associated in Thoreau's effort to analyze the origins of the modern American fall. The Indian's primal participation in nature must be reconstructed from the fragments of a vanishing culture: arrowheads, bits of pottery, the buried brands of a hunter's campfire. "Sunday" carefully subverts Christian orthodoxy by arguing that Christ's doctrinal "conformity to tradition" initiated a systematic metaphysics that violates the infinite variety of natural creation. The Christian's "cut and dried" ideology is explicitly related to the American colonist's clearing of the wilderness. Thoreau's American Adam *plants* "the civil apple tree," whose "perfume" invades the wilderness: "Some spring the white man came, built him a house, and made a clearing here, letting in the sun, dried up a farm, piled up the old gray stones in fences, cut down the pines around his dwelling, planted orchard seeds brought from the old country, and persuaded the civil apple tree to blossom next to the wild pine and the juniper, shedding its perfume in the wilderness" (*Week*, 64–65). Throughout the narrative, the apple tree functions as an emblem of this American fall. It is the tree against whose trunk the brains of Hannah Dustan's infant child are dashed by Indians and yet from which "many . . . in later times have lived to say that they have eaten of the fruit" (426–27). Only at the very end of the voyage does the poet transform it back into "the wild apple-tree" to which the brothers may fasten their craft (518).

The corruption of the white colonists and the indiscriminate progress of the modern age compel Thoreau to substitute a spiritual frontier for the vanishing physical wilderness. History has generated a split between the spiritual and the actual that violates the wholeness of divine creation and signifies nineteenth-century Americans' falling away from their true being. The superficiality of Thoreau's generation is the result of the incapacity to relate apparent oppositions, to see the spiritual depth blossoming in the actual surface of things. Being is not merely concealed from man, but divided and fragmented by Thoreau's contemporaries themselves, who have purchased their own fall. The poet must be more than an inspired explorer who discovers what is present; the poet must also be a visionary who will redeem Being by restoring the active relation of surface and depth, time and eternity, the particular and the universal:

> The frontiers are not east or west, north or south, but wherever a man *fronts* a fact, though that fact be his neighbor, there is an unsettled wilderness between him and Canada, between him and the setting sun, or, farther still, between him and *it*. Let him build himself a log house with the bark on where he is, *fronting* IT, and wage there an old French war for seven or seventy years, with Indians and Rangers, or whatever else may come between him and the reality, and save his scalp if he can. [*Week*, 401]

"Building" is dramatized in the language of the passage itself, which allows the unnameable Being ("IT") to be "fronted" through language. If direct participation in the language of nature is no longer possible for the fallen nineteenth-century American, Thoreau attempts to open a path homeward by reflecting on the nature of language.

The literary form of *A Week* appears to be modeled after the natural flow of the river journey. Thoreau seems to elide any basic distinction between writing and experience by elaborately developing the voyage as a metaphor for composition. I have already suggested how his brother's death disrupts the easy equation of literary form and natural order. But there is other evidence to indicate that the experience of the voyage is inadequate to capture the presence of Being. The ecstatic moment of transcendental vision atop Saddleback Mountain is interpolated into the narrative from a later excursion, which Thoreau had made to the Berkshires and Catskills in 1844. The addition is motivated by the writer's description of the morning mists that obscure the sunrise for the brothers in the opening paragraphs of "Tuesday": "Though we were enveloped in mist as usual, we trusted that there was a bright day behind it" (*Week*, 233). Thoreau tells the Saddleback anecdote in order to demonstrate the limits of such "fogs," which in the given context must be taken figuratively for the obscurity in which we ordinarily live. Thoreau even playfully suggests that the narrative itself has been obscured by such fog: "As we cannot distinguish objects through this dense fog, let me tell this story more at length" (234).

These contextual clues indicate the story's importance as a supplement to the voyage, which at this moment at least leaves the poet in obscurity rather than offering him clear vision. Once the solitary traveler has experienced "the gracious god" rising above the fog and mists of temporal existence, he must descend Saddleback "in the region of cloud and drizzling rain" (*Week*, 248). This emblematic reentrance into time provides an appropriate transition for the writer back to the original "Tuesday" morning: "But now we must make haste back before the fog disperse the blithe Merrimack water." Brought together in the poet's composition of *A Week*, the foggy morning in 1839 and the excursion to Saddleback in 1844 offer an integrated presentation of the relation of temporal illusion and obscurity to eternal reality and clarity. Yet, it is an eminently "literary" achievement, which Thoreau makes no effort to disguise. Nature may be sufficient unto itself, but Thoreau suggests here the need for a poetic composition that will allow us entrance into the complex structure of the natural order. The Saddleback episode argues against the ability of any immediate experience to bring the truth of nature into proximity with man.

The poetic form of *A Week* is also made explicit by the week that Thoreau deletes from his narrative of the 1839 voyage. This omission is especially significant because it occurs at the precise end of the outward voyage, at the moment when the literal and metaphorical origin of the rivers is anticipated: "Thus, in fair days as well as foul, we had traced up the river to which our native stream is a tributary, until from Merrimack it became the Pemigewasset that leaped by our side, and when we had passed its fountainhead, the Wild Amonoosuck, whose puny channel was crossed at a stride, guiding us toward its distant source among the mountains, at length, without its guidance, we were enabled to reach the summit of AGIOCOCHOOK"

(*Week,* 414). The "fountainhead" is "crossed at a stride" and the "guidance" of the rivers is left behind as the travelers head for yet another "summit."

This casual reference to both the source of the rivers "among the mountains" and the summit of Agiocochook undercuts the relation between the actual and spiritual voyages Thoreau has developed so carefully in the preceding narrative. Whatever the brothers "discover" in the mountains is deleted from the text. One suspects that this is the same kind of temporal condensation to be found in *Walden,* the single week offering a more unified structure for Thoreau's philosophic reflections and his parody of measured time. Historically, the second week's journey was conducted "alternately by foot and stage," which may have caused Thoreau to omit the week as disruptive of the purer and simpler fluvial excursion.[18] These formal and biographical explanations are certainly acceptable enough to account for the deletion.

However, within the context of Thoreau's philosophic and poetic aims, this omission is as significant and literary as the interpretation of the Saddleback episode, which has attracted such extended critical attention. In fact, the content of the "Tuesday" vision may tell us something about Thoreau's reasons for omitting the significant approach to the origin in "Thursday." On Saddleback, the full vision of the sun-god at his fullest radiance is denied the lonely traveler:

> But, alas, owing, as I think, to some unworthiness in myself, my private sun did stain himself, and
> > "Anon permit the basest clouds to ride
> > With ugly wrack on his celestial face," —
> for before the god had reached the zenith the heavenly pavement rose and embraced my wavering virtue, or rather I sank down again into that "forlorn world," from which the celestial sun had hid his visage. [*Week,* 247–48]

In this passage the distinction between "my private sun" and the "celestial face" of the eternal god is caused by an "unworthiness" in the mortal who yearns for divine vision. Thoreau's "unworthiness" appears to be a conventional reference to his limited mortal capacity for apprehending the universal. Yet, in the preceding paragraph he offers a clue to a precise notion of this "stain" that obscures his vision. The dawn itself is a full, untranslatable presence: "As there was wanting the symbol, so there was not the substance of impurity, *no spot nor stain.* It was a favor for which to be forever silent to be shown this vision" (*Week,* 246; my italics). Thoreau is clearly incapable of remaining silent, however, especially during the literary moment in which he reconstructs his experience on the mountain. Purity is associated with the absence of symbolism in the spiritual "fact" of divine presence. Even so, such mystery can only be recaptured through language, and Thoreau offers a gaudy panoply of rhetorical figures and classical references to approximate his vision. He concludes such "unworthy" literary flights by qualifying what the reader has been allowed to see: "But my muse would fail to convey an impression of the gorgeous tapestry by which I was surrounded, such as men see faintly reflected afar off in the chambers of the east" (247). The verbal effort to "front" the unspeakable purity of "IT" ends by dividing and obscuring its presence. Writing becomes an act of displacing the god in the very struggle to awaken us to his Being.

Thoreau's "unworthiness" in this moment need not, however, be taken as an indication of the essential inadequacy of language. His "stain" is caused by a particular mode of expression that distorts the true poeticality of nature and thus of language itself. William Bysshe Stein sees Thoreau's response to the vision on Saddleback as flawed by the style it employs: "Instead of responding spiritually to the sight, he affects an aesthetic enthusiasm, even as the trite verbal expression of his emotion implies. . . . The pedantry of a bookworm underscores the insincerity of the rapture." [19] In fact, the dominant presence in Thoreau's account is not the concealed divinity arising to view, but the central "I" imposing its will on all that it sees. The moment of vision is transformed into a self-conscious paean: "As the light in the east steadily increased, it revealed to me more clearly the new world into which I had risen in the night, the new terra firma perchance of my future life" (*Week,* 245). The "snowy pastures" spread out "all around beneath me," and the vain "I" sees divinity as a guarantee of immortality: "As I had climbed above storm and cloud, so by successive days' journeys I might reach the region of eternal day, beyond the tapering shadow of the earth" (246). Thus, *"my private sun did stain himself"* marks the failure of such inauthentic poetizing. Because his muse failed, the traveler is condemned to return to the rain and mist surrounding the mountain.

Throughout *A Week* Thoreau insists on a poetry inspired by the divinity in nature and bearing the traces of the god. This is not a simply theory of inspiration, but a complex notion of the play between one's temporal being and the concealed immanence of the divine: "When the poet is most inspired, is stimulated by an *aura* which never even colors the afternoons of common men, then his talent is all gone, and he is no longer a poet. The gods do not grant him any skill more than another. They never put their gifts into his hands, but they encompass and sustain him with their breath" (*Week,* 451). But what is the nature of such poetic saying? The effort of the poet to recollect the Saddleback experience fails when he attempts to transform the divine into his own private possession. Thoreau's "poetic description" is closely related to the technological impulse of the white colonial, who brings his fall into a New World:

> The white man comes, pale as the dawn, with a load of thought, with a slumbering intelligence as a fire raked up, knowing well what he knows, not guessing but calculating; . . . building a house that endures, a framed house.

> He buys the Indian's moccasins and baskets, then buys his hunting-grounds, and at length forgets where he is buried and ploughs up his bones. And here town records, old, tattered, time-worn, weather-stained chronicles, contain the Indian sachem's mark perchance, an arrow or a beaver, and the few fatal words by which he deeded his hunting grounds away. He comes with a list of ancient Saxon, Norman, and Celtic names, and strews them up and down this river.
> [*Week,* 66]

Like the white man's "load of thought" and "framed house," his very "names" represent a desire to possess and control the wilderness. In a similar sense, the poet's insistence on naming the divine reflects his own participation in the original sin of the white settlers. True poetic saying ought to be that language in which the divine is made to abide in its own proper dwelling, not displaced either by the "commonsensical" truths of reason or the "egotistical sublime" of the vain poet.

The failure to recollect the full presence of the divine on Saddleback helps explain the omission of the week's journey to the source in the mountains. In his essays on Hölderlin, which investigate the proximity of poetry and thinking, Heidegger refers to the poetic "measure" whereby man is enabled to span the dimension of "the between of sky and earth": "Man exists as mortal. He is called mortal because he can die. To be able to die means: to be capable of death as death. Only man dies — and indeed continually, so long as he stays on this earth, so long as he dwells. His dwelling, however, rests in the poetic. Hölderlin sees the nature of the 'poetic' in taking of the measure by which the measure-taking of human being is accomplished." [20]

For Heidegger, this measure is both an assertion of man's mortality and a way of thinking of that mortality as man's relation to Being. Poetry constitutes the difference whereby Being is disclosed as the Being of beings. It is a relation that allows Being to appear in its nature, rather than in the form of what we desire from or impose on it. [21] And this nature is disclosed only as the concealment of Being, which is fundamental to the difference constituting Being and beings:

> The measure consists in the way in which the god who remains unknown, is revealed *as* such by the sky. God's appearance through the sky consists in a disclosing that lets us see what conceals itself, but lets us see it not by seeking to wrest what is concealed out of its concealedness, but only by guarding the concealed in its self-concealment. Thus the unknown god appears as the unknown by way of the sky's manifestness. This appearance is the measure against which man measures himself. [22]

The language that insists on disclosure falsifies the nature of language for both Thoreau and Heidegger. The origin of the rivers (and thus the "goal" of the voyage) is not simply *omitted* from the narrative; the text itself becomes a way of disclosing the concealedness of the origin as its very nature. The authentic philosophic origin — Being-in-itself — is allowed to emerge only in the narrative of the journey itself, which preserves the mystery in the production of its signs.

The subsequent discussion of Thoreau's poetics will attempt to demonstrate that this apparently paradoxical manner of "fronting" Being is an essentially poetic activity. It is the aim of such poetry to open the way to an authentic human dwelling: the establishment of human being-in-common in the world. Perhaps this is why Thoreau selects the first stanza from George Herbert's "Vertue" to open the section immediately following the deferred week in "Thursday":

> Sweet days, so cool, so calm, so bright,
> The bridal of the earth and sky,
> Sweet dews shall weep thy fall to-night,
>   For thou must die.[23]

Herbert's lament about the transience of nature and its association with the inevitability of man's death effects the narrative entrance back into time.[24] But the lines of the poem resonate with other associations in *A Week* to suggest a spiritualized human temporality that differs from the measured time of "common men" or meaningless seasonal repetition. The days are "sweet" because they are the "bridal of the earth and sky." And yet this marriage of earthly and divine is the result of the days' relation to the night. Thoreau's misquotations, "Sweet days" and "Sweet dews," are telling, because they make more explicit the subtler equation in Herbert's alliteration of "Sweet day" with "The dew." The metaphysical pun "to-night" and "to [unto] night" suggests how the dews fulfill their nature by bringing the "days" into relation to the night. The concealed divine, in the form of the night, brings the nature of the day into its own by virtue of the divine's self-concealedness. Time and nature are made "bright" by the measure that relates them to their own temporality. Herbert's "Vertue" minimizes the emphasis I have placed on "day[s]" by adding stanzas concerning the same evanescence in the "Sweet rose" and "Sweet spring," only to end with lines that superficially would seem more appropriate for the conventional interpretation of Thoreau's transcendentalism:

> Onely a sweet and vertuous soul,
> Like season'd timber, never gives;
> But though the whole world turn to coal,
>   Then chiefly lives.

The origin in the mountains is displaced by the poetic voyage itself, whose source is to be discovered in this ever-renewed "fronting" of time and eternity, beings and Being, being in the world and death. My emphasis on these lines from Herbert would be excessive were it not that they are so clearly associated with Thoreau's own conception of spiritual voyaging. One recalls that the brothers' boat has been artfully constructed with an eye to "The bridal of the earth and sky." It is "painted green below, with a border of blue, with reference to the two elements in which it was to spend its existence." As Thoreau interprets such iconography: "If rightly made, a boat would be a sort of amphibious animal, a creature of two elements, related by one half its structure to some swift and shapely fish, and by the other to some strong-winged and graceful bird" (*Week,* 16). Yet, this boat is merely a painted symbol, whose true "art is all . . . but the wood" (17). The vehicle of spiritual voyaging—of human dwelling in time—is what the paint only crudely represents: the poetry of being that is the essential subject of the writer's journey. Perhaps this conjunction of voyaging and dwelling, transience and endurance, openness and concealment is closer to the true architecture of the "House Beautiful" Thoreau had built in his dreams at Walden.

In both *A Week* and *Walden,* "wildness" is the word Thoreau uses to indicate the unnameable in nature that the modern American has forgotten. Critics frequently refer to the "wild" as the element of nature's potential energy: the possibility of regeneration and transformation. This inner-structuring principle of nature cannot be itself measured or named; it is the presence of the divine which is forever absent, like the elusive loon in *Walden.* In *A Week* the Indian epitomizes the individual who can dwell by "fronting" this wildness, and thus it is the life of the Indian that gives us some further hint of the nature of poetry. When Thoreau writes that "gardening is civil and social, but it wants the vigor and freedom of the forest and the outlaw," there seems to be a clear distinction between the conventional polarities of city and frontier, form and openness, law and freedom. But these oppositions are resolved in the Indian's mode of being, itself an "intercourse with Nature": "We would not always be soothing and taming nature, breaking the horse and the ox, but sometimes ride the horse wild and chase the buffalo. The Indian's intercourse with Nature is at least such as admits of the greatest independence of each. If he is somewhat of a stranger in her midst, the gardener is too much of a familiar" (*Week,* 69–70).

The savage is not closer to nature in a conventional Romantic sense, but rather is "somewhat of a stranger." [25] I am reminded of how Thoreau's familiarity with the divine on Saddleback quickly turned into a desire for possession. Instead, the Indian or the poet participates in nature by virtue of a certain strangeness, which is in the nature of each person's relation to Being as the disclosure of what is concealed *as* concealment. This reciprocal difference—self-recognition through strangeness—is what makes possible being-in-common and human dwelling. It is not alienation in an existential sense, but an "intercourse" that "admits of the greatest independence of each." [26] In such a manner man "fronts" his own strangeness as the measure of his relation to the "wildness" of Being. What appears to be a polar opposition ought to be considered the ontological difference (in the Heideggerean terms I have employed) in which man takes up his poetic vocation on earth.[27] True poetry speaks endlessly this difference, because it is the enduring saying of the measure-taking of being human.

Most would agree that for Thoreau history is not the mere crudity of what happened, but the natural emergence and evolution of Being. It would seem to be a simple step to assert that Being in its essence is its "coming into being," but much is lost by such shortcuts of thought. Being is what endures in its own withholding and is disclosed as such by thinking. *Understanding* as the "possession" of Being in ideas or words is a falsification, indeed *the* violation perpetrated by "white men" and their Christian theology. In *A Week* Thoreau searches the classics in an effort to retrieve the original wholeness of the relation of Being and beings, Being and thought, as the essence of history:

> The fable, which is naturally and truly composed, so as to satisfy the imagination ere it addresses the understanding, beautiful though strange as a wildflower, is to the wise man an apothegm and admits of his most generous interpretation. When we read that Bacchus made the Tyrrhenian mariners mad, so that they leapt into the sea, mistaking it for a meadow full of flowers, and so became dolphins, we are not concerned about the historical truth of this, but rather a higher poetical truth. We seem to hear the music of a thought, and care not if the understanding be not gratified. [*Week*, 72-73]

The fable makes possible a thinking prior to ordinary cognition, a thinking that is able to step outside the concern for understanding "literal" distinctions. By establishing a primary relationship between Being and thinking, *mythus* (of which fable is but a part) is the authentic saying: the opening of the way to the conversation of Being among men.

Heidegger puts the problem in the following terms in "Hölderlin and the Essence of Poetry": "The poet himself stands between the former — the gods, and the latter — the people. He is one who has been cast out — out into that *Between*, between gods and men. But only and for the first time in this Between is it decided, who man is and where he is settling his existence. 'Poetically, dwells man on this earth.'"[28] As I have already suggested, this is not simply "mediation" but what I have chosen to call "fronting," which in Thoreau's own usage retains the sense of the frontier. For Heidegger, this is the place of *emergence* of the measure of the between of earth and sky, of Being and beings in the world. Thoreau's conception of *mythus* establishes a similar site for human dwelling:

> The hidden significance of these fables which is sometimes thought to have been detected, the ethics running parallel to the poetry and history, are not so remarkable as the readiness with which they may be made to express a variety

of truths. As if they were the skeletons of still older and more universal truths than any whose flesh and blood they are for the time made to wear. It is like striving to make the sun, or the wind, or the sea symbols to signify exclusively the particular thoughts and dreams of men as its hieroglyphics to address men unborn. In the history of the human mind these glowing and ruddy fables precede the noonday thoughts of men, as Aurora the sun's rays. The matutine intellect of the poet, keeping in advance of the glare of philosophy always dwells in this auroral atmosphere. [*Week,* 76]

Mythus, "authentic poetry," is itself the facilitation of the language of Being, not a mere symbolic product or representation. *Mythus* endures only through change and transformation, by the perpetual renewal of the reciprocal difference that makes the project of human dwelling possible and necessary. An "ancient fable" achieves its "completeness and roundness" only by means of a ceaseless history of interpretation, in itself the essence of the historical situation of one's being as temporal:

> By such slow aggregation has mythology grown from the first. The very nursery tales of this generation were the nursery tales of primeval races. They migrate from east to west, and again from west to east; now expanded into the "tale divine" of bards, now shrunk into a popular rhyme. This is an approach to that universal language which men have sought in vain. This fond reiteration of the oldest expressions of truth by the latest posterity, content with slightly and religiously retouching the old material, is the most impressive proof of a common humanity. [*Week,* 74]

Thoreau underscores the transience of contemporary values by suggesting how mythology endures through diverse migrations and cultural appropriations. If ancient poetry has "now shrunk into a popular rhyme," it reflects the destitution of our age.[29] But Thoreau's characteristic verbal play implies a rebirth in the "nursery" that would bring about the "popularity" of true poetic saying as that which relates the social self to being. In this way poetry informs the ontological movement of beings in time as historical.[30] This process suggests that the realization of *mythus* is the project of human dwelling on earth, the realization of being with others, not only the "proof" but the *constitution* of a "common humanity." Poetry as an entrance into man's being in time establishes the foundation on which Thoreau bases his subsequent attacks on the expectations of "common men" for "heaven": "What is this heaven which they expect, if it is no better than they expect? Are they prepared for a better than they can now imagine? Where is the heaven of him who dies on a stage, in a theatre? Here or nowhere is our heaven" (*Week,* 501).

"We have need to be earth-born as well as heaven-born, γηγενεῖς, as was said of the Titans of old, or in a better sense than they," Thoreau warns those who long for an eternal life out of time. And this "earth we till and love" is more truly cultivated through our "music," which allows us to constitute ourselves as other than the mere animal: "With our music we would fain challenge transiently another and finer sort of intercourse than our daily toil permits. The strains come back to us amended in the echo, as when a friend reads our verse. Why have they so painted the fruits, and freighted them with such fragrance as to satisfy a more than animal appetite?" (*Week*, 503). This is a remarkable passage, bringing together poetry and friendship as well as suggesting a contradiction of Thoreau's earlier remarks about the inferiority of word to deed. Such epigrammatic saws as "A sentence should read as if its author, had he held a plough instead of a pen, could have drawn a furrow straight and deep to the end" seem to imply that writing is a mere representation of what could have been more authentically lived (*Week*, 136). Yet, the distinction between the immediacy of experience and the secondary mediation of words is part of the modern fall — the misinterpretation of Being and beings — that Thoreau has outlined in *A Week*. "The poet sings how the blood flows in his veins" is neither metaphorical nor representational, but a saying that is simultaneous with human action (*Week*, 117). Authentic poetry *is* action, in itself what constitutes action as such. Modern "civilization" has degraded the Muse:

> We cannot escape the impression that the Muse has stooped a little in her flight, when we come to the literature of civilized eras. Now first we hear of various ages and styles of poetry; it is pastoral, and lyric, and narrative, and didactic; but the poetry of runic monuments is of one style, and for every age. The bard has in great measure lost the dignity and sacredness of his office. Formerly he was called a *seer*, but now it is thought that one man sees as much as another. He has no longer the bardic rage, and only conceives the deed, which he formerly stood ready to perform. [*Week*, 484]

For both Heidegger and Thoreau, the divorce of word and deed is the subject of the true poet in "a destitute time." It is a separation that points toward a fundamental violence: the distinction between Being (*physis*) and thinking (*logos*) that is the target of Heidegger's destruction of Western metaphysics and Thoreau's more modest criticism of civilization and its discontents. Heidegger's attempt to recapture the original pre-Socratic meaning of the identity-in-difference of *physis* and *logos* has some remarkable affinities with the poetics outlined in *A Week*. In his analysis of the thought of Heraclitus and Parmenides, Heidegger attempts to restore the original bond between these two aspects of Being. In this originary sense, *physis* is the Being of nature as unfolding and emergence:

> *Physis* as emergence can be observed everywhere, e.g. in celestial phenomena (the rising of the sun), in the rolling of the sea, in the growth of the plants, in the coming forth of man and animal from the womb. But *physis*, the realm of that

which arises, is not synonymous with these phenomena, which today we regard as part of "nature." This opening up and inward-jutting-beyond-itself [in-sich-aus-sich-hinaus-stehen] must not be taken as a process among other processes that we observe in the realm of the essent. *Physis* is being itself, by virtue of which essents become and remain observable. . . .

 . . . *Physis* means the power that emerges and the enduring realm under its sway. This power of emerging and enduring includes "becoming" as well as "being" in the restricted sense of inert duration. *Physis* is the process of a-rising, of emerging from the hidden, whereby the hidden is first made to stand.[31]

Heidegger speaks of *physis* as "scattering" and "opening" in order to establish a functional relationship with *logos* as "gathering" and "bringing together," but only "in the sense of 'permanent gathering.'"[32] Interpreted subsequently as "thinking," "word," "logic," "meaning," *logos* gradually drifted apart from its originary bond with *physis*: "In thus maintaining a bond, the *logos* has the character of permeating power, of *physis*. It does not let what it holds in its power dissolve into an empty freedom from opposition, but by uniting the opposites maintains the full sharpness of their tension."[33] The reciprocal difference of *physis* and *logos* is falsified by substituting such terms as "object" and "subject," "nature" and "mind." Their originary bond depends upon the permeation of *physis* and *logos*, each of which finds its power in and through the other.[34]

The conventional formulation of Thoreau's transcendentalism depends upon polarities — subject and object, individual and nature, time and eternity — that lead to the critical conclusion that "he is not a writer with settled or comfortable views but one committed to forcing together opposites in the hope they will mesh."[35] Much of our literary criticism still relies on the traditional distinction between immediate experience and its secondary representation. In this view, any system of signs operates only in reference to a prior "reality": an object or event. In the originary sense that links *physis* and *logos*, however, action and word are integrally bound together. The event does not precede its representation, but is constituted as event only through the signs that situate the event in time. Writing about Sir Walter Raleigh, Thoreau remarks:

The word which is best said came nearest to not being spoken at all, for it is cousin to a deed which the speaker could have better done. Nay, almost it must have taken the place of a deed by some urgent necessity, even by some misfortune, so that the truest writer will be some captive knight, after all. And perhaps the fates had such a design, when, having stored Raleigh so richly with the substance of life and experience, they made him a fast prisoner, and compelled him to make his words his deeds, and transfer to his expression the emphasis and sincerity of his action. [*Week,* 134]

Raleigh's natural and fluent style opened the possibility of a "new world" of poetic dwelling, which ironically did not flower in the American colony he never visited. When Thoreau refers to "some urgent necessity, even some misfortune" by which one is compelled to substitute words for deeds, he implies a more fundamental imprisonment than Raleigh's political captivity. He recalls the destitute time of America's origin, when the white man arrived without the poetic vision of Raleigh. The transient and ephemeral events of American history have not been constituted by that poetry of being which "contains only enduring and essential truth" (*Week*, 75). The culture that distinguishes poet and hero, word and deed, undermines its own history. Raleigh stands as the lost figure of the true New World discoverer, whose bonding of experience and word might have restored the "new beginning," the "origin," violated by the actual white settlers long before their arrival: "There have been some nations who could do nothing but construct tombs, and these are the only traces which they have left. They are the heathen" (220).[36]

A Week is an attempt to think poetically and thus retrieve this lost origin: the ontological bond of man and nature, time and eternity, being in the world and Being. The apparently discursive form of the work is designed to call forth this identity-in-difference that is approximated in Heidegger's interpretation of the pre-Socratic understanding of Being as *physis* and *logos*. In its effort to come to terms with the fact of John Thoreau's death, *A Week* both reflects upon and employs a poetry that opens the possibility of a true dwelling on earth. Poetry discloses man's destitution in order to "put him on the way" to the being of language: the language of being.[37] Attempts to analyze the unity of *A Week* are inevitably restricted by the Western philosophic heritage that Thoreau attacks in this work. "Examine your authority," Thoreau insists, "you did not invent it; it was imposed on you. . . . Your scheme must be the framework of the universe; all other schemes will soon be ruins" (*Week*, 88). Do we imagine that our naive categories of thought could lead to anything but contradiction, confusion, and paradox? We have lacked *deliberate* method all along.

In his introduction to the Rinehart edition of *A Week*, Walter Harding casually remarks the diversity of subjects incorporated into the work: "Thus he introduces into the text essays on fables, the Christian religion, poetry, Sir Walter Raleigh, reform movements, history, friendship, Aulus Persius Flaccus, Goethe, cattle shows, and Chaucer, to name only a few of the more important ones. Each of these essays is basically independent and can stand alone."[38]

Harding's list offers an appropriate contemporary example of what Thoreau argues the "modern" has done to the harmony of classical thought. I have already demonstrated how Thoreau's subversion of Christian theology opens the way for an originary poetry or *mythus* that might constitute our being in time. I have insisted with Thoreau that *mythus* is the inauguration of history in its nature, not merely the record of isolated events. The call for a renewed poetic saying is particularly urgent for Thoreau, who finds himself in an alienated time that has been created by modern American society. Mythology, Christianity, poetry, history, social reform, and friendship: these are the generic topics of Harding's list. They all have their places — are "situated" — in Thoreau's poetic thinking. "Friendship" alone remains to be accounted for, and it adds a final support to Thoreau's dynamic structuring of a "hypaethral" dwelling: "I thought that one peculiarity of my 'Week' was its hypaethral character, to use an epithet applied to those Egyptian temples which are open to the heavens above, under the ether. . . . I trust it does not smell so much of the study and library, even of the poet's attic, as of the fields and woods, that it is a hypaethral or unroofed book, lying open under the ether, and permeated by it, open to all weathers, not easy to be kept on a shelf." [39]

Thoreau's discussion of friendship in "Wednesday" seems self-evident in terms of the conventional interpretation of his transcendentalism: true friendship is a simulacrum of the Ideal for which human beings yearn. The relation of the brothers on the voyage is a microcosm of the social communality Thoreau desires. And yet, for many critics this episode remains one of the most troubling in his writings, betraying as it does an underlying anxiety concerning the transience of human relations and the inability of the individual to discover an enduring relation with others. [40] A certain nostalgia and sense of loss dominate this section, and the importance of John's death as a controlling concern cannot be overemphasized. When Thoreau writes that "friendship is evanescent in every man's experience, and remembered like heat lightning in past summers," one senses that Thoreau's own identity has been threatened by his brother's absence (*Week*, 344).

What is most remarkable, however, is the extent to which friendship is related to the ideals of poetry discussed in the rest of the volume. Thoreau makes little attempt to relate friendship and poetry directly; in fact, there seems to be far less analysis of interpersonal communication than we might expect on such a subject. Emerson's "Friendship," however, does repeatedly stress the relation between poetry and friendship: "We seek our friend not sacredly, but with an adulterate passion which would appropriate him to ourselves. In vain. We are armed all over with subtle antagonisms, which, soon as we meet, begin to play, and translate all poetry into stale prose." [41] Emerson stresses the ideal self-consciousness that is merely shadowed in the temporal friend: "Thou art not Being, as Truth is, as Justice is, — thou art not my soul, but a picture and effigy of that." [42] Thoreau suggests that it is the longing for the Ideal that may corrupt authentic friendship, just as it had perverted his "poetry" on Saddleback: "When they say farewell, then indeed we begin to keep them company. How often we find ourselves turning our backs on our actual Friends, that we may go and meet their ideal cousins. I would that I were worthy to be any man's Friend" (*Week*, 350).

In my analysis of Thoreau's poetics, I have argued that human dwelling depends upon the interdependence of *physis* and *logos*, the constitution of Being in and through the poetic saying of beings. Unlike *Walden*, the text of *A Week* is not merely a metaphor for a fuller, more immediate experience of the divine, but the "bringing-into-being" of the nature of such experience. The endurance of friendship shares this recollective or cognitive quality, for the words of love may be "few and rare indeed, but, like a strain of music, they are incessantly repeated and modulated by the memory" (*Week*, 354). The truly universal friendship enters *mythus*, revealing and completing itself only in its temporal transformations. The "presence of loss" is a necessary aspect of the path that leads to an understanding of the essence of friendship; only in this way is the friend constituted as friend. Evanescence is not so much transcended as *related* to the enduring and universal aspects of human interrelation. In a curious monologue addressed to a hypothetical friend, Thoreau insists: "I love thee not as something private and personal, which is *your own*, but as something universal and worthy of love, *which I have found*. . . . I did not think that humanity was so rich. Give me an opportunity to live." Thoreau appears to establish a hierarchy of ideal love and secular friendship in the manner of Emerson, but he continues in the following way: "You are the fact in a fiction, you are the truth more strange and admirable than fiction. Consent only to be what you are. I alone will never stand in your way" (355). The "fiction" refers to the desired ideal, which appears to be realized as a possibility through the "fact" of the secular friend, which revises the Emersonian apothegm: "Friends such as we desire are dreams and fables." [43]

In this context we may recall the prose that prefaces "The Atlantides" in *A Week:* "The Friend is some fair floating isle of palms eluding the mariner in Pacific seas. Many are the dangers to be encountered, equinoctial gales and coral reefs, ere he may sail before the constant trades. But who would not sail through mutiny and storm, even over Atlantic waves, to reach the fabulous retreating shores of some continent man?" (345). The quest may be governed by a transcendental ideal, but it is finally man in time who is the goal of such a journey. Thoreau recognizes that the elusive fiction of ideal Friendship may be constructed only on the basis of human differences, which are essential to being in the world itself: "We must accept or refuse one another as we are. I could tame a hyena more easily than my Friend. He is a material no tool of mine will work" (*Week*, 374).

This is more than a simple assertion of the radical individualism that Emerson reaffirms at the end of his essay: "I do then with my friends as I do with my books. I would have them where I can find them, but I seldom use them." [44] The friend points toward the divine by virtue of his own self-preservation, thus disclosing the ground of human dwelling as the difference between Being and beings in the world and also between being and being. Like the poet who would appropriate the divine as a guarantee of his own identity or the white settlers who subordinate natural wildness to their Anglo-Saxon names, we violate our friends if we attempt to make them our property. In this regard, Thoreau does agree with Emerson, who writes, "Leave to girls and boys to regard a friend as property, and to suck a short and all-confounding pleasure, instead of the noblest benefit." [45]

The ontological implications of friendship are constantly emphasized. As we have seen, ordinary language may suffice for the exchange of news or goods, but only poetry speaks of our spiritual situation in time. The ratio holds as well for mere neighbors and true friends: "We do not wish for Friends to feed and clothe our bodies, — neighbors are kind enough for that, — but to do the like office to our spirits" (*Week*, 351). Like poetic saying, the language of friendship is universal to the extent that it makes individuality possible. The friend expresses the truth of man's being in the divine love that springs from human difference: "To his Friend a man's peculiar character appears in every feature and in every action, and it is thus drawn out and improved by him." Only by understanding this pervasive notion of "identity-in-difference" as the ontological basis of Thoreau's poetics may we begin to resolve the apparent contradictions in *A Week*. Critics have been too hasty in leaping to the conclusion of the essay on friendship to quote: "My Friend is not of some other race or family of men, but flesh of my flesh, bone of my bone. He is my real brother. I see his nature groping yonder like mine. We do not live far apart" (*Week*, 375). This vision of human dwelling in common has been achieved poetically by the entire discourse on friendship. "Brotherhood" springs from the recognition of differences and the necessity of our social condition. Thoreau realizes in this essay the full implications of what Emerson had termed "a sort of paradox in nature": "I who alone am, I who see nothing in nature whose existence I can affirm with equal evidence to my own, behold now the semblance of my being, in all its height, variety and curiosity, reiterated in a foreign form." [46]

As most commentators have noticed, the essay on friendship prefigures the more general social vision of *Walden*. Emerson privileges the "law of *one to one*" as the basis of a transcendental poetic, which seems to be at odds with social intercourse: "The high freedom of great conversation . . . requires an absolute running of two souls into one." [47] By stressing the difference of self and other as the principle of friendship, Thoreau makes a more viable connection between brotherhood and wider social relations. The ideal of brotherly love achieved at the end of this digression is not merely a representation of the natural relation of John and Henry during the voyage, but a more enduring constitution of what eludes us in ordinary experience. *A Week* returns us to time by means of a journey into poetry, the language of which is itself a reflection on the nature of language and the social intercourse it initiates.

Walden mocks measured time by finding the signs of divinity in all seasons, in every weather. *A Week* demonstrates how Thoreau struggles not to transcend the temporal but to enter it more authentically than either clocks or unreflective experience allow. *A Week* is a way of thinking the being of poetry as the poetry of being. The experience of nature — of human nature, of nature in itself — is always on the way to language, to the poetic saying that constitutes it as human history. Much of this seems lacking in *Walden;* Thoreau seems to give up the reflection on language that organizes *A Week* for a more immediate dialogue with the sound of nature.

I have already suggested how *Walden* appears to suffer from the same dualistic mentality that is the source of modern alienation for the poet of *A Week*. Perhaps the failure of *A Week* made Thoreau impatient for clarity and understanding, and he sought a form and order that would permit his readers to see in more accustomed ways. Yet, such accommodation has its inevitable costs, and Thoreau has paid richly as the prophet of posters, the politician's poet, the soothesayer. The "rambling," "discursive," "disjointed," "contradictory" qualities of *A Week* tell us more about our criticism, our culture, and our language than they express the truth of Thoreau. What Heidegger says of Hölderlin's timeliness seems equally appropriate for the poet of *A Week on the Concord and Merrimack Rivers:* "It would thus be mistaken to believe that Hölderlin's time will come only on that day when 'everyman' will understand his poetry. It will never arrive in such a misshapen way; for it is its own destitution that endows the era with forces by which, unaware of what it is doing, it keeps Hölderlin's poetry from becoming timely."[48]

3.

The Metaphysics of Imagination: Narrative Consciousness in Hawthorne's *The Blithedale Romance*

Like a respectable woman turned harlot, I must constantly try to overcome the reserve that makes a gentleman reluctant to talk about himself. This book, however, is made up of nothing else. I did not foresee this sudden complication, which may cause me to abandon the whole project. I foresaw no other difficulty than that of having the courage to tell the truth about everything. But that is the least of my problems.
— Stendhal, *Souvenirs d'égotisme*

Far in the woods they sang their unreal songs,
Secure. It was difficult to sing in face
Of the object. The singers had to avert themselves
Or else avert the object. Deep in the woods
They sang of summer in the common fields.
— Wallace Stevens, "Credences of Summer"

Recent studies of Nathaniel Hawthorne have attempted to show how the genetic development of his imaginative consciousness unifies and structures his works. Psychoanalytical and psychobiographical critics have stressed the apparently close relations between Hawthorne's existential anxieties and the respective attitudes of his various narrative personae in the tales, sketches, and romances.[1] Formalist and phenomenological critics have relied on the repetition and continuity of certain central images, motifs, and themes to investigate either the coherence of Hawthorne's literary forms or what a phenomenological critic like Edgar Dryden would term "the form of Hawthorne's presence in his work."[2] Each of these varied critical approaches has tried to determine a particular principle of cohesion that would account for the apparent rhetorical, thematic, stylistic, and intellectual repetitions in Hawthorne's collected works.

A few recent critics, however, have attempted to investigate the apparent continuity and repetition in Hawthorne's works in terms of an ever-renewed and often contradictory struggle to redefine the central issues of individual identity, the function of the imagination, the nature of history, and the structure of society. For example, Kenneth Dauber argues that the traditional reliance on the thematic unities in Hawthorne's texts has caused us to simplify the intellectual issues involved by assuming "the unity of the material at issue" and by mistaking paraphrased "images as ideas."[3] Dauber warns us that by concentrating on the apparent resemblances in Hawthorne's works we may have minimized his variety and originality.

The inadequacies of the various critical perspectives that rely on criteria of formal unity and coherence or genetic development and continuity are most evident in considerations of Hawthorne's three major romances. The historical succession of *The Scarlet Letter* (1850), *The House of the Seven Gables* (1851), and *The Blithedale Romance* (1852) would seem to warrant the view that they constitute a trilogy, whose parts are related by an extraordinarily intense and concentrated act of creative imagination. Formally and thematically, these works revolve around the same problems of freedom, interpersonal and social relations, imagination, and history that are also at issue in the earlier tales. The images seem to be drawn from the same source and in themselves would seem to be variant expressions of the same perspectives. Mirrors and masks, portraits and photographs, moonlight and sunlight, enclosed spaces and open spaces, heights and depths, obscurity and clarity: all suggest a unified poetic that enables Hawthorne to deploy his figures with an almost predictable regularity and rigor. Formalist readings of Hawthorne such as Richard Harter Fogle's *Hawthorne's Fiction: The Light and the Dark* (1952), Hyatt Waggoner's *Hawthorne: A Critical Study* (1955), Roy Male's *Hawthorne's Tragic Vision* (1957), and Richard Brodhead's *Hawthorne, Melville, and the Novel* (1976) rely upon the consistency and organic development of Hawthorne's themes and images in his various works. And yet, even these critics are unwilling to conclude that the formal continuities in Hawthorne's collected writings, especially in the three central romances, reflect a unified attitude toward God, man, consciousness, imagination, and society. This apparent discrepancy between form and content threatens the very assumptions on which formalist criticism is based. In response to this dilemma, these critics and others like them tend to establish one of Hawthorne's romances (usually *The Scarlet Letter*) as a model for the proper marriage of form and content. Hawthorne's other works are then measured in terms of such an achievement, and their divergences from this critical ideal are offered as indications of Hawthorne's failure to realize his intellectual aims. I am tempted to say that such "self-fulfilling prophecies" are especially prevalent in formalist literary criticism, but I ought to qualify this judgment by adding that Hawthorne's stylistic and thematic consistencies seem to invite formalist methods of analysis and evaluation.

The Blithedale Romance in particular has been considered the least successful of the three romances, primarily because its characters seem undeveloped and its dramatic action confused by conflicting interests. When the failure of *Blithedale* has not been determined according to certain vague critical criteria of "felt life," "tone," or "realistic" representation, it has been attributed to the divergence of this work from Hawthorne's romantic idealism in *The Scarlet Letter* and *The House of the Seven Gables*.[4]

Even more interesting than these critical judgments of *Blithedale* are those interpretations that seek to restore the romance to its rightful place in Hawthorne's canon. Roy Male's sympathetic reading of *Blithedale* still insists upon subordinating the work to the major themes of the two preceding romances by arguing that the very failure of the characters to attain "tragic vision" reflects the psychic and emotional superficiality of their era: "The implication seems to be that once the normal rhythms of time, the seasons, and love are rejected, they will reassert themselves in ugly distorted forms."[5] The pessimism of *Blithedale* is thus viewed as the negative side of the more vital, positive engagements of humanity's tragic destiny that are dramatized in the two preceding books. As appropriate as such a view is for the historical situation in *Blithedale*, Male bases it on the questionable assumption that Hawthorne still embraces the values suggested by *The Scarlet Letter* or *The House of the Seven Gables*.

Dauber's fertile suggestion that the thematic and imagistic similarities in Hawthorne's works might be the very resource of his originality and vitality ought to be the starting point for a revaluation of Hawthorne's vision in *The Blithedale Romance*. Richard Brodhead notes that "there is a striking degree of continuity in Hawthorne's work — indeed he seems to be telling the same story over and over. But when we look at the ways he tells his story and at the fictional worlds in which he sets it, what is equally striking is how remarkably little his books have in common."[6] As most critics recognize, the story that Hawthorne repeatedly tells primarily concerns the relation of imagination to experience. Hawthorne struggles endlessly to define the nature of the imagination and to determine its function in relation to consciousness, the emotions, and the objective world. In order to understand Hawthorne's shifting use of what are often the same figures, images, and themes, we must first investigate the fundamental conceptual differences among these works. In particular, we must explore Hawthorne's anxiety concerning the relation of the imagination and reality.

In *The Scarlet Letter*, the imagination serves primarily to mediate between the individual and the universal, sensuous particulars and abstract generalities, the phenomenal and the noumenal. The world of sense is constructed of appearances, which in themselves deceive and alienate the perceiving consciousness. Natural objects are no less hieroglyphic and mysterious than the Governor's Hall, whose surface "glittered and sparkled as if diamonds had been flung against it" with the "brilliancy" that "might have befitted Aladdin's palace, rather than the mansion of a grave old Puritan ruler."[7] In the Puritan community, however, there is a marked division between surface appearances, such as the high officials' ruffles and ruffs that Hester sews, and the general moral principles on which the community is established. Hawthorne attributes the failure of this community to its inability to reconcile individual identity and moral law, the particulars of temporal experience and the universal truth of God. This society no longer directly and personally experiences the meaning of original sin, but simply accepts conventional doctrine as it is preached from the pulpit. Dimmesdale's hypocrisy is, of course, an indication of his personal duplicity, but it also reflects the hypocrisy of a spiritual community that maintains its laws at the expense of individual freedom and sustains the eternal by trivializing the temporal and experiential.

Undirected and unchecked, the imagination becomes mere "fancy" or uncontrolled passion that simply contributes to the illusions on which the characters base their lives and values. Hester recognizes the dangers of imaginative license in her own passionate nature, and thus in the first twelve chapters of the romance she remains exiled from society and herself. However, the imagination becomes equally destructive when it is employed primarily for the purposes of stripping away the outer wrappings of the soul to penetrate a "human heart." Thus, Chillingworth's cold rationality offers another version of the misuse of the imagination because it serves to violate the shapes and masks whereby nature or the individual appears in the world. For Hawthorne, the primary conflict does not involve "appearance" and "reality," because the sensuous appearances ought to be understood as inextricably involved in a higher "reality." Like Hegel, Wordsworth, and Emerson, Hawthorne wants to demonstrate the dynamic interrelation of the particular and the universal, the temporal and the eternal.

Like Kant's "schematism" of the pure concepts of understanding, Hawthorne's imagination in *The Scarlet Letter* ought to mediate the eternal "truths of the human heart" and their sensory appearances.[8] Hawthorne is more Hegelian, however, in his analysis of the psychological processes involved in this mediation between the mind and its sensible objects. In keeping with the *felix culpa* structure of the narrative, Hester's exile enables her to achieve that self-consciousness which seems excluded by the very organization of Puritan society. The psychological drama in the second half of *The Scarlet Letter* depends primarily on Hester's awakening self-consciousness which closely follows the basic stages of self-consciousness outlined by Hegel in the *Phenomenology*.[9] The dialectical becoming of Hester's self-awareness in and through others (Pearl, Chillingworth, Dimmesdale) enables her to recognize in her own experience certain psychological universals that have been obscured by the "artifice" of Puritan society.

Central to Hawthorne's spiritual argument, of course, is Hester's discovery of original sin in herself and in others. In Hawthorne's psychic conception of original sin, redemption and sin are dialectically related as the necessary complements of humanity's spiritual nature. Imagination enables the individual to relate his or her own experience to those others through whom he or she has accomplished a self-conscious constitution. In the sympathy or compassion achieved, the individual can identify his or her existential situation with that of others and thus establish a renewed basis for human community. Thus, alienated self-consciousness is actually the necessary stage in a larger process of being, whereby the individual discovers personal meaning and intention in the organic interrelation of individual, family, society, and spirit. Like Hegel's *Geist,* the "spiritual truth" of *The Scarlet Letter* does not displace appearances but synthesizes their variety into a "historical consciousness" wherein alienation, suffering, and ambiguity are placed in the service of a primary spiritual intention. Thus, the narrator of "The Custom-House" employs his own imaginative act of creation to identify with the truth of Hester's self-consciousness. His own narrative method is itself an act of self-consciousness that is frequently compared to Hester's. In reviving the "burning heat" of the scarlet letter, the narrator achieves an imaginative identification with Hester's emblematic education that promises to provide an antidote to the torpor and ennui of his own unspiritual age. In his imaginative rendering of Surveyor Pue's record of the various accounts of Hester's life, the narrator enters into a dialectical relation with the "Hester Prynne" constituted by these diverse historical representations; as a result, the narrator achieves a renewed sense of his own relation to a general historical consciousness.

In *The House of the Seven Gables,* Hawthorne's conception of the imagination still betrays its romantic origins, but the imagination no longer serves simply to mediate between mind and matter, abstract form and sensuous appearance. The imagination itself has become an alchemical force that transmutes inert matter into spiritual gold. Rather than attempting to demonstrate the dialectical interrelation of the sensuous objects of experience and our categories for understanding, Hawthorne relies on a fundamental dualism between the substance of the empirical world and the "aery fancies" of the mind. The opposition between Judge Pyncheon and Clifford that organizes the dramatic action epitomizes this dualism, even though both characters represent extremes of materialism and spiritualism that the narrative ultimately moderates through Hepzibah, Phoebe, and Holgrave. Hawthorne's happy ending seems to reconcile the material wealth of Judge Pyncheon with the imaginative values of his heirs, but these secular goods are clearly subordinated to the triumphant powers of the imagination. As Alfred Marks suggests, it is the imagination itself — as represented by both Clifford and Hawthorne — that "kills" Judge Pyncheon.[10]

In *The Scarlet Letter,* the imagination enables Hester and Dimmesdale to bring to self-consciousness their own hidden natures and to internalize their own sin. Hester's recognition of sin is the basis of her discovery of a relation to a universal spirituality based on the capacity for evil shared by everyone. In *The House of the Seven Gables,* however, an individual's secret sins are signs of a lack of imaginative vitality and spiritual sensibility. "Maule's Curse" itself suggests that the greatest delusion and thus the most profound sin involves the confidence in the world as a substantial "property" that may be owned or possessed. The "original sin" of the Pyncheon family is passed on by a typical historical necessity to the succeeding generations, but Clifford, Holgrave, and Phoebe realize their "innocence" once they have escaped the curse of the fathers. Touched by the sins of the past, they ultimately confront those sins and redeem the past with their own imaginative goodness and love.

However we interpret the final movement of *The Scarlet Letter,* it seems undeniable that Hester has progressed from alienation to some sort of social action as a result of her own experience and recognition of sin. In *The House of the Seven Gables,* however, the promise of love and marriage that ends the text offers less a hope for social reform than an alternative to social corruption. Holgrave's vague and uninformed zeal for social reform is displaced by his love for Phoebe. In *The House of the Seven Gables,* the imaginative construction of reality reveals the superficiality of the world of substance and action. Writing the romance is not a preparation for a more meaningful return to the social world but an alternative to the ineluctable corruption of humanity's social and historical condition. Hester achieves a difficult and tragic love at the end of *The Scarlet Letter,* a love that argues for the bond of sin and redemptive grace. There is little similarity between this anguished love and the "Flower of Eden" that blossoms for Holgrave and Phoebe in the house of death: "They transfigured the earth, and made it Eden again, and themselves the first two dwellers in it. The dead man, so close beside them, was forgotten. At such a crisis, there is no Death; for Immortality is revealed anew, and embraces everything in its hallowed atmosphere." [11] Hester, Pearl, Dimmesdale, and Chillingworth are all transfigured in a moment that is entangled with Dimmesdale's emblematic death. Indeed, Hester's transformation is unthinkable outside the concept of original sin, which couples life and death, fall and redemption. In contrast, in their moment of renewed "innocence," Holgrave and Phoebe "forget" death, and "Immortality . . . embraces everything."

In *The Blithedale Romance,* however, the imagination neither mediates between the mind and its objects nor serves as a simple alternative to the empirical world. The complexity of Hawthorne's vision in this work is formally represented by the chaos of conflicting stories and intentions. Each of the stories in *Blithedale* relies on a different literary form and thus on a different conception of the imagination. In *The Scarlet Letter* and *The House of the*

Seven Gables, Hawthorne's general intention is to synthesize the apparent oppositions between such different narratives as "The Custom-House" and Hester's history, "Maule's Curse" and the love affair of Phoebe and Holgrave. In *The Blithedale Romance,* however, different narrative strategies constantly threaten to subvert one another: Westervelt's and Old Moodie's "romances" invade the presumed "realism" of the Blithedale experiment; Coverdale's own narrative offers an imaginative freedom that displaces the utopians' project; Hollingsworth's philanthropic scheme subverts the communal experiment. Hawthorne makes it quite clear that each of these stories relies on a certain conception of human understanding intimately related to the problems of writing and imaginative representation at the center of the work. *The Scarlet Letter, The House of the Seven Gables,* and *The Blithedale Romance* are all expressly metaliterary works, each of which employs its dramatic action to comment on how and why one writes. Yet, more than the others, *Blithedale* subordinates the substance of what is told to problems inherent in the method of telling.

The Blithedale Romance is composed of three conflicting narratives, each of which has a particular place in Hawthorne's hierarchy of imaginative values. The story of Zenobia, Priscilla, Westervelt, and Old Moodie is a popular romance of the most conventional and often mechanical sort. Wizards and devils, dark and fair ladies, hidden origins, secret compacts, mesmeric machinations, mistaken identities are all characteristic of the form. As a literary mode, such romance employs airy fancy to construct insubstantial worlds for the sake of a certain diversion. As harmless as such fancies might at first appear, however, they are associated throughout *Blithedale* with the sleight-of-hand diabolism of Westervelt and the mesmeric sham of "The Veiled Lady." Just as the popular romance relies on a certain suspension of disbelief in order to maintain its hold over the reader, so Westervelt would substitute his own illusions for reality in order to enchant and possess others. Playing upon his audience's dissatisfaction with its ordinary experience, Westervelt promises to substitute a glittering illusion that hints at a truth hidden from ordinary perception.

On the other hand, the second narrative — the story of the Blithedale experiment and Hollingsworth's competing philanthropic project — depends upon a sort of naive realism, whereby the utopian reformers depart the illusions and corruptions of the city to make direct contact with nature. More importantly, the reformers presume to escape the burden of history and establish a new Arcadia, a fresh and innocent origin for their world of the future. Both their falsification of the past and their anticipation of the future corrupt the immediacy and contact with the present that they seek at Blithedale. Proposed as a quest for a higher and purer reality, the utopian project subtly shares the mesmerist's or popular romancer's yearning to disguise the circumstances of our human situation behind a veil of illusion. Unlike Westervelt, however, the reformers remain largely unaware of their manipulation of the actual and continue to delude themselves by mistaking their own fancies for the most substantial realities.

The third story in *Blithedale* is, of course, Coverdale's struggle to untangle the psychological and supernatural mysteries that govern the two other stories. The reformers' utopian ideals are darkly shadowed by the romance of Zenobia's past, which Hawthorne employs as a parable within the larger narrative to suggest the hidden corruptions that secretly erode hopes for a reformed community. Whatever ills or artifices the reformers had hoped to leave behind in the city have been transported with them to Blithedale. The material circumstances of social man actually hide deeper psychic motivations that the reformers either have refused to acknowledge in themselves or believe they have escaped by virtue of their geographical detachment.

Coverdale's narrative ought to be the means whereby the reader discovers the relation between these two stories, serving as the mediation that enables us to interpret the parable of "The Silvery Veil" in the context of the Blithedale experiment. However, Coverdale's first-person involved narration has always seemed the principal obstacle to such an end. Dramatically involved in both narrative actions and psychologically prone to the same weaknesses as the other characters, Coverdale would seem to provide us with little more than a repetition of the same blindness and delusion. Following Hawthorne's own hints, critics have associated Coverdale with a manipulator like Westervelt, who uses others either for his own entertainment or to enhance his sense of power.[12] Coverdale's idle curiosity and dilettantism contrast markedly with Hollingsworth's social commitment. Hollingsworth's fall is the result of his obsessive concern with his philanthropic scheme, and many critics tend to agree with Zenobia that Hollingsworth's fatal egotism is the tragic liability of a noble nature: "But a great man — as, perhaps you do not know — attains his normal condition only through the inspiration of one great idea" (*BR*, 153). Incapable of substantive action and unwilling to expose himself to others, Coverdale appears to substitute cold inquiry for love, detached and inviolate individuality for social involvement, and witty chatter for meaningful communication. According to such a reading, Coverdale ironically mediates the two narratives by expressing in his own person and narrative the same corruptions that are exposed in the other characters. Identified with "Theodore" in Zenobia's parable, "The Silvery Veil," Coverdale shares Chillingworth's primal sin of violating the sanctity of a human heart and Young Goodman Brown's failure to place his trust in his fellows.

Unquestionably, Coverdale suffers from all these liabilities, but his narration does not describe a simple and unchanging personality. The twelve years that separate his narrative from the events at Blithedale would appear to suggest that he is left only with the impotent and unproductive repetition of a story whose moral continues to escape him. Unable to resolve any of the substantive mysteries at the heart of the romance, Coverdale seems merely to represent his younger follies with the skepticism of a disappointed man. Indeed, offering us an unlikely confession in his final words — "I — I myself — was in love — with — PRISCILLA!" — Coverdale seems to be trying desperately to supplant the emptiness of his psychic and literary life with some surrogate truth or simulated secret. As Philip Rahv suggested long ago, the confession is a "psychological detour" perfectly in keeping with Coverdale's willing self-blindness; it "permits him to covet Zenobia and to pry into her affairs without in any way committing himself to her — for how could he, a paleface poet with overcharged scruples, make up to a woman who is 'passionate, luxurious, lacking simplicity, not deeply refined, incapable of pure and perfect taste'?" [13] Manipulating the reader in much the same way as he manipulates other characters in the narrative, Coverdale seems intent on preserving the very position of detachment that most critics single out as his highest crime. Yet, Coverdale repeatedly reminds us that his act of narration is hardly a passive act of recollection. The narrative itself describes Coverdale's education in the imagination and his exploration of the varieties of imaginative representation. Coverdale's complicated mode of narrative detachment only superficially resembles his reluctance as a character in the drama to commit himself to his fellows.

What complicates Coverdale's story of his story is that it develops through several negative stages of knowledge, each of which risks repeating mistakes of the other characters. Coverdale is identified with virtually every character at one point or another; his eclectic personality has led critics to generalize that he epitomizes this superficial culture, whose members perform a perpetual masquerade to avoid the deeper feelings and more frightening passions that secretly drive them. However, Coverdale's moments of imaginative identification with Hollingsworth, Priscilla, Zenobia, Westervelt, Old Moodie, and Silas Foster enable him to transcend the personae that trap and imprison the other characters. Like Pound's Mauberley or Stevens's Crispin, Coverdale is defined less by the masks he wears than by the successive roles that he has been able to cast off. For Coverdale, the imagination serves neither to mediate between appearance and reality nor to subordinate the world of substance to the mind, but to negate the stubborn substance of the world as the means of discovering human freedom. The "freedom" that is made possible as the result of Coverdale's understanding of the imagination's nature and function is posed as an alternative to the inadequate efforts of utopians, philanthropists, feminists, and mesmerists to liberate us from servitude to our physical, sexual, and social circumstances. And it is precisely because Coverdale situates human freedom in terms of the very contradictions between body and mind, appearance and reality, self and others, the past and the future that the other characters seek to transcend that his conception of the imagination is ultimately identifiable with Hawthorne's.

The various conceptions of the imagination in *Blithedale* are focused economically by the parable of "The Veiled Lady," which is told in a number of different versions and complemented by the predominant veil and mask imagery in the rest of the narrative. The significance of "The Veiled Lady" has caused critics endless trouble. A number of studies attribute the work's failure to Hawthorne's inability to give the veil the symbolic centrality and clarity that he accomplishes with the scarlet letter or the house of the seven gables.[14] The frustrating ambiguity of the veil's "meaning" has led Richard Harter Fogle to conclude equivocally: "The veil is somehow true as well as false, beautiful in its own right, an embodiment as well as a concealment or a mere deception."[15] The veil serves variously as an uncannily suggestive figure for the problems in the dramatic action, a metaphor for Coverdale's name and narration, and a theatrical device for Westervelt and Zenobia. Hawthorne certainly designs the veil to evoke a symbolic ambiguity, which we might compare with that of Melville's doubloon or James's wings of the dove. Its primary symbolic function is to prompt an interpretive response from the viewer, who thereby betrays his own character in the method of his reading. Whereas Westervelt uses the veil to manipulate others, Hawthorne transforms the veil into a point of reference for psychological reflection.

Most critics concentrate on the version of "The Veiled Lady" told by Zenobia in the interpolated story, "The Silvery Veil." As the most extended version of the parable, Zenobia's narrative naturally draws the reader's attention, but it is hardly a reliable indication of Hawthorne's outlook. Unlike Holgrave's legend of "Alice Pyncheon," the story is told by a character who represents attitudes that Hawthorne criticizes throughout the remainder of the narrative. Thus, the frequent critical analogy drawn between the skeptical young Theodore, who seeks the identity of "The Veiled Lady" to settle a wager and scornfully disregards her warnings, and the prying Coverdale tells us less about Hawthorne's judgment of Coverdale than about Zenobia's highly prejudiced view of the dilettantish young poet. Zenobia's legend, however, does suggest a point of departure for evaluating the various interpretations of the veil in the romance. Mysteriously appearing to Theodore in her "private withdrawing-room," "The Veiled Lady" offers to satisfy his curiosity in two different ways:

> "Thou canst go hence and think of me no more; or, at thy option, thou canst lift this mysterious veil, beneath which I am a sad and lonely prisoner, in a bondage which is worse to me than death. But, before raising it, I entreat thee, in all maiden modesty, to bend forward, and impress a kiss, where my breath stirs the veil; and my virgin lips shall come forward to meet thy lips, and from that instant, Theodore, thou shalt be mine, and I thine, with never more a veil between us! . . . Dost thou hesitate . . . while the veil yet hides my face? Has not thy heart recognized me? Dost thou come hither, not in holy faith, nor with

a pure and generous purpose, but in scornful scepticism and idle curiosity? Still, thou mayst lift the veil! But from that instant, Theodore, I am doomed to be thy evil fate; nor wilt thou ever taste another breath of happiness!" [*BR*, 104–5]

Theodore lifts the veil without offering the kiss of faith and thus discovers only his own sense of loss as "the apparition vanished, and the silvery veil fluttered slowly down, and lay upon the floor" (106).

Zenobia's tale is appropriate to the context in which it is told; it is a rather transparent moral exemplum with all the intellectual subtlety of a tableau or a parlor charade. Told as it is shortly after Zenobia's secret meeting with Westervelt in the woods, the tale takes on added significance for Coverdale and the reader. But Hawthorne does not want us to forget that this story is told to conclude an evening of entertainment by a woman who is repeatedly described as "theatrical" or as a "tragic actress." The "moral" itself is perfectly in keeping with the general themes of most of Hawthorne's works, but this should not mislead the reader into designating Zenobia's legend as the key to Hawthorne's own moral conclusions in *Blithedale*. Richard Brodhead provides an intelligent summary of the tale's moral: Theodore "must choose between 'holy faith' and 'scornful scepticism and idle curiosity'; and his choice mirrors the larger one offered to all the characters in the book between a generous and loving commitment that frees others and a selfish intention that enslaves others to their own purposes." [16] The only problem is that each of the characters has his or her own idea of what constitutes "holy faith" or "scornful scepticism and idle curiosity" and of what distinguishes freedom from servitude.

Hollingsworth's project for the reformation of criminals betrays a particular conception of human freedom and man's servitude to "selfish intentions." Although he "preaches" to Zenobia, Priscilla, and Coverdale at Eliot's Pulpit, Hollingsworth hardly shares the Puritans' sense of original sin. Hollingsworth roughly approximates the "privation" theodicy of Augustine and subsequent theologians, who would argue that man's sinfulness is defined by his straying from the good. For Hollingsworth, human nature is fundamentally good; it has been obscured, however, by selfishness, pride, and lack of charity. His entire project depends upon the possibility of "eradicating" such "blackness of man's heart" by means of "spiritual discipline." Unlike Fourier, Hollingsworth is repelled by the idea of human progress improving on nature and harnessing self-interest to the task of accomplishing an earthly paradise. For Hollingsworth, the reform of criminals is a matter of negating the corrupt influences of the material world that have led them astray from the purer impulses of their spiritual natures. As Coverdale summarizes Hollingsworth's scheme, it proposes "the reformation of the wicked by methods moral, intellectual, and industrial, by the sympathy of pure, humble, and yet exalted minds, and by opening to his pupils the possibility of a worthier life than that which had become their fate" (*BR*, 122). Human wickedness and sinfulness are the illusions that prevent us from seeing the good and the true; the reformer recalls the fallen to their better natures in order to lift the veil that blinds them to their spiritual destinies. Deluded by the appearances of this world, we stray even further from the truth of our own hearts, which is at once the truth of all humanity and the common foundation for a reformed society.

Coverdale and ultimately Zenobia recognize that Hollingsworth's ideology is little more than a mask for the very egotism that Hollingsworth himself considers the "Unpardonable Sin." Coverdale indirectly rebukes Hollingsworth for equating his own *idée fixe* with divine truth when he remarks of Fourier: "He makes no claim to inspiration. He has not persuaded himself — as Swedenborg did, and as any other than a Frenchman would, with a mission of like importance to communicate — that he speaks with authority from above. He promulgates his system, so far as I can perceive, entirely on his own responsibility" (*BR*, 50). For Hollingsworth, such presumption is precisely Fourier's sin; for Coverdale, Hollingsworth's sin is his insistence that his ideology has a unique claim to spiritual truth. Hollingsworth cries out to Coverdale, "Be with me . . . or be against me! There is no third choice for you" (125). Although Hollingsworth appeals to Coverdale to be his "brother" in this "great scheme of good," he suggests that Coverdale will be one of the first whom he shall reform: "Strike hands with me; and, from this moment, you shall never again feel the languor and vague wretchedness of an indolent or half-occupied man! There may be no more aimless beauty in your life; but, in its stead, there shall be strength, courage, inmitigable will — everything that a manly and generous nature should desire" (124). Hollingsworth is more than contemptuous of Coverdale's reputation as a poet; for him, Coverdale's ballad-making is merely a sign of his idle and misdirected life. For Hollingsworth, "exalted minds" only achieve their true purpose in the quest for the good and the reformation of the wicked.

As Hollingsworth subsequently demonstrates when he leads Priscilla away from Westervelt, the reformer seeks to lift the veil of illusion so that human beings may see the hidden truth and discover a "worthier life." In this regard, Hollingsworth's conception of the proper use of mental faculties is not substantively different from the basic principles of the Blithedale utopians. He objects, of course, to these dreamers who hope vainly to bring about social reform indirectly through their own example; Hollingsworth insists upon a more practical and less symbolic method of reform, one that would proceed according to a rational plan and achieve tangible results. Yet, Hawthorne employs Hollingsworth to suggest some of the dangers implicit in the utopians' general conception of social reform. As Irving Howe notes, "It is clearly Hawthorne's intention to show in Hollingsworth the utopian impulse as it has hardened into an inhumane ideology." [17]

In a similar fashion, the unrealistic scheme of the utopians helps illustrate how Hollingsworth's pragmatic plan for social action is actually the vainest of fancies. Like Hollingsworth, the utopians hope to lift the veil of social and urban illusions in order to regain some contact with their own natures. Disregarding for the moment the impossibility of any such "new beginning" for Hawthorne, I would point out that the utopians' plan for achieving direct participation in the "real" world is governed by a number of a priori assumptions about both human nature and the objective natural order. Coverdale summarizes the general principles of this new community early in the narrative:

> And first of all, we had divorced ourselves from Pride, and were striving to supply its place with familiar love. We meant to lessen the laboring man's great burthen of toil, by performing our due share of it at the cost of our own thews and sinews. We sought our profit by mutual aid, instead of wresting it by the strong hand from an enemy, or filching it craftily from those less shrewd than ourselves, (if, indeed, there were any such, in New England,) or winning it by selfish competition with a neighbor; in one or another of which fashions, every son of woman both perpetrates and suffers his share of the common evil, whether he chooses it or no. And, as the basis of our institution, we purposed to offer up the earnest toil of our bodies, as a prayer, no less than an effort, for the advancement of our race. [*BR*, 19]

Like the moral of "The Silvery Veil" and Hollingsworth's philanthropic scheme, this utopian project depends upon extremely general principles, which could lead to radically diverse results if enacted by different personalities. Further, these principles involve certain assumptions about human nature that seem based on "common sense" but that are in no way consistent. Coverdale claims that they have "left the rusty iron frame-work of society behind . . . for the sake of showing mankind the example of a life governed by other than the false and cruel principles, on which human society has all along been based" (18–19). Somewhat later, however, Coverdale suggests that both this corrupt society and man's "brute" nature are based on the principle of the survival of the fittest. Reflecting on Hollingsworth's "brotherly attendance" during his illness, Coverdale notes: "Most men — and, certainly, I could not always claim to be one of the exceptions — have a natural indifference, if not an absolutely hostile feeling, towards those whom disease, or weakness, or calamity of any kind, causes to faulter and faint amid the rude jostle of our selfish existence." These remarks seem to be directed at the selfishness of the corrupt social order that the utopians have left behind, but Coverdale continues: "The education of Christianity, it is true, the sympathy of a like experience, and the example of women, may soften, and possibly subvert, this ugly characteristic of our sex. But it is originally there, and has likewise its analogy in the practice of our brute brethren, who hunt the sick or disabled member of the herd from among them, as an enemy. It is for this reason that the stricken deer goes apart, and the sick lion grimly withdraws himself into his den. Except in love, or the attachments of kindred, or other very long and habitual affection, we really have no tenderness" (*BR*, 38–39). The artifices of society, then, accurately reflect the natural condition of humanity, which these pastoral reformers are attempting to recapture in their experiment in agrarian communism. Far from being a return to nature, their project betrays from the beginning a desire to supplant a brutish and selfish human nature with the higher ideals of nineteenth-century progressive politics. What they would accomplish "at the cost of our own thews and sinews," these reformers have already fabricated in their dreams. Their pastoral retreat has no more contact with nature than the walls and streets of the city.

Like Thoreau, the utopians would "reduce life down to its lowest terms" in order to purify themselves of those delusions of city-dwellers that prevent them from seeing the truth. Like Hollingsworth, the reformers consider the veil that hides the truth to be merely an illusion that may turn invisible once the senses have been properly honed. But the dreams of mutual aid and brotherly love involve more than just the violation of fundamental human nature; in the interpersonal relations dramatized in *Blithedale*, such ideals serve to mask and repress deeper psychic motives. This experiment in freedom is actually governed by human relations that replicate more subtly and thus more subversively the brute law of the survival of the fittest. Love is the highest spiritual aim of both the utopians and Hollingsworth, but love is often a mask in *Blithedale* for the most selfish manipulation and control of others. Hawthorne makes it quite clear that the possessiveness of Hollingsworth, Westervelt, Zenobia, Old Moodie, and even Coverdale stems from a confusion between imagination and the actual. Just as the reformers confuse their ideals with the actual state of nature, so the individual characters equate their own mental constructions of the world with things as they are. In a moment of remarkable lucidity and self-consciousness, Coverdale recognizes this tendency in himself. Aloft in his woodland hermitage, Coverdale fancifully casts "a message for Priscilla" to a passing bird:

"Tell her," said I, "that her fragile thread of life has inextricably knotted itself with other and tougher threads, and most likely will be broken. Tell her that Zenobia will not long be her friend. Say that Hollingsworth's heart is on fire with his own purpose, but icy for all human affection, and that, if she has given him her love, it is like casting a flower into a sepulchre. And say, that, if any mortal really cares for her, it is myself, and not even I, for her realities — poor little seamstress, as Zenobia rightly called her! — but for the fancy-work with which I have idly decked her out!" [*BR*, 93–94]

As I shall attempt to demonstrate, Coverdale's recognition that he does not love Priscilla for herself, but rather in the image of his own desire, informs his final confession. In the course of his narrative, Coverdale learns not only how fanciful all conceptions of reality are but also how they disguise our most egotistical drives.

Hawthorne suggests that more than egotism is involved in his characters' efforts to make the world agree with their mental conceptions of it. The fatal pride of such characters as Zenobia and Hollingsworth is not merely self-assertiveness, but also the delusion that they can control their own wills. The reformers believe that they can throw off the shackles of society and willfully begin anew in their "counterfeit Arcadia." As the romance concerning Zenobia and Priscilla suggests, however, one may forget the past but still never escape its influence. For all her aggressive independence, Zenobia dramatizes the incapacity of any man or woman to remain aloof from the influences of others. In this world of masks, pseudonyms, aliases, disguises, and secrets, it seems especially inappropriate that the "theatrical" Zenobia should insist on remaining "true" to herself.

Although Hawthorne exposes the false realism of the utopians' project and Hollingsworth's ideology, he does not embrace a purely nominal world of dizzying illusion. The reformers may confuse mental objects with actual objects, but this does not lead Hawthorne to refute the substance of the world beyond consciousness. Westervelt is a character of mere surfaces, whose counterfeit appearance seems to Coverdale a token of an increasingly apparitional world. Westervelt's performance of "The Veiled Lady," however, is not a demonstration of the apparitional character of the substantial world; it is a systematic manipulation of people's tendency to confuse their perceptual and imaginative faculties. Hawthorne makes a clear distinction between Westervelt's subtler art and the stage effects of more contemporary performers:

> Now-a-days, in the management of his "subject," "clairvoyant," or "medium," the exhibitor affects the simplicity and openness of scientific experiment; and even if he professes to tread a step or two across the boundaries of the spiritual world, yet carries with him the laws of our actual life, and extends them over his preternatural conquests. Twelve or fifteen years ago, on the contrary, all the arts of mysterious arrangement, of picturesque disposition, and artistically contrasted light and shade, were made available in order to set the apparent miracle in the strongest attitude of opposition to ordinary facts. In the case of the Veiled Lady, moreover, the interest of the spectator was further wrought up by the enigma of her identity, and an absurd rumor (probably set afloat by the exhibitor, and at one time very prevalent) that a beautiful young lady, of family and fortune, was enshrouded within the misty drapery of the veil. [*BR*, 5–6]

The modern mesmerist tricks the senses in such a way that any viewer with sufficient patience might work out the scientific laws employed to produce the illusion. Westervelt relies primarily on the imagination of his audience, especially as it is fed by rumors, gossip in anticipation of the show, and the presentation of a woman who is in fact hidden. In terms of the novel's primary themes, Westervelt manipulates the very confusion between imagination and perception that dooms the utopians' quest for an authentic pastoral existence and destroys Hollingsworth's philanthropic dream.[18] Anticipating as they do miraculous and supernatural events, the viewers are more than willing to supply mentally the voices and movements, the portents and prophecies that constitute "The Veiled Lady's" story.

Hollingsworth and the utopians read the parable of "The Veiled Lady" in terms of a simple opposition between appearance and reality. If the veil prevents us from seeing the truth, as Theodore suggests in "The Silvery Veil," then it is only a matter of developing a method for removing the veil. Hawthorne rejects this naive opposition of appearance and reality. Life at Blithedale is no less a masquerade than is the corrupt and artificial life of the city-dweller. For Hawthorne in *The Blithedale Romance,* there is absolutely no way to escape the sensory, perceptual, imaginative, and rational mental functions that veil objective reality from us. Nevertheless, Hawthorne does not for this reason subscribe to a naive theory of human subjectivity and the inevitable relativity of all our conceptions of the real. The primary source of delusion in *Blithedale* is not simply the result of our cognitive limitations, but of our failure to understand the different functions of our own minds. Repeatedly confusing the mental images of the imagination with the sensations and perceptions that we draw from the objective world, we become prey to the most dangerous illusions. Westervelt's viewers do not acknowledge that his "magic" is the result of their own imaginations, and thus they attribute a power to him that properly belongs to them.

In a similar sense, the other characters in the novel frequently submit themselves to the presumed authority of another that is in fact their own secret power. What Zenobia "loves" in Hollingsworth is his forceful and aggressive commitment to his philanthropic cause, a characteristic that is of course entangled with his masculinity and sexual presence. Yet, it is precisely these "masculine" personality traits that distinguish Zenobia, but that she seems unwilling or unable to use in the service of a feminist cause. Representing as it does all that Zenobia fights against, such virility seems the very thing she ought to repress in her own nature. But such a contradiction is only operative if one assumes that "virility," aggression, and self-assertiveness are qualities defined by their physical referent — man. In fact, it is merely the custom of this patriarchal society that has enforced such an interpretation. Hawthorne himself repeatedly suggests in *The Blithedale Romance* as well as in *The Scarlet Letter* that human nature is androgynous and that the association of certain psychological qualities with particular physical referents — power with the phallus, submission with the vagina — is to confuse the psychical with the biological.[19]

Hollingsworth, of course, epitomizes masculine power, but what principally attracts Coverdale to him in their early relationship is Hollingsworth's capacity for a "feminine" tenderness and compassion: "But there was something of the woman moulded into the great, stalwart frame of Hollingsworth; nor was he ashamed of it, as men often are of what is best in them, nor seemed ever to know that there was such a soft place in his heart. I knew it well, however, at that time; although, afterwards, it came nigh to be forgotten" (*BR*, 39). Hollingsworth is not "ashamed" of this tenderness, because he never seems "to know that there was such a soft place in his heart." Just as Zenobia is confused and troubled by her own "masculinity," Hollingsworth represses the "femininity" in his nature that unpredictably and irregularly manifests itself in his behavior.

Clearly, Hawthorne does not equate our higher spiritual nature with our physical and biological natures. Our true nature for Hawthorne, of course, is defined by our imaginative and cognitive faculties — by the consciousness that distinguishes each of us from the beasts and promises us the possibility of redemption from the brutish "survival of the fittest." We define our own nature by virtue of the meaning we create in and through our conscious acts; to understand the "truths of the human heart" is not a pastoral experiment, but an investigation into the possibilities and limitations of human consciousness. The function of the romance is neither to provide an entertaining and temporary escape from our unsatisfactory lives nor to displace the actual with the promise of some higher, supernatural reality hidden from the senses. As all of Hawthorne's prefaces suggest, the truth of the romance lurks in its capacity to employ the imagination in order to reflect upon the process of consciousness itself. For Hawthorne, the imagination is not a means of giving a greater latitude to the "objects" of sensation, but rather of performing a special cognitive function: to enable us to make consciousness itself an object for reflection.

Hawthorne's effort in *Blithedale* to draw certain clear distinctions among imagination, perception, and the objects of the world constitutes his most sustained and sophisticated attempt to justify his activity as a romancer. Hawthorne's repeated concern in all his writings is to demonstrate the truth of the imagination, but most critics have interpreted this to indicate primarily the mythic or archetypal "truths of the human heart" conventionally associated with literary expression. In *Blithedale*, however, the truth of the imagination is closely related to understanding the phenomenology of one's own consciousness.

Many critics have noticed the marked similarities between Hawthorne's complex psychological analyses and twentieth-century developments in psychology.[20] In this regard, Hawthorne's conception of the imagination in *Blithedale* seems to prefigure the efforts of phenomenologists like Brentano and Husserl and existential psychologists like Sartre to study our cognitive processes in terms of the intentional acts of consciousness and the intentional objects of such acts (Husserl's noetic-noematic correlation). And yet, despite several "phenomenological" studies of Hawthorne, few critics have attempted to relate Hawthorne's thinking to the phenomenological descriptions offered by these philosophers and psychologists. Sartre's two works on the imagination — *L'Imagination* (1936) and *L'Imaginaire, psychologie phénoménologique de l'imagination* (1940) — helps focus much of the twentieth-century work on the phenomenology of the imagination.[21] By reading Hawthorne's exploration of the function of the imagination in relation to the central issues raised by Sartre, we ought to be able to measure the extent to which Hawthorne's thinking approximates a phenomenological outlook.

Sartre's primary aim in *L'Imagination* is to refute theories of the imagination that base the image on a sensory content that refers to an object beyond consciousness. Criticizing philosophers and psychologists from Descartes to Bergson, Sartre insists that the associationism of most theories primarily relies on what he terms a "naive ontology of images," whereby the image is considered "a reviving sensation, a solid fragment snapped off from the external world" (*I*, 25). Sartre argues that the notion of the image as merely a "fainter" and less permanent "sensation" provides us with no means of "distinguishing images from the other things belonging to the world" (*I*, 117). By assuming the "basic identity of images and perceptions," these theorists risk finding themselves in the same phantasmal world that deceives and subverts Hawthorne's utopians, Hollingsworth, and the audience for Westervelt's performances. Continually confusing their sensations with the phantoms of their own minds, Hawthorne's characters continue to veil the truth they seek to reveal. Assuming the concordance of the images of thought and the objects of the external world, these characters insist that delusion may be transcended by means of properly refined senses and that we may be "trained" to "see" the truth.

Sartre's preliminary distinction between the objects of perception and the image asserts the superabundance of the objects given to perception and the essential "poverty" of the image: "In a word, the object of consciousness overflows consciousness constantly; the object of the image is never more than the consciousness one has; it is limited by that consciousness: *nothing can be learned from an image that is not already known*" (*PI*, 12; my italics). Pursuing Husserl's notion of the "margin" or "horizon" that bounds every intentional act of consciousness, Sartre argues that our perception of an object is never complete and always open to an "infinity of determined relationships with the infinity of other things" (*PI*, 11).[22] The act of vision continually leads to new impressions that are limited only by the need for reflection and conceptualization. The image, on the other hand, derives its "poverty" from the intentional act of consciousness, which *appears as an image*. The image is not some free, fanciful variation on the possibilities inherent in sensation; the image always *realizes* what is *already known* in consciousness. Thus, the image is not associated with a certain quest for knowledge, but is itself the appearance or the becoming-objective of what is already known: "It cannot be said that an image clarifies our knowledge in any manner whatsoever for the very reason that it is the knowledge that constitutes the image" (*PI,* 121). In furthering this distinction, Sartre argues that the perceptual consciousness "appears to itself as being passive," whereas the "imaginative consciousness presents itself to itself . . . as a spontaneity which produces and holds on to the object as an image" (*PI,* 18). The spontaneity of the imaginative consciousness is what assures us that it is not sparked by an external referent, but itself constitutes an intentional structure of consciousness.

Sartre's main aim in these two works is to use the image to demonstrate Husserl's fundamental definition of consciousness as an intentional act, which can be investigated only through its intentional objects: "The image is defined by its intention" and "in the imaginative consciousness, knowledge and intention can be distinguished only by intention" (*PI,* 81). Husserl's primary *epoché* puts the "world as such" in brackets and compels us to seek our meanings only within the noetic-noematic correlation that is the intentional structure of consciousness.[23] For Husserl, phenomenology claims as its eidetic aim "the presentation of invariant structural systems without which perception of a body and a synthetically concordant multiplicity of perceptions of one and the same body as such would be unthinkable."[24]

Sartre devotes two volumes to the technical differences between the objects of sensation and the intentional objects of the imaginative consciousness in order to provide a basis for his own existential phenomenology and the metaphysics of nothingness. The primary distinction between the perceptual and imaginative consciousness depends upon the *presence* of the object required for perception and the *absence* of the referential object that characterizes the imaginative act: "Let us recall *the essential characteristic of the mental image:* it is a certain way an object has of being absent within its very presence" (*PI,* 104). The very absence of the referential "object" is itself what prompts the mental image. It is for this reason that the imagination, in contrast to perceptual consciousness, is not an aid to the understanding, because the image itself already indicates the understanding that is implicit in the intentional act with which it is identified: "The *image* . . . is a consciousness that aims to produce its object: it is therefore constituted by a certain way of judging and feeling of which we do not become conscious as such but which we apprehend *on* the intentional object as this or that of its qualities. In a word, the function of the image is *symbolic*" (*PI,* 138).

For Sartre, the image is a mode of symbolizing what we already comprehend but which has not yet become manifest to us. The truth that is symbolized in the image-object has nothing to do with the empirical truth, but is in fact the psychic truth of our own natures: "Understanding is not a pure reproduction of a meaning. It is an act. In making itself manifest, this act envisions a certain object and this object is, in general, a truth of judgment or a conceptual structure" (*PI*, 147). To reflect upon the symbolic process is to perform phenomenologically a transcendental reduction that takes the entire process of the imagination as an object for reflection. In this way, both Husserl and Sartre suggest that we may begin to investigate the principles governing our judgments and concepts. Granting that the objects of the world exist as hyletic data that can never be known purely in themselves, the phenomenologist situates truth and meaning exclusively in those intentional acts of consciousness whereby we make our world.

This brief summary of some of Sartre's main points suggests a number of interesting ramifications for Coverdale's education in *The Blithedale Romance*. On the one hand, Hawthorne carefully works through the inadequacies of the various epistemologies governing the ideology of the utopians and Hollingsworth as well as the artistry of Westervelt. By reading "The Veiled Lady" as a simple problem involving the illusions of the senses and the objective truth that is hidden, both the utopians and Hollingsworth situate the truth of human nature in an objective realm only shadowed in consciousness. On the other hand, Westervelt plays on this very confusion of the different cognitive functions of the imagination and perception in order to effect the "miracle" of "The Veiled Lady" on a "stage" that is in fact the viewer's own consciousness.

For Hawthorne and ultimately for Coverdale, however, the veil represents, not the illusions of the senses, but the imagination itself. A veil is in fact constituted by its capacity to hide or negate what lies behind it. Westervelt's performance of "The Veiled Lady" negates the ordinary world of sensation by directing the audience's interest to something that is expressly hidden and must be imagined in order to be present in its sensory absence. Westervelt, of course, manipulates his stage props in order to control his audience, just as he plays upon Zenobia and Priscilla in order to work his will. But Hawthorne enacts his own drama of "The Veiled Lady" in Coverdale's narration. Most critics assume that Coverdale's name suggests the phantasmal obscurity in which these characters live, but in fact Hawthorne's own method of "covering" the "dale" reveals the process of the imagination as an intentional structure of consciousness.

In Hawthorne's version of "The Veiled Lady," the imagination veils or negates the world of sense in a way that is quite similar to Husserl's *epoché* of the objective world. In fact, we have already seen how much of this work is devoted to demonstrating the hopelessness of ever trying to escape the "illusions" of consciousness. Granting the existence of the world as such but negating it as a possible origin for human understanding, Hawthorne turns his glance inward to explore the methods whereby consciousness constructs its meanings and makes its judgments. This seems perfectly in keeping with

Coverdale's "unreliable" first-person confessional narration; in fact, Hawthorne thereby announces that "romance" ought to begin with the investigation of a particular subjective consciousness as the only proper phenomenological basis for any description of consciousness.[25] By hiding or veiling the world as such, the imagination directs our attention to those intentional acts that have constructed the "phantoms" that manifest our hidden desires and needs. Simply put, the work of the imagination is an effort to make visible what is already known on the affective level. The image symbolizes our desires and psychic needs rather than some elusive realm of sensible objects. The imagination is a process of psychic rememoration: "Every word in terms of which I can make an effort to understand is therefore shot through and through with a knowledge that is nothing other than the recollection of past understandings" (*PI,* 147).

Husserl argues that the perceptual consciousness operates by means of retentions and protentions that determine the spatio-temporal location of the object of consciousness. Every perception involves the retention of a past that immediately precedes the "now" and the anticipatory intention (protention) of which ought to follow. In a way, the perception fulfills or satisfies retention and protention by establishing its object in a temporal sequence. The perceptual consciousness that originates the "now" judges and evaluates the retentions and protentions according to their adequacy in facilitating the perception. What Husserl terms the "originary presentation" of perception synthesizes retentions and protentions in its intentional structure. Husserl offers the example of a melody: "In the 'perception of a melody,' we distinguish the tone *given now,* which we term the 'perceived,' from those which *have gone by,* which we say are 'not perceived.' On the other hand, we call the *whole melody* one that is *perceived,* although only the now-point actually is."[26] What actually survive or are retained, however, are the particular notes that *are no longer.* The synthetic aim of the perception of the melody as a whole negates this absence of the notes in order to preserve them for the perception of the melody as a unified form. In a similar sense, the remainder of the melody that is *not yet present* is synthesized by perception in the protentional anticipation of what is to come. Perceptual consciousness thus situates the past, present, and future by means of retention and protention in order to provide the "originary presentation." The "absences" that are represented by these retentions and protentions are thus canceled by the perceptual presentation.

As Sartre recognizes, the dependence of retention and protention on what is *absent* closely associates these functions with the imaginative consciousness. The image, moreover, is characterized by its presentation of what is absent; thus, the formation of the image is accomplished by retentions and protentions that in themselves are intentional objects. In an effort to confirm his metaphysical principles, Sartre defines the image as the objective structure of desire. This desire is prompted on the affective level by emotions that are retained and made present by virtue of the absence of that which would satisfy them. In other words, the object of the imaginative act is not the same as the sensory or perceptual object, but it is the affective state that itself has given rise to this longing:

> In a word, *desire* is a blind effort to possess on the level of representation what I already possess on the affective level; through the affective synthesis it envisions a "beyond" which it pursues without being able to know it; it directs itself upon the affective "something" which is now given to it and apprehends it as the representative of the desired thing. So the structure of an affective consciousness of desire is already that of an imaginative consciousness, since here, as in the image, a present synthesis functions as a substitute for an absent representative synthesis. [*PI,* 102]

Sartre's inevitable conclusion is that the imagination not only depends upon the absence of the sensory objects that prompt perceptual consciousness but also excludes or negates those objects. Imagination and perception "represent the two main irreducible attitudes of consciousness. It follows that they exclude each other" (*PI,* 171). The imagination constitutes a distinct realm of "unreal objects" that negates the substance of the world and thereby affirms the freedom of consciousness, which is no longer exclusively tied to the determining laws of the substantial world: "Thus the unreal — which is always a two-fold nothingness: nothingness of itself in relation to the world, nothingness of the world in relation to itself — must always be constituted on the foundation of the world which it denies, it being well understood, moreover, that the world does not present itself only to a representative intuition and that this synthetic foundation simply demands to be lived as a situation" (*PI,* 270).

On the basis of these observations, we ought to be able to read more clearly Hawthorne's own version of "The Veiled Lady" in *The Blithedale Romance.* Hawthorne himself negates the "facts" of the Brook Farm episode in order to concentrate on a romance, in which the structure of his own desire might become manifest. In a similar fashion, Coverdale wearies of ever untangling the perceptual "truth" from mental fabrication and turns instead to the structure of his imagination as a key to his own psychological motives. The veil that he uses to "cover" the "dale" is in fact his imaginative expression of his own self-knowledge. *Blithedale* images what Coverdale has always already known about himself and his relations with others but which he has repressed or avoided. More important than Coverdale's discovery of his own psychic motives, however, is the general truth that his shift from a perceptual to an imaginative consciousness provides: Coverdale discovers in and through the imagination the possibility of freedom that eludes the utopians, Hollingsworth, Westervelt, Zenobia, and Priscilla. Westervelt claims that the veil carries its bearer beyond time and space: "Slight and ethereal as it seems, the limitations of time and space have no existence within its folds" (*BR*, 186). For Hawthorne, only the imagination is capable of negating the spatio-temporal world and permitting us entrance into the duration of consciousness, which in its pure form remains undetermined by either spatial or temporal particularity.[27] Sartre also defines the realm of the imagination — the unreal — in terms of its negation of perceptual space and time: "Thus the time of unreal objects is itself unreal. It has no characteristics whatever of perceptual time: it does not run off (as does the duration of this piece of sugar which is melting), it can expand or contract at will while remaining the same, it is not irreversible. It is a shadow of time, like the shadow of the object, with its shadow of space. Nothing separates the unreal object from me more surely: the world of imagery is completely isolated, I can enter it only by unrealizing myself in it" (*PI*, 188).

By lifting the veil of the imagination to perceive the "truth" behind it, Hawthorne's characters find the mute and meaningless substance of the world beyond consciousness. In Zenobia's version of "The Silvery Veil," Theodore lifts the veil only to discover his own loss and thus remain condemned to the futile effort to capture what he can never possess: "His retribution was, to pine, forever and ever, for another sight of that dim, mournful face — which might have been his life-long, household, fireside joy — to desire, and waste life in a feverish quest, and never meet it more!" (*BR*, 106). The knowledge that desire is by its nature unsatisfiable may well lead to the despair that drives Zenobia to suicide and the other characters into mental labyrinths. However, Hawthorne himself seems to affirm desire as the structural principle of human consciousness, the very element that distinguishes man. By requesting him to place his faith in the veil by means of an emblematic kiss, "The Veiled Lady" asked Theodore to acknowledge the unreality of the imagination as the token of human freedom and the essence of our higher nature. In Hawthorne's version, "The Veiled Lady" becomes a metaphor or an image of our own psychic truth, rather than the key to some objective mystery lurking in the forest of life. Zenobia (or is it Coverdale?) prefaces her (his?) legend by warning us that it is an "unreal" drama of the self viewing its own consciousness: "Now, listen to my simple little tale; and you shall hear the very latest incident in the known life — (if life it may be called, which seemed to have no more reality than the candlelight image of one's self, which peeps at us outside of a dark window-pane) — the life of this shadowy phenomenon" (100). If, as I have suggested, "The Veiled Lady" is a metaphor for the essential freedom of consciousness, then to cast aside the veil in the quest for truth is to abandon "her" entirely. "The Veiled Lady" is the very figure of desire, that lack or nothingness that makes human being possible *for itself* (*être-pour-soi*). As Sartre writes, "If man adopts any particular behavior in the face of being-in-itself . . . it is because he is *not* this being. We rediscover non-being as a condition of the transcendence toward being." [28]

The detachment or negation that characterizes the imaginative consciousness is therefore not a masking or hiding of our paradoxical situation in the world. Indeed, the negation of the imaginative consciousness places us in relation to the objective world that is negated. More importantly, imaginative detachment is a mode of symbolizing what we have been — our historical essence — in the very effort to negate that identity and achieve a renewed liberty. Thus, the imagination for Hawthorne and Sartre is hardly "escapist," and its freedom is by no means unconditional. The imagination teaches us that we have the freedom to choose what we shall become, just as it reveals to us what our prior choices have constituted as our selves. The freedom discovered is equally the full responsibility that we take for ourselves. Sartre's moral rigor seems perfectly in keeping with Hawthorne's puritanical insistence upon the "moral value" of the romance: "I do not have nor can I have recourse to any value against the fact that it is I who sustain values in being. Nothing can ensure me against myself, cut off from the world and from my essence by this nothingness which I *am*." [29]

I must return to the details of Hawthorne's narrative in order to place Coverdale's education in the imagination within this phenomenological context. Throughout my analysis of *Blithedale*, I have employed "The Veiled Lady" as a point of reference for various epistemological and cognitive attitudes. Coverdale, of course, participates in most of the episodes that involve "The Veiled Lady" as either metaphor, legend, or theatrical performance. Yet, he himself enacts his own version of the cognitive problem represented by "The Veiled Lady" in a series of scenes that have some remarkable structural similarities. I am thinking of those moments in which Coverdale detaches himself from the dramatic action in order to reflect upon events, regain his self-composure, or, in some instances, do what most critics consider some furtive spying. The following sites are the most crucial: Coverdale's sick-chamber on his arrival at the farm; his "hermitage" in the woods; his hotel room, which overlooks the back of the boardinghouse in the city; and his visit with Old Moodie in the saloon.

A number of minor scenes could be added to this list, such as Coverdale's secret return to Blithedale and his unaccountable slumber at the foot of Eliot's pulpit while Zenobia commits suicide, but these moments lack the descriptive details that so specifically relate these four episodes to a single paradigm for the activity of the imaginative consciousness. Each place of imaginative detachment involves some influence that suspends ordinary consciousness: Coverdale's fever yields strangely prophetic dreams and mutterings; his hermitage in the woods is discovered during Coverdale's private "holiday," expressly designed to preserve "the better part" of his "individuality" (83); he drinks a sherry cobbler during his first observation of the boardinghouse windows (139); and he and Old Moodie share a bottle of particularly fine claret as Moodie tells his story in a private room in the intoxicating atmosphere of the saloon. Each moment is associated with reading, storytelling, interpreting, or the general furnishings of a study. In his sick-chamber, Coverdale reads "interminably in Mr. Emerson's Essays, the Dial, Carlyle's works, George Sand's romances, (lent me by Zenobia), and other books which one or another of the brethren or sisterhood had brought with them," including the works of Fourier (48). His observations of the boarding-house from his hotel room are prompted by his boredom with a "novel" that "was of the dullest, yet had a sort of sluggish flow, like that of a stream in which your boat is as often aground as afloat" (136–37). His meeting with Old Moodie, who provides the germ for Coverdale's romance of "Fauntleroy," is preceded by Coverdale's consideration of the various paintings that decorate the saloon, which constitute a short history of western theories of representation.

All these references to literary and imaginative activities have a central relation to Coverdale's hermitage in the woods, which resembles nothing so much as Hawthorne's own study in the Old Manse:

> It was an admirable place to make verses, tuning the rhythm to the breezy symphony that so often stirred among the vine-leaves; or to meditate an essay for the Dial, in which the many tongues of Nature whispered mysteries, and seemed to ask only a little stronger puff of wind, to speak out the solution of its riddle. Being so pervious to air-currents, it was just the nook, too, for the enjoyment of a cigar. This hermitage was my one exclusive possession, while I counted myself a brother of the socialists. It symbolized my individuality and aided me in keeping it inviolate. . . . So there I used to sit, owl-like, yet not without liberal and hospitable thoughts. [*BR,* 92]

Hawthorne's "little nook of a study" in the Old Manse is also a place for scholarly composition and the private contemplation of nature:

> There was in the rear of the house the most delightful little nook of a study that ever afforded its snug seclusion to a scholar. It was here that Emerson wrote Nature; for he was then an inhabitant of the Manse, and used to watch the Assyrian dawn and Paphian sunset and moonrise from the summit of our eastern hill. . . . A cheerful coat of paint and golden-tinted paper-hangings light up the small apartment; while the shadow of a willow-tree that swept against the overhanging eaves attempered the cheery western sunshine.[30]

Not only do the two spaces suggest some of the same reading and writing, but the view that these sites afford is almost identical. Coverdale describes the view from his perch:

Ascending into this natural turret, I peeped, in turn, out of several small windows. The pine-tree, being ancient, rose high above the rest of the wood, which was of comparatively recent growth. Even where I sat, about midway between the root and the topmost bough, my position was lofty enough to serve as an observatory, not for starry investigations, but for those sublunary matters in which lay a lore as infinite as that of the planets. Through one loop-hole, I saw the river lapsing calmly onward, while, in the meadow near its brink, a few of the brethren were digging peat for our winter's fuel. [*BR,* 92–93]

Hawthorne's view from the study in the Old Manse is extraordinarily similar:

The study had three windows, set with little, old-fashioned panes of glass, each with a crack across it. The two on the western side looked, or rather peeped, between the willow branches down into the orchard, with glimpses of the river through the trees. The third, facing northward, commanded a broader view of the river at a spot where its hitherto obscure waters gleam forth into the light of history. [*OM,* 14]

These similarities between Coverdale's hermitage and Hawthorne's study permit me to suggest certain conceptual associations. The Manse was formerly inhabited by a clergyman, who died a "twelvemonth" before; Hawthorne judges it the perfect spot for a clergyman's residence: "In its near retirement and accessible seclusion it was the very spot for the residence of a clergyman — *a man not estranged from human life, yet enveloped in the midst of it with a veil woven of intermingled gloom and brightness*" (*OM,* 12; my italics). Hawthorne implies an association between himself and the clergyman whom he has replaced. The obscure theological treatises and other traces of the holy life that Hawthorne discovers in "the Saint's Chamber" in the garret indicate how remote spiritual reality and authority are for the modern man. Despite Hawthorne's confession that he has failed to accomplish in his own work the "intellectual good" he had planned, his account of the interior of the Old Manse recalls the spirituality that the man of imagination ought to represent. Indeed, the decline of Puritan faith is attributed in part to the divines themselves, who in the obscurity of their works excluded themselves from the natural world framed by the study's bright windows and enjoyed by the author in his garden. In "The Old Manse," Hawthorne reapproximates the former inhabitant's supposed mode of detachment by weaving in his own works that "veil . . . of intermingled gloom and brightness" that facilitates his involvement "in the midst" of life rather than his "estrangement" from it.

The four structurally similar moments of Coverdale's detachment are metaphors for a parallel activity of the imagination: they are in themselves the scene of writing for both Hawthorne and Coverdale. For Sartre, of course, such detachment is the alienation or negation that is given with consciousness itself, as its essential characteristic and the token of its freedom. J. Hillis Miller discovers the same sort of detached self-constitution in Hardy's works: "The separation which is natural to the mind may be lost by a man's absorption in the world or it may be maintained by a willful standing back, but initially it is given with consciousness itself. To be conscious is to be separated. The mind has a native clarity and distinctness which detaches itself from everything else it registers."[31] The imagination is man's means of discovering his own freedom as a being and thus of affirming his "higher" nature. I noted earlier how three of these scenes are set in artificial places: a sick-chamber, an urban hotel room, and a saloon. Hawthorne goes to some lengths in his descriptions of the view from the hotel room window and the furnishings of the saloon to provide some curiously "natural" landscapes. The interval separating his room from the boardinghouse "was apportioned into grass-plots, and here and there an apology for a garden. . . . In two or three places, grape-vines clambered upon trellises, and bore clusters already purple, and promising the richness of Malta or Madeira in their ripened juice" (*BR,* 137–38). The grape vines, with their promise of rich and intoxicating liquor, recall the vine that has entangled itself among the branches of Coverdale's pine-tree hermitage at Blithedale: "A hollow chamber, of rare seclusion, had been formed by the decay of some of the pine-branches, which the vine had lovingly strangled with its embrace, burying them from the light of the day in an aerial sepulchre of its own leaves" (92). Yet, this apparently deadly vine, which figures in part the possessiveness of the other characters in the narrative, also promises a rich harvest: "I counted the innumerable clusters of my vine, and fore-reckoned the abundance of my vintage. It gladdened me to anticipate the surprise of the community, when, like an allegorical figure of rich October, I should make my appearance, with shoulders bent beneath the burthen of ripe grapes, and some of the crushed ones crimsoning my brow as with a blood-stain" (92).

Hawthorne's style and imagery in these passages achieve extraordinary depth and complexity. Fertility and death, intoxication and annihilation, freedom and servitude are all simultaneously expressed in his description of the vine. And its promise of rich liquor links both the vine of the hermitage and the vine that grows upon the boardinghouse walls to the intoxicating atmosphere of the saloon, where Coverdale himself reflects upon liquor and wine as poor simulacra for a higher and more enduring form of intoxication: "Human nature, in my opinion, has a naughty instinct that approves of wine, at least, if not of stronger liquor. The temperance-men may preach till doom's day; and still this cold and barren world will look warmer, kindlier, mellower, through the medium of a toper's glass; nor can they, with all their efforts, really spill his draught upon the floor, until some hitherto unthought-of discovery shall supply him with a truer element of joy" (160–61). Certainly it is the aim of the utopians and Hollingsworth to provide some surrogate for

Hawthorne's "truer element of joy." Their reforms will never touch man's secret need, however, if they are solely directed at abolishing the corrupt ways in which he attempts to realize such joy or freedom.

Man's "naughty instinct" for intoxicating drink is an indication of his need for an alternative to the "weary world" that might promise "the renewed youth and vigor, the brisk, cheerful sense of things present and to come" (*BR*, 163). What is this but the possibility of freeing oneself from the burdens of the past and the exercise of a desire that brings both the present and the future into relation? The imagination allows us to reflect upon what we have become, and it is equally the means of liberating us from the past by offering us the possibility of perpetually remaking the self. Sartre writes: "Freedom is the human being putting his past out of play by secreting his own nothingness. . . . Consciousness continually experiences itself as the nihilation of its past being." [32] As we have seen, such a nihilating movement is not an escape from the past but a recognition of the essence that is man's past in relation to the future wherein he projects his desire as freedom.

In his moments of imaginative self-reflection, Coverdale discovers a different sort of veil that separates us from the world. The metaphor of the vine suggests both the intoxication and the negation that are reconciled in the imaginative consciousness. For Hawthorne, the unreality of the imagination is that which nihilates the substantial world, just as the vine emblematically strangles the pine and threatens to cover the boardinghouse walls. Hawthorne himself is reminded that his seemingly timeless tenure at the Old Manse is coming to an end when carpenters and gardeners begin to renovate the house for the returning owner. Among other changes, Hawthorne regrets the removal "of the veil of woodbine which had crept over a large portion" of the Manse's "southern face" (*OM*, 44). This "sacrilege" marks the end of his imaginative detachment and his departure "from the Old Manse into a custom house." Hawthorne and Coverdale use their own narratives to reweave the veil or vine of the imagination in order to maintain the distance and desire that govern the dialectical process of knowing. Unlike Westervelt, Coverdale and Hawthorne weave this veil in order to recognize the nothingness on which their own consciousness and being depend. This nothingness is at once the nihilating movement of the imagination, the fundamental alienation of the for-itself from the in-itself, and death as "the absolute non-value" with respect to which "all value is determined." [33]

In contrast with Coverdale's authentic mode of "living-in-the-face of death," Zenobia's attempt to engage death directly ends in the rudest theatrics. [34] Attempting to break through all the veils and screens that imprison her, Zenobia merely confirms the inauthentic existence that she has lived. Unlike the drowned man in the fifth book of Wordsworth's *Prelude*, Zenobia offers no intimations of immortality but only the most grotesque parody of such spiritual intentions: [35]

> She knelt, as if in prayer. With the last, choking consciousness, her soul, bubbling out through her lips, it may be said, had given itself up to the Father, reconciled and penitent. But her arms! They were bent before her, as if she struggled against Providence in never-ending hostility. Her hands! They were clenched in inmitigable defiance. Away with the hideous thought! The flitting moment, after Zenobia sank into the dark pool — when her breath was gone, and her soul at her lips, was as long in its capacity of God's infinite forgiveness, as the lifetime of the world. [*BR,* 217]

Coverdale constitutes his relation to the world by means of the veil of imagination, which reconciles negation and freedom. Zenobia fulfills her promise to assume the black veil: "When next you hear of Zenobia, her face will be behind the black-veil; so look your last at it now — for all is over! Once more, farewell" (*BR,* 210). Miming the gestures of a tragic actress playing a star-crossed character, Zenobia at the very last still fails to meet even the reality of death. Her suicide is one more desperate effort to escape the truth of her own consciousness, which she has always repressed behind her own covering veils: "Zenobia, I have often thought, was not quite simple in her death. She had seen pictures, I suppose, of drowned persons, in lithe and graceful attitudes. And she deemed it well and decorous to die as so many village-maidens have, wronged in their first-love, and seeking peace in the bosom of the old, familiar stream. . . . But, in Zenobia's case, there was some tint of the Arcadian affectation that had been visible enough in all our lives, for a few months past" (218).

I have argued that Coverdale's moments of detachment represent his development of an imaginative power that liberates him from the determinants of the substantial world and directs his gaze toward his own mental processes. I shall now return to these four formally similar scenes in order to analyze the content of Coverdale's vision. What the imagination enables him to recognize in himself and his relations with others governs my understanding of Hawthorne's argument in *Blithedale.* In general, these moments of detachment describe neither the activities of a petty voyeur nor the *isolato's* refusal to engage life. Coverdale is prone to both sins, as is Hawthorne, who fears that his own imaginative detachment might transform him into one of those madmen in "The Hall of Fantasy" who no longer distinguishes the substantial world from his own fancies.[36] However, Coverdale's reflection upon his own consciousness enables him to sympathize with the plight of others as well as to anticipate the psychic destiny that the characters have made for themselves. Coverdale is strangely prophetic, a quality that many critics have simply attributed to his narrative distance. But his prophetic powers go beyond the wisdom of hindsight. In each of his moments of vision, Coverdale accurately predicts developments in the subsequent narrative action. At the height of his illness, for example, he whispers to Hollingsworth: "Zenobia is an enchantress! . . . She is a sister of the Veiled Lady! That flower in her hair is a talisman. If you were to snatch it away, she would vanish, or be transformed into something else!" (*BR,* 42). Zenobia does turn out, of course, to be Priscilla's stepsister, and she is associated with the enchantments of Westervelt, at whose command she drops the veil once again over Priscilla. And in a final gesture of renunciation, she takes the jeweled flower from her hair and sends it to Priscilla.

Both Hawthorne and Sartre consider the dream to be homologous with the imaginative consciousness: "In fact, what constitutes the nature of the dream is that reality eludes altogether the consciousness which desires to recapture it; all the effort of consciousness turns in spite of itself to produce the imagery" (*PI,* 255). Since the image symbolizes that which we already know by virtue of its intentional structure, Coverdale's feverish prediction reveals what he has already dimly sensed in his relations with Zenobia, Priscilla, and Hollingsworth. This is not to say that the imagination may be used to predict future events, but it does reveal the ways in which we have conceptualized the world and thus what we might reasonably anticipate on the basis of such an attitude of consciousness. Coverdale's clairvoyance is *not* an insight into Zenobia's essential personality; like most women in this patriarchal culture, Zenobia is a series of masks and pseudonymous identities that she has been forced to assume because of her femininity. Zenobia is *reactive:* her identities are either rebellions against or surrenders to the male authorities that govern her social and ontological situation. Coverdale's prophecy to an extent indicates the ways in which Zenobia will be intended by others: in particular, by those males who fear her passionate intensity. She represents a threat to the masculinity of men like the dilettantish Coverdale and the monomaniacal Hollingsworth — a threat which they liken to the mystery of an enchantress or "dark lady." Zenobia playfully develops Coverdale's reference to her as Eve: "As for the garb of Eden, . . . I shall not assume it till after May-Day," and Coverdale promptly imagines "a picture of that fine, perfectly developed figure, in Eve's earliest garment." But he checks this reflection by noting: "Her free, careless, generous mode of expression often had this effect of creating images which, though pure, are hardly felt to be quite decorous, when born of a thought that passes between man and woman" (*BR,* 17).

"Pure" images that are "hardly decorous" suggest the sort of conflict at work in Coverdale's own mind. In his description of Zenobia's "mode of expression" as "free, careless, generous," Coverdale links freedom and charity — the twin goals of both Hollingsworth and the utopians — with irresponsibility. Zenobia's passionate, sexual, and self-assertive nature ought to be given full range, but in this society such characteristics in woman are "indecorous" and subliminally associated with a sort of license. It is no coincidence that the feminist Zenobia kills herself in despair over the ways in which she has been defined by such men as Hollingsworth, Westervelt, and Coverdale. Just as Hollingsworth would lift the veil from Priscilla only to insure his own control, so he metaphorically transfers Zenobia's "flower" to Priscilla by appropriating her enchantment. Coverdale's prediction is realized and fulfilled in the subsequent narrative by means of his own conscious intentions as well as those of Hollingsworth and Westervelt.

Coverdale's vision in his hermitage is more directly prophetic and thus less problematic. I have already quoted the message that he tosses to a passing bird for Priscilla, in which he warns her of Zenobia's jealousy and Hollingsworth's egotism. More importantly, he sees in himself the same possessiveness toward Priscilla that passes for "love" with Hollingsworth and "magic" with Westervelt: "And say, that, if any mortal really cares for her, it is myself, and not even I, for her realities — poor little seamstress, as Zenobia rightly called her! — but for the fancy-work with which I have idly decked her out!" (*BR,* 94). Coverdale's self-rebuke complements his clairvoyance concerning the ways in which the other men will use Zenobia and Priscilla for their own selfish purposes. The importance of this recognition in relation to Coverdale's final confession cannot be overemphasized: "I — I myself — was in love — with — PRISCILLA!" (228). In at least one way, this confession is Coverdale's admission of complicity in the possessive plots that destroy Zenobia and imprison Priscilla. Like Hollingsworth and Westervelt, Coverdale manipulates Priscilla to meet the requirements of his own desire. Coverdale's detachment in his hermitage enables him to recognize, through the imagination, man's fundamental estrangement from the world and his primary desire to overcome such alienation. In this regard, Coverdale resembles Stendhal's Fabrizio in *The Charterhouse of Parma,* who discovers in his imprisonment in the Farnese tower the dialectic of distance and desire whereby the imagination is liberated. Communicating with his beloved Clélia by means of cryptograms and glimpses through the holes in his boarded window, Fabrizio finds supreme happiness by possessing Clélia in his imagination and yet still maintaining the "virginity" of her unviolated otherness.[37] In a similar sense, Coverdale thinks his hermitage the ideal place for a honeymoon: "Had it ever been my fortune to spend a honey-moon, I should have thought seriously of inviting my bride up thither, where our next neighbors would have been two orioles in another part of the clump" (92).

Coverdale's view from his hotel room also involves a prophetic vision fulfilled by the dramatic action. On the day following his first observation of the general life in the boardinghouse, he awakens from a sleep disturbed by the most tormenting dreams. Coverdale associates these dreams with the detached perspective on events at Blithedale he achieved by returning to the city: "It was not till I had quitted my three friends that they first began to encroach upon my dreams." His dream anticipates the ways in which Priscilla will be increasingly victimized by others: "In those of the last night,

Hollingsworth and Zenobia, standing on either side of my bed, had bent across it to exchange a kiss of passion. Priscilla, beholding this — for she seemed to be peeping in at the chamber-window — had melted gradually away, and left only the sadness of her expression in my heart" (*BR,* 142). Priscilla takes Coverdale's usual post at the window as a displaced image of Coverdale's own exclusion from Hollingsworth's and Zenobia's passion. The kiss ironically recalls the legend of "The Silvery Veil." In this case, however, the kiss itself is what causes Priscilla gradually to melt away, whereas the Veiled Lady vanishes only after Theodore refuses the kiss of faith and lifts the veil. Read in this context, Zenobia's and Hollingworth's kiss is not merely a sign of Coverdale's expectation that both he and Priscilla will be excluded from the passion of these two lovers; it is equally an indication of how both Coverdale and Priscilla are dominated or enchanted by the passion of others. Coverdale recognizes in the dream that the "love" between Hollingsworth and Zenobia is equivalent to the pact between Westervelt and Zenobia.

In the next paragraph, Coverdale tries to grasp the meaning of the "unreasonable" sadness that Priscilla's oneiric disappearance has left in his mind by reflecting on his own involvement in these matters. He promptly accuses himself of having avoided his responsibilities and having thus resigned his friends to their fates: "That cold tendency, between instinct and intellect, which made me pry with speculative interest into people's passions and impulses, appeared to have gone far towards unhumanizing my heart" (142). Reproaching himself with that sin for which he is most often condemned by the critics, Coverdale achieves self-knowledge as a result of his dreams. And yet, he himself qualifies this self-condemnation: "But a man cannot always decide for himself whether his own heart is cold or warm. It now impresses me, that, if I erred at all, in regard to Hollingsworth, Zenobia, and Priscilla, it was through too much sympathy, rather than too little" (142–43). Coverdale realizes that "too much sympathy" for others often results in the same possessive egotism that motivates Hollingsworth or Westervelt. His argument closely resembles Emerson's and Thoreau's objections to philanthropy, but Coverdale offers his own imagination in the place of Emerson's self-reliance as the best defense against such self-delusion. Because the imagination offers some shadowy access to what we ordinarily repress, it suggests a possible solution to the paradox of romantic self-consciousness. The imaginative reflection on self teaches us how every act of "self-reliance" depends upon forces over which we have little control.

What Coverdale sees through the boardinghouse windows confirms his dream of Priscilla's victimized life. Westervelt has now replaced Hollingsworth, as if to make the destiny of Priscilla even more explicit. Indeed, when Coverdale confronts Priscilla in Zenobia's drawing room and asks her: "Does Hollingsworth know that you are here?" Priscilla answers, "He bade me come" (*BR,* 158). When Westervelt detects Coverdale at his observation post and Zenobia drops "the white linen curtain . . . like the drop-curtain of a theatre, in the interval between acts," the veil of illusion is once again thrown over the secrets of these characters (147). However, what Coverdale's dreams and imagination have allowed him to see does not prevent him from acting. If Zenobia, Westervelt, and Hollingsworth have once again dropped the veil over Priscilla, Coverdale offers her the opportunity to free herself. Reenacting the legend of "The Silvery Veil," Coverdale does not refuse the "kiss" of faith that preserves the integrity of others by acknowledging our inevitable estrangement. Just before he decides to present himself in Zenobia's drawing room, Coverdale again reflects upon his own status as an observer and potential judge of his fellows: "Zenobia . . . should have been able to appreciate that quality of the intellect and the heart, which impelled me (often against my own will, and to the detriment of my own comfort) to live in other lives, and to endeavor — by generous sympathies, by delicate intuitions, by taking note of things too slight to record, and by bringing my spirit into manifold accordance with the companions whom God assigned me — to learn the secret which was hidden even from themselves" (*BR,* 148). Indeed, Coverdale's awakened imagination has made it possible for him to bring his "spirit into manifold accordance" with his companions.

Critics may consider this passage to be one more indication of Coverdale's inflated egotism; the extent to which Coverdale has literally attempted to "live in other lives" *is* a measure of his own possessive instincts. Yet, in those moments of detachment when he has sympathized with the plight of his fellows — recognizing Hollingsworth's weaknesses as his own, Westervelt's superficiality as a reflection of his own dilettantism, and Priscilla's abandonment as his own "unreasonable sorrow" — Coverdale has approached a compassion notably absent in the behavior of others. Coverdale has some right to lay claim to the position of a judge, whose understanding might not redeem the others from the fates they have chosen but which might nonetheless be an expression of love:

> Had I been judge, as well as witness, my sentence might have been as stern as that of Destiny itself. But still, no trait of original nobility of character; no struggle against temptation; no iron necessity of will, on the one hand, nor extenuating circumstance to be derived from passion and despair, on the other; no remorse that might co-exist with error, even if powerless to prevent it; no proud repentance, that should claim retribution as a meed — would go unappreciated. True, again, I might give my full assent to the punishment that was sure to follow. But it would be given mournfully, and with undiminished love. [*BR,* 148]

Coverdale's apparent vanity and pretension in this passage are greatly mitigated by the difference between his proposed judgment of others and Hollingsworth's ruthless judgment of Zenobia at Eliot's Pulpit. Coverdale promises compassion and human understanding, even though he cannot offer to save others from their own willful acts; Hollingsworth ignores those very traits in Zenobia that Coverdale promises would not go unappreciated by him.

Thus, when Coverdale does recognize what he terms his "duty" and acts upon what he has seen from his hotel window, he does not offer Priscilla his own authority in the place of Hollingsworth's, Westervelt's, or Zenobia's. These three characters echo each other's commandments by variously ordering: "Come, Priscilla." Instead, Coverdale merely offers her the opportunity to make her own decisions, to achieve the freedom that would truly liberate her from her veiled past:

> "Priscilla," said I, in the hearing of them all, "do you know whither you are going?"
> "I do not know," she answered.
> "Is it wise to go? — and is it your choice to go?" I asked. "If not — I am your friend, and Hollingsworth's friend — tell me so, at once!" [*BR*, 159]

Commanding Priscilla to *tell him*, Coverdale orders her to act for herself for the first time in the narrative. Yet, Westervelt answers the question for her, in a mockery of the free will that Coverdale has tried to evoke: "'Priscilla sees in me an older friend than either Mr. Coverdale or Mr. Hollingsworth. I shall willingly leave the matter at her option.' While thus speaking, he made a gesture of kindly invitation; and Priscilla passed me, with the gliding movement of a sprite and took his offered arm" (159).

Like his literary successor, the narrator of James's *Sacred Fount*, Coverdale learns that he must not assume the role of either the effaced observer or the author of others' destinies.[38] A great distance separates *this* Coverdale from the character who perversely questions Priscilla about her feelings as they observe Zenobia press Hollingsworth's hand to her bosom in a moment of uncontrollable passion. Indeed, Coverdale recalls this interrogation in terms that unmistakably suggest rape and the general violation of others figured in the legend of "The Silvery Veil": "No doubt, it was a kind of sacrilege in me to attempt to come within her maidenly mystery. But as she appeared to be tossed aside by her other friends, or carelessly let fall, like a flower which they had done with, I could not resist the impulse to take just one peep beneath her folded petals" (*BR*, 116). Coverdale learns that the deepest sin and greatest vanity is the effort to appropriate and possess the other, even in the interests of what appears to be good or true. The power of the imagination may enable one to sympathize with others and even identify with their circumstances, but the imagination is also an indication of each person's fundamental alienation from the world. The distance between self and other may never be breached without violating the integrity of both.

Communication becomes the means of offering others those signs whereby they may discover their own truths.

In a sense, this mode of narrational being is what Coverdale approximates in the "romance" he composes out of Old Moodie's talk in the saloon. The story of "Fauntleroy" is ostensibly an effort to fill in the details of Zenobia's and Priscilla's backgrounds. However, Coverdale's account is deliberately ambiguous and fictionalized; it refuses to provide us with the "facts" that have been so perversely veiled in the preceding drama. What Coverdale's story does accomplish is still another repetition of the main themes of the narrative, especially those concerning the misuse of the imagination. Sparked by Fauntleroy's stories of "his former wealth, the noble loveliness of his first wife, and the beautiful child she had given him," Priscilla's imagination "tended upward, and twined herself perseveringly around this unseen sister; as a grape-vine might strive to clamber out of a gloomy hollow among the rocks, and embrace a young tree, standing in the sunny warmth above" (*BR,* 171). The very idea of love is born in Priscilla as the product of this desire, which in itself offers the freedom of "a higher and imaginative life within" (172). Priscilla achieves that inner spirituality whose lack has been her father's distinguishing characteristic. A man of surfaces and "false glitter," Fauntleroy is "a mere image, an optical delusion, created by the sunshine of prosperity," who seems to vanish as his wealth is exhausted (168–69). Priscilla's imaginative nature offers some redemption of her father's sinful past, but Fauntleroy continues to control her nature as he had once manipulated both his wives and his first daughter, Zenobia. For Hawthorne, the imagination is a mode of self-recognition, but Priscilla's imagination is directed by her father's stories toward its realization in Zenobia. The image of a higher, more spiritual life that ought to be Priscilla's image of herself is incarnated and thus falsified by Zenobia, whose material wealth and advantages take the place of the spiritual riches that Priscilla desires. Priscilla's own future is already invaded by her father's nostalgia; Priscilla is "possessed" by her father's *idea* of Zenobia long before she has been imprisoned by Westervelt. The imaginative vitality that ought to be Priscilla's resource and freedom becomes the means by which she is placed in greater bondage, not only to her father and Westervelt but to Zenobia as well. Embodying Priscilla's own desire, Zenobia steals the very essence of Priscilla's identity.

Readers are generally bewildered by Priscilla's initial attachment to Zenobia at the farm, a situation that apears to be clarified by the gradual unfolding of Old Moodie's history. But Priscilla's attachment to Zenobia goes beyond sisterly love; Priscilla unwittingly loves what she has imagined Zenobia to be. Like all of the other characters in this work, Priscilla projects her own desire for self-identity onto others and thus loves not the other, but an alter ego. All of this is dramatically suggested by the reversal of the women's roles at the end of the work. Offering her jeweled flower to Coverdale as a token to be given to the victorious Priscilla, Zenobia transfers her distinguishing mark to the sister who has now taken her place in Hollingsworth's affections. Priscilla has triumphed through the perversity of her misdirected imagination by taking the place of the one who has always been for her the object of her own desire for selfhood. Thus, Priscilla's quiet but pervasive authority over the broken Hollingsworth seems less inconsistent with her personality. As tempting as it is to imagine that Priscilla has finally achieved a level of willful action and choice, we must conclude that she remains consistently blind to the psychic mechanisms that have governed her life from the beginning. Fulfilling her own desire by assuming Zenobia's role, Priscilla surrenders herself to a delusory world of appearances. Instead of the higher, spiritual freedom that her imagination had at first offered her, Priscilla discovers the possessive authority over others by which she herself has always been victimized. In the end, neither Hollingsworth nor Priscilla has any measure of the freedom that Coverdale approximates in his own narrative. D. H. Lawrence's classic judgment of Priscilla as a "little psychic prostitute" economically expresses this perverse truth.[39]

In these four structurally similar moments of imaginative detachment, Coverdale sees himself in and through the other characters in the narrative. These scenes constitute Coverdale's inside narrative — the story of his story — wherein the power of the imagination is reaffirmed as man's only access to freedom. Despite the pastoral dream of the utopians, their experiment at Blithedale simply repeats the same illusions that in the urban world condemn men and women to the endless reenactment of the drama of master and servant. Despite Hollingsworth's promethean effort to make man acknowledge his fallen condition and discover his better nature, he himself repeats the very crimes that he had hoped to reform. And despite Westervelt's appeal to the imagination, he merely exploits the confusion between the sensory and the imaginative in order to secure his own power and authority. At the heart of all these characters' lust for power and mastery there is the hidden fear that human beings are by nature alien and contingent. Only Coverdale approaches the freedom that such nothingness permits and the responsibility that it entails.

Coverdale's education in the imagination, however, remains incomplete and equivocal. When he claims to have "nothing" to tell, we may read this either as his relapse into his original diffidence or as a pun on the "nothingness" that is the essential discovery of the imagination. He yearns nostalgically for the failed utopian project: "More and more, I feel that we had struck upon what ought to be a truth." We may read his subjunctive either as a desperate effort to salvage the past or as an affirmation that the only true utopia is that no-place of the imagination. Although he claims to have given up poetry, he reminds us that the volume he published two years after his departure from Blithedale has achieved some popular success and brought him some small stature "among our minor minstrelsy" (*BR*, 226). Perhaps Coverdale shares Hawthorne's knowledge that the imaginative life does not depend on publication or fame, but Hawthorne also knows that the imagination requires the "otherness" of the world that redeems it from sheer fancy. It is just this otherness that seems so woefully lacking in Coverdale's concluding confession, which reveals his drift back to mere sensory gratifications: "Being well to do in the world, and having nobody but myself to care for, I live very much at my ease, and fare sumptuously every day." Coverdale's world-weary tone is, of course, understandable as his final expression of what he has seen of himself and the other characters in the course of his narration. Contrary to what popular psychology may assure us, self-knowledge is not always a cure for human weakness, fear, or evil. Coverdale has recognized in himself a will to mastery that is both the essence of Hawthorne's Unpardonable Sin and fundamental to human consciousness. The reader might well "charitably suppose" Coverdale "to blush," when he confesses to a "love" that in all the other dramatic circumstances of this work has been a double for egotism.

Yet, if Coverdale's confession indicates in part his acceptance of responsibility for the events at Blithedale, his final equivocation may reveal his inability to accept the full implications of what his imagination has shown him of human nature. In his analysis of the imagination's construction of an "image" of what we already know on an affective level, Sartre virtually transforms the unconscious into a function of consciousness. There is certainly a difference between our "knowledge" of that which has not yet been made present to consciousness and that which we have objectified as an image. The process of constructing such an image cannot be accomplished without distortion or "translation." For Sartre, the goal of the argument is the discovery of human freedom, so it is not surprising that he ignores those aspects of imaginative activity that would limit its freedom and purity. In a similar sense, those critics who understand literary narration as an educational process in which the self discovers its freedom must minimize the repressions by which such a consciousness is achieved.

Hollingsworth surrenders his own power to Priscilla's deceptive love as a consequence of his guilt. As he tells Coverdale, "Ever since we parted, I have been busy with a single murderer!" (*BR*, 224). Perhaps it is also Coverdale's destiny to remain a prisoner of his knowledge of sin, a character incapable of transforming its truth for the sake of his own freedom. Beyond the "time" of his narrative, Coverdale reverts to the superficial figure introduced in the early chapters. However, what allows his narrative to "tell" him is precisely its dependence on others, whose very strangeness the imagination allows Coverdale to discover. Coverdale's final confession of love might also be read as his desperate bid to return to the romance: that is, the family romance in which the struggle between self and other requires both a language of power and an imagination of freedom.

The "Priscilla" imaged by Coverdale in the absence of her character merely repeats the basic intention of the preceding narrative, recalling us to the circuit of Coverdale's desire, sin, and sympathy. It is just this absence — of Priscilla, of the narrative as Coverdale's other — that grants the reader entrance to the text. Hawthorne does not offer a history of Brook Farm "for the behoof of future experimentalists"; he offers the romance of Blithedale as an ambiguous tale whose moral must be constructed by an active, imaginative reader. Sartre suggests that the act of writing is an appeal "to the freedom of the readers" without whom the work ceases to exist.[40] Coverdale's alienation and apparent lack of direction at the end of this work involve a certain anticipation and desire. He awaits his reader, the only "other" who can now liberate the character from the past of his narration. Sartre writes: "To write is thus both to disclose the world and to offer it as a task to the generosity of the reader. It is to have recourse to the consciousness of others in order to make one's self be recognized as *essential* to the totality of being; it is to wish to live this essentiality by means of interposed persons; but, on the other hand, as the real world is revealed only by action, . . . the novelist's universe would lack thickness if it were not discovered in a movement to transcend it."[41]

Dryden has argued that the relation of writer and reader in Hawthorne's works in certain ways resembles the relation of lovers. Yet, he distinguishes the "spontaneous commitment" of lovers from the dialectical struggle between Hawthorne's writer and reader: "For Hawthorne the fascination of reading like the fascination of love is the result of the irresistible lure exerted by another person's existence, but, unlike the relation between the beloved and the lover, that between author and reader is generated by a will to power."[42] A Sartrean existentialist would be quick to argue that the power struggle between writer and reader differs from the endless cycles of master and servant insofar as it engages the freedom of both. However, such freedom is extraordinarily problematic if one acknowledges the dependency of the imagination on those unconscious influences that have motivated it. The moral ambiguity of *The Blithedale Romance* hardly guarantees the freedom of its readers. Such readers may, of course, choose to find whatever they wish in the text, but Coverdale remains to warn us that neither our choices nor our wishes are ever free. In the imaginative space of the romance, the reader will, as Coverdale has, see himself, which is to say the history of what he has become. Such a reader may deny this knowledge or behold his own image with joyous dread, but his very act of reading condemns him to the prison of his interpretation. Like Sartre's Roquentin, who has vanished except for his edited notebooks, Coverdale exists at the very last only in this narration, which both depends upon and is threatened by an imaginative, usurping other. If Coverdale concludes fadedly:

> Fickle and fumbling, variable, obscure,
> Glozing his life with after-shining flicks,
> Illuminating, from a fancy gorged
> By apparition, plain and common things,
> Sequestering the fluster from the year,
> Making gulped potions from obstreperous drops,
> And so distorting, proving what he proves
> Is nothing, . . .

then:

> So may the relation of each man be clipped.[43]

4.

Writing and Truth
in Poe's *The Narrative*
of Arthur Gordon Pym

Language, as sense that is sounded and written, is in itself suprasensuous, something that constantly transcends the merely sensible. So understood, language is in itself metaphysical.
    — Heidegger, "A Dialogue on Language," *On the Way to Language*

That the signified is originarily and essentially (and not only for a finite and created spirit) trace, that it is *always already in the position of the signifier,* is the apparently innocent proposition within which the metaphysics of the logos, of presence and consciousness, must reflect upon writing as its death and its resource.
    — Derrida, *Of Grammatology*

In the past two decades, critical interest in Poe's *Narrative of Arthur Gordon Pym of Nantucket* (1838) has resulted in various interpretations of the work's coherence and organization. Most commentators basically agree with Edward Davidson's summary of Pym's spiritual education: "It is a study of emerging consciousness, a very special intelligence and awareness which is Arthur Gordon Pym's (and, to an extent, Poe's). . . . The self-as-imagination begins with the real, substantial world, follows the poetic direction of penetrating and destroying the world, and then goes even farther in order to set up on 'the other side' certain symbols and keys to the mind's perception of reality." [1] Davidson's general characterization of the work as *Bildungsroman*, however, has been challenged by a host of ingenious critics, each offering some historical or contextual key that will unlock the secret of *Pym*'s form and meaning. In particular, recent American criticism either relentlessly tries to fit *Pym* into some predetermined generic category or marshals impressive evidence to demonstrate the basic flaws and inconsistencies in the text. In both cases, the same critical standard continues to operate: a good work of literature ought to demonstrate internal coherence and narrative consistency.

Such an attitude implies that criticism is a process of making difficult or extraordinary texts intelligible. The degree to which a work meets the criteria of unity and coherence is more often than not a measure of its conventionality, or at least its susceptibility to analytic "translation." Since literature depends upon its ability to disrupt and violate accepted meanings and ordinary expectations, the most original work characteristically frustrates established methods and categories of interpretation. It does not, of course, follow that the text's resistance to interpretation is a guarantee of its literary value, but more attention ought to be paid to the ways in which our critical traditions tend to privilege certain "major works" and exile other "eccentric" texts. One need only review the various generic characterizations of *Pym* to realize that this work is either a monumental bungle or the achievement of transcendent genius. The title of Joseph Ridgely's review of the criticism suggests some of the prevailing confusion: "Tragical-Mythical-Satirical-Hoaxical: Problems of Genre in Pym."[2]

Contemporary French critics find *Pym* and Poe's works in general appropriate pretexts for the consideration of basic literary and theoretical questions. The *Tel Quel* theorist Jean Ricardou closely examines the episode on the island of Tsalal as an exemplary demonstration of how all writing is basically concerned with its own inscription. *Pym* is a "Journey to the Bottom of the Page" that explores the possibility of its own textual existence at the same time that it prefigures its own erasure: "No text is more complete than *The Narrative of Arthur Gordon Pym,* for the fiction it presents points to the end of every text, the ultimate establishment of 'blank paper defended by whiteness.'"[3] Ricardou's interpretation, however, concentrates on one restricted part of the narrative and disregards the formal strategies of the narration. Focusing on the hieroglyphs carved in the chasms and the "singular character" of the water on the island, Ricardou only hints at a comprehensive reading of the metaliterary possibilities in *Pym*.

In "Le tombeau d'Edgar Poe," Maurice Mourier adds some important remarks on the "Preface" and "Note" in relation to the inscriptions in (and of) the chasms. Mourier parodies the critical desire for hidden meaning by forcing the shapes of the chasms to spell out "E. A. Poe" and deciphering the alphabetical characters carved in the marl as "A. G. Pym" and "E. A. P." He concludes that the narrative displaces and hides any narrating subject, an idea that relies on Derrida's concept of *écriture* as the graphic mark of the "trace" or *différance* that characterizes the productive play of all signification: "The text of *The Adventures of Arthur Gordon Pym* mimes/refuses/exorcises the death of the narrator (of any narrator), the death of the *I* and its text wherein the narrator-character conceals the languishing scriptor who slips away, childishly placing onto the character all responsibility for the fictional *mise-en-scène* (it does not belong to *I*)."[4]

The metaliterary character of *Pym* clarifies a number of problems concerning the work's form and thematic intention. In its fundamental investigation of the problematics of writing, *Pym* also questions the nature and possibility of literary form. What critics have considered difficulties and inconsistencies in the text may also be considered self-conscious disruptions of the impulse toward coherent design and completed meaning. Forever holding out the promise of a buried signified, *Pym* offers a sequence of forged or imitation truths: delivered messages, deciphered hieroglyphs, a penultimate vision. And yet, the inability of each successive sign to present its truth is ironically disclosed, increasingly entangling any reading in the signifying web it attempts to unravel.

Poe's writings have also provided the occasions for Lacan's reading of Freud in "Seminar on 'The Purloined Letter'" and Derrida's deconstruction of Lacan in "The Purveyor of Truth."[5] Derrida's objections to Lacan's psychoanalytic treatment of "The Purloined Letter" might be applied generally to certain implicit assumptions made by literary critics. Derrida demonstrates how Lacan's disregard for the formal strategies of the narrator of the tale tends to reduce the text to an "exemplary content" in the analyst's own argument. Thus, Derrida suggests how all criticism (psychoanalytic, literary, historical) tends to neutralize the constraints of the pretext that continue to operate in the critical discourse. What Derrida terms Lacan's "ideality of the signifier" — the "indivisible" presence of the signifier — subtly shares the "ideality of a meaning" that governs the critical tendency to employ texts to illustrate general laws.[6] The violence of interpretation — the displacement of the signifier by a supplementary signifier — is repressed in the history, formalist scholarship, psychoanalysis, or psychobiography that presumes to make the historical event of the pretext semantically present. The work in question must always be the differential relation of pretext and criticism, a work produced in the interpretative supplementation of its ostensible subject. If any "literary history" is to be salvaged, then it ought to be a narrative of this disguised critical appropriation (neither by authors nor critics, but *in* language), an unveiling of the ways in which a signifying potential is generated and used.

In the introductory chapter, I suggested why traditional literary history so often seems insensitive to the idea of literary expression. In part, criticism fails when it refuses to respond to the interpretative imperatives that constitute the very meaning of such self-conscious authors as Poe. Reading and writing are so often doubled in Poe's writings that we falsify the main impulse of his poetics when we attempt either to reconstruct the author's meaning or to assign a historical context to his truth. Dupin's "understanding" of any of the three crimes he attempts to solve is a function of poetic reconstruction, which simulates the bare facts only to transform them. If we refuse to follow Dupin's own method of poetic interpretation, then we are left with nothing but the empty significance of the actual crimes. The center or bottom of any Poe text is either a frustrating indeterminacy (the white curtain at the end of *Pym*) or a useless and contrived "unity" (the conventional solution of the detective novel).

The French *Symbolistes* were attracted to Poe's works precisely because these writings demand an active, imaginative reader, who would imitate the method of Dupin's poetic understanding by displacing the bare fact of the literary text. Thus, Poe's writings ought to be viewed primarily as evocative and suggestive, which are crucial poetic qualities for the *Symbolistes*. In one sense, of course, this poetic impulse to awaken the reader's imaginative faculties is inscribed within the romantic tradition that still governs Poe and his symbolist heirs. Yet, both Poe and the *Symbolistes* give up the ultimate *telos* of romantic intersubjectivity and the implicit goal of that universal self-consciousness in which all acts of interpretation and expression might ultimately be reconciled. In Poe, it is the absence of the principle of unity for which poet and reader long that prompts the perpetual wandering of the text; for the *Symbolistes* the "abyss" itself would prompt the delicious agonies of the alienated poet longing for an impossible ideal. The anxiety of such desire may lead to an aestheticism in which Mallarmé's "Book," or the imagination, is celebrated as a simulated ideal. However, the artifice of such transcendental principles is the constant reminder of the poet's self-conscious yearning, whose truth is manifest only in the repeated expression of poetic desire. As Joseph Riddel writes, "Poetry is textuality that can only reflect an absence of the ideal."[7]

The characteristic self-reflexivity of symbolist aestheticism — which mediates the romantic irony of Poe and the high modernism of Pound, Eliot, Joyce, and Stevens — is both its resource and the beginning of its subversion. As an incestuous production, this autotelicism attempts to mark the boundaries of a "palace" of art remote from the tedious repetitions of *la vie quotidienne*. The logic of such metaliterary reflection, however, demands a supplementary act of reading that will break down its formal boundaries, one that requires the interpretative violation of the text as its own justification. Such a "moment" is, of course, a particular instance of what de Man has described as the dialectic of modernity; it is the moment in which the poet's longing for free and original self-expression lapses into the inevitable historicity of tradition, culture, and language. It is this "modern" Poe, both the father and son of the *Symbolistes,* whose writings may be said to reveal our own critical situation by dramatizing the inescapable dilemma of modernism. In Joseph Riddel's analysis, it is the Poe who "carried his discourse into an aestheticism which brought itself into such severe question and subjected itself to such acute guilt that only an utterly idealistic aestheticism could reconstitute the world with a center. It was this Poe whom the *Symbolistes* discovered, an implicit Poe who most crucially realized the Modernist rupture in an art which accentuated the center as the presence of an absence, the music of nothingness." [8]

The "idealistic aestheticism" that seems to control most of Poe's writings is precisely what is threatened by *The Narrative of A. Gordon Pym*. This text enacts the deconstruction of representation as the illusion of the truth and prefigures the contemporary conception of writing as the endless production of differences. In its main outlines, *Pym* appears to follow the basic argument of Poe's poetry and to prefigure the gnostic cosmology of *Eureka* (1848). In the course of his sea voyage, Pym proves himself to be one of Poe's least perceptive characters. Pym's lack of insight in his early adventures is comparable to the myopia of the narrator in "The Fall of the House of Usher"; both characters epitomize the dangers of relying on the illusory world of sense impressions and misleading empirical data. Repeatedly baffled and frustrated by his experiences, Pym is forced to rely on various helpers and companions during his voyage. In the poetry, psychic guides generally assist the persona to interpret the cosmic message obscurely inscribed in nature. Nesace is charged by the deity with conveying his Word to the world in "Al Aaraaf," Psyche reads "What is written" on the "legended tomb" for the "I" in "Ulalume," and the "pilgrim shadow" points the way toward "Eldorado" for the "gallant knight." Pym's companions, however, are far less effective in helping him to understand either the progress or purpose of his voyage. Augustus dies of gangrene as the survivors drift aimlessly on the wreck of the *Grampus,* Tiger the Newfoundland dog simply disappears shortly after he has served his narrative function, Parker is eaten by the others, and Captain Guy and his crew are buried alive by the natives on the island of Tsalal. Dirk Peters alone accompanies Pym to the furthest limit of the voyage and returns alive, but not to tell the tale. Daniel Hoffman sees Peters as the "resilient dwarfish savage" who replaces the "rational Prefect of Police side of Pym's mind" represented by his earlier friend and guide, Augustus.[9] Peters calls Pym's attention to the "singular looking indentures in the surface of the marl," and Peters rather than Pym judges them to have "some little resemblance to alphabetical characters." [10] Although Peters has a basic intuitive sense of natural order, he can neither articulate nor communicate this understanding. To the end of the voyage, Pym remains blind to the metaphysical and spiritual implications of his adventures.

The failure of Pym's companions to help him understand his journey gives special importance to his editorial relationship with Mr. Poe, who must be considered another character in the drama and distinct from the historical Poe. The elaborate framing devices of Pym's "Preface" and the appended editorial "Note" have generally been viewed as part of Poe's parody of the scientific voyage narratives that were in such vogue in the nineteenth century. The deliberate confusion of Pym and Mr. Poe as narrative voices also seems to reinforce the parabolic character of the tale and its relation to Poe's own inner voyagings. Mr. Poe, however, is neither a simple *Doppelgänger* of Pym nor identical with Edgar Allan Poe. As the writer of the adventure, Mr. Poe transforms the "facts" provided by Pym into the poetic expression that constitutes Pym's education and understanding. Pym explains why he has not undertaken the writing of his own story: "A distrust of my own abilities as a writer was, nevertheless, one of the principal causes which prevented me from complying with the suggestion of my advisers" (724). And in spite of the encouragement from Mr. Poe "to prepare at once a full account of what I had seen and undergone," Pym fears he "should not be able to write, from mere memory, a statement so minute and connected as to have the *appearance* of that truth it would really possess. . . ." Thus, Pym's lack of talent as an imaginative writer is intimately bound up with his failure to understand the significance of his voyage. Pym's claim at the end of the "Preface" must be taken as a ruse to deceive the unwary reader: "This exposé being made, it will be seen at once how much of what follows I claim to be my own writing; and it will also be understood that no fact is misrepresented in the first few pages which were written by Mr. Poe. Even to those readers who have not seen the Messenger [*Southern Literary Messenger*], it will be unnecessary to point out where his portion ends and my own commences; *the difference in point of style will be readily perceived*" (725; my italics). Pym's contribution to the text remains simply the germ of Mr. Poe's poetic idea, which is the true story behind this improbable romance.[11] Pym still plays a crucial role in this drama of poetic composition; Mr. Poe's story is an interpretation of what is already part of Pym's psychic experience. Narrative authority is in question from the beginning, because the writing must rely on both the formlessness of Pym's unconscious and the poetic interpretation of Mr. Poe.

As we shall see, there are several other writers involved in Pym's story, all of whom are controlled by the poetic composition. The multiple authorities for the narration appear to contradict Poe's general concern in his works with poetic unity. For Poe, poetic expression moves toward the origin and end of all language: the energetic cosmic unity described in the pseudo-science of *Eureka:* "In sinking into Unity, it [Matter] will sink at once into that Nothingness which, to all Finite Perception, Unity must be — into that Material Nihility from which alone we can conceive it to have been evoked — to have been *created* by the Volition of God."[12] In its referential function, language sustains the spatial and temporal dimensions of our material condition. Poetry does violence to this mode of representation and attempts to constitute itself as a self-referential system of signs. The poem imitates cosmic design and symmetry rather than offering a reflection of empirical phenomena. Thus, poetic expression strives for a physical presence in the word itself as the embodiment of psychic and cosmic truth. The poetic aim is essentially formalist: to construct the poem *in* its being rather than *through* its meaning. In his analysis of "Tamerlane," Davidson summarizes the transcendental intention of Poe's poetry as the effacement of the self-conscious Ego; thus, the "annihilation of self" ironically becomes the ground for one's identity in Being. The poem approximates this spiritual completion by transforming the self into a full poetic image rather than a mere "name." [13]

Straining against ordinary temporality and its materiality, poetic writing imitates the cosmic dialectic of "Attraction and Repulsion," the consolidation and dispersion which together define the "throb of the Heart Divine." [14] Writing inaugurates a desire for completion that its own inscription is destined to frustrate. Unity is nowhere present for Poe, because the original act of creation "was that of a determinate irradiation — one finally *dis*continued." [15] Bearing as it does both nostalgia and desire for divine silence, writing substitutes the idea of order and unity as a simulacrum for the lost presence. The poetic act may prefigure a reconciliation of all things, but in so doing it only asserts more fully its own lack. Thus, the poetic image presents itself as a complex play between the extremes of self-conscious alienation and the dissolution of self in metaphysical unity. Such writing embodies the essential doubleness of Poe's cosmic metaphor: both irradiation and decentralization. Recall at this point Poe's definition of the "Poetic Principle" as "strictly and simply, the Human Aspiration for Supernal Beauty. . . ." The dialectic of desire and repression informs Poe's idea of "the Poetry of words as *The Rhythmical Creation of Beauty*." [16]

In *The Narrative of A. Gordon Pym,* the differential process of writing is enacted as the subject and object of the work. The tale "progresses" from an ordinary referential discourse to a poetic expression in which the metaphoric structure of language materializes in a landscape of signs. For both Pym and Mr. Poe, the true journey is into the text itself, in which a paradoxical kind of self-definition might be found. Their mutual silence at the end opens the play of writing to its necessary interpretation, marked by the appended Note penned by yet another hand. Neither in form nor content does this Note satisfy our expectation of a conclusion. We learn of "the late sudden and distressing death of Mr. Pym," only to discover "that the few remaining chapters which were to have completed his narrative . . . have been irrecoverably lost through the accident by which he perished himself." The limit of the voyage is itself the incompletion of writing, which must be supplemented by the author of the Note or by Peters, who is "still alive, and a resident of Illinois, . . . and will, no doubt, afford material for a conclusion of Mr. Pym's account" (852). Yet, Mr. Poe declines "to fill the vacuum," as if the disclosure of the absence that grounds all writing has been the end and the beginning of his poetic task. Thus, the Preface and Note formally define Pym's metaphysical adventure by questioning beginnings and endings.

Within this frame, the text explores the nature of writing in such a way as to render ambiguous what we thought we had understood to be Poe's gnostic philosophy of composition.

Pym's motivation for going to sea originates with the stories told by his friend and occasional bedfellow, Augustus Barnard. Their brief voyage on the *Ariel* and their rescue by the *Penguin* prefigure their subsequent adventures at sea. It is Augustus's "manner of relating his stories of the ocean" that reinforces Pym's "somewhat gloomy although glowing imagination." Pym later suspects these stories "to have been sheer fabrications," but it is just this air of unreality that sparks the boys' desire for adventure. Both of them seem to long for some alternative to the superficially ordered world of Edgarton. Thus, it seems especially appropriate that their "scheme of deception" enables them to escape as well as to expose the illusion of control and order maintained by this conventional society. Augustus forges a note to Pym's father, which purports to be a formal invitation for Pym to spend a fortnight with the sons of a family friend, Mr. Ross. Augustus thus displaces the proper signified of such a message and calls into question the habitual methods of reference supporting social intercourse. Like all forgeries, this note plays upon the notion that we read a text according to a specific author, in this case the authorizing signature of "Mr. Ross." The deception threatens the fundamental rules of social behavior and communication; their departure is made absolute by this act of forgery. At first they anticipate sending a second, corrective letter, written at such a time as all possibility of "any turning back" would be "a matter out of the question." Pym confidently believes that "vessels enough would be met with by which a letter might be sent home explaining the adventure to my parents" (733). But Augustus's violation of social language suggests that such an explanation might involve a more difficult task than Pym envisions. The mutiny on board the brig makes it technically impossible to send such an explanation. And yet, it is the writing of the note that demonstrates the arbitrariness and ambiguity of reference implicit in any text. The plot itself is initiated by a reflection on language that has already been suggested in the Preface and will be the primary concern of the final Note.

There is a curious sequential relation between writing and performance in this tale. No sooner is the note "written and delivered" than Pym acts out its deception of his family. On his way to the wharf, Pym runs into his grandfather who calls him by name: "'Why, bless my soul, Gordon . . . why, why — *whose* dirty cloak is that you have on?'" (734). Pym answers him "in the gruffest of all imaginable tones," disguising his voice with a jackson's jargon. Predictably enough, Pym's manner of speech affects the vision of his grandfather, who complains: "'Won't do — *new glasses* — thought it was Gordon — d— —d good-for-nothing salt water long Tom'" (my italics). This error of perception is, of course, partially attributable to the morning fog, under the cover of which Pym is stealing to the brig. Like the white curtain at the Pole and all the figures of blankness or darkness in the story, however, the fog is an objective correlative for the formlessness that motivates the desire for definition and discrimination. The grandfather's perception is also determined by the class structure coded in the social language of Edgarton. This small episode dramatizes a central issue in the entire narrative. Jacques Derrida claims that "from Plato and Aristotle on, scriptural images have regularly been used to *illustrate* the relationship between reason and experience, perception and memory."[17] Augustus's note and Pym's deception question this classical conception of language as a mediating representation, suggesting instead that language constitutes reason and experience, perception and memory in a differential play of which the mark of writing is a sign.[18]

From the obscurity of the morning fog, Pym quickly slips into the darkness of the ship's hold. When he boards the *Grampus,* he enters a space that is implicitly textual. Before he enters this darkness, Pym has a glimpse of Augustus's spacious stateroom and notices "a set of hanging shelves full of books, chiefly books of voyages and travels" (734). In the hold, Pym finds that his coffinlike "iron-bound box" is also equipped with "some books, pen, ink, and paper." Thus, Pym enters the realm of romance through a succession of intertwined metaphors of textuality: preface, fabricated stories, forged note, books, writing implements, paper, ink. Derrida remarks that in the opening of "The Purloined Letter," "Everything begins 'in' a library: among books, writing, references. Hence nothing begins. Simply a drifting or a disorientation from which one never moves away."[19] The voyage in *Pym* is only nominally conducted by sailors, ships, and oceans. These are mere figures for the writing itself, which is characterized by a "drifting" and "disorientation" from its own origin or end. Every effort at representation discloses only another representation, and we are quickly entangled in an inescapable metaphoric play. *Pym* is a narrative about a journey toward a metaphysical and geographical center, but in the very effort of writing such a story that center is displaced, disrupted, deferred.

The hidden textuality of Pym's voyage gradually emerges from the darkness to enter the body of the world. Shortly after he accustoms himself to his cramped quarters, Pym falls into a deep sleep that intensifies the discontinuity of Edgarton and the poetic space of the voyage. Pym dozes off while reading "the expedition of Lewis and Clark to the mouth of the Columbia," another voyage in quest of origins and ends.[20] Pym reads and dreams in a site that is variously described as a cloacal womb, a tomb, and a library. Riddel notes that Roderick Usher's library stands directly above the subterranean vault in which Madeline is entombed: "Moreover, the library is not only a central room, but another closure that stands outside or over the central tomb. The texts that stand for one idea signify its absence. They are signs of death."[21] From the beginning, Pym's confinement is associated with the doubleness of writing, which secretes its own exhaustion and death in the very effort to discover the truth. During his first lapse into unconsciousness, Pym crosses the border separating ordinary temporality from the psychological time of writing that will govern the subsequent voyage. Augustus has left his watch with Pym, but it runs down while Pym is asleep. When he awakens, he can only guess that he has slept "for an inordinately long period of time" (737). Despite frequent references to dates in the remainder of the narrative, Pym's temporal disorientation in the hold continues throughout the rest of the voyage. Measured time is gradually replaced by a temporal sense closely related to the length of particular episodes and other kinds of narrative emphasis.

Pym's fears multiply when Augustus fails to appear. Falling into another deep sleep, Pym dreams of being "smothered to death between huge pillows, by demons of the most ghastly and ferocious aspect" and strangled by "immense serpents." Like many of Poe's characters, Pym reacts psychically to darkness and confinement as anticipations of death and burial. In this episode, dreaming is explicitly associated with "reading, writing, or conversing." Pym's confused dreams not only recall Augustus's tales of adventure and the volume of Lewis and Clark's voyages, but also prefigure the poetic goal of the narrative. At first smothered and strangled, Pym then finds himself in "deserts, limitless, and of the most forlorn and awe-inspiring character" or confronted with "immensely tall trunks of trees, gray and leafless" with roots "concealed in wide-spreading morasses, whose dreary water lay intensely black, still, and altogether terrible beneath" (738). Suffocating enclosure and unbounded expanse, like the colors black and white, are only apparent oppositions in this narrative; such contraries are actually doubles for the same absence that motivates both the writing of dreams and poetic narratives. Pym's anxieties represent Poe's own double fear: the self-annihilation that is the ultimate entropy of any writing that strains toward the undifferentiated unity of spiritual absence.

Imprisoned by the mutineers, Augustus manages to scrawl a note to Pym. Pym's Newfoundland dog, Tiger, conveniently materializes in order to deliver the message. Pym is awakened from his delirious dreams of monsters, demons, and ferocious beasts by "some huge and real monster . . . pressing heavily upon my bosom" (738). Only after an elaborate attempt to escape from the hold does Pym discover the note that is buried beneath the fur of Tiger's left shoulder. The contiguity of the dog with both Pym's dream images and Augustus's note suggests a more general movement in the narrative from a conception of language as a system of abstract referential signs to the material facts of a poetic landscape. In his search for the entrance to Augustus's cabin, Pym follows a "whipcord" attached to the trap door cut in the stateroom floor. Even when his passage is blocked by "boxes and ship-furniture," Pym is reluctant to leave this cord and strike out on his own.

Holding to this lifeline, Pym reaches the trap door only to find it blocked by "some immense weight." Failing in his Thesean labor, Pym returns to the hold where only two paragraphs later he is "tracing" the string around Tiger by means of which Augustus has attached his note. Augustus's message is intended to serve as a substitute for the freedom promised by the trap door. As the message ultimately indicates, the freedom beyond the hold has been replaced by the brutal rule of the mutineers. The only clew of thread that will lead Pym out of his labyrinth is that which ends in Augustus's cryptic scrawl.

Tiger may bear the message, but he destroys the means by which it might be read. Pym finds that the dog has "mumbled" the candles and scattered most of Pym's phosphorus. Left in the dark as a result of Tiger's ravenous appetite, Pym contrives a "multitude of absurd expedients for procuring light" before finally deciding to rub the paper with his few remaining fragments of phosphorus: "Not a syllable was there, however — nothing but a dreary and unsatisfactory blank; the illumination died away in a few seconds, and my heart died away within me as it went" (743). Pym's frustration and growing delirium cause him to tear the note into three pieces and cast them aside. Only after this impetuous act does he realize that he has looked at only one side of the paper. Once again, Pym's consciousness proves inadequate to interpret the message carried by language. Pym must appeal to Tiger and his sensitive nose to fetch the pieces from the dark recesses of the hold. Pym then carefully feels each one in hopes that the letters might show "some unevenness." What he discovers instead is an "exceedingly slight, but discernible glow, which followed as it proceeded" (744). Assuming that the glow must emanate from the traces of phosphorus he had earlier rubbed on the blank side of the note, Pym easily finds the proper combination by turning each piece dark side up. In his excitement, Pym is unable to read the entire message, even though "there would have been ample time enough for me to peruse the whole three sentences before me." Nevertheless, the seven-word fragment he does read is sufficient to convey the urgency of Augustus's warning: "*blood — your life depends upon lying close*" (745).

Pym's personal concern for his own survival blinds him to the philosophic implications of this written message. The entire episode, from Tiger's arrival to the reading of the fragment, is an education in language and its expressive function. The blank side of the note at first exasperates Pym, but it is in fact the means whereby the message itself is made legible. Like the "white curtain" at the end of the narrative, blankness and silence motivate human discourse. Unlike reflected light, the phosphorescent glow is an internal radiation analogous to the illumination of the poetic imagination. Augustus's note deals with man's fundamental situation, stressing as it does both "blood" and "life." Pym ought to have already learned the arbitrariness of human expression, which has been suggested by both the forged note from "Mr. Ross" and Pym's own willful scattering of Augustus's warning. Subject to myriad combinations and the intentions of endless "authors," language generally disseminates its truth.

Everything in this episode contributes to the materialization of the text of Augustus's note. Pym feels each piece of paper for "some unevenness," only to see the glow of the phosphorus. Tiger smells the first piece of note in order to retrieve the other two. Although these sensory acts concentrate only on the paper itself, the words themselves are related to the physicality of the note. The crucial word "blood" is, of course, the very medium in which Augustus has been forced to write; the "red ink" perceived by Pym is a synecdoche for the body of Augustus. Augustus's first note employs the false reference of familiarity and social custom — Mr. Ross's invitation — to cover the boys' escape. In this second message, the key word "blood" refers to the writing of the note itself: *"I have scrawled this with blood. . . ."* Augustus's communication is carried by the second clause: *"your life depends upon lying close"*; but Pym, Mr. Poe, and the reader concentrate on the disjointed word "blood."

The narrative makes the association between these two notes explicit. Pym learns from Augustus that "Paper enough was obtained from the back of a letter — a duplicate of the forged letter from Mr. Ross. This had been the original draught; but the handwriting not being sufficiently well imitated, Augustus had written another, thrusting the first, by good fortune, into his coat-pocket, where it was now opportunely discovered" (755). This coincidence of the two notes contradicts Pym's earlier perception of the blank obverse of Augustus's message. Yet, what critics have generally considered an error made in the haste of composition offers an important illustration of Poe's conception of the doubleness of writing. Poe's poetic theory seems to argue that human discourse is grounded in a principle of unity that is silence: a paradoxical emptiness and fullness. In *Pym* the act of writing carries the trace of a prior representation, which defers the desired approach to an undifferentiated meaning or central signified. This minor textual "error" helps to illustrate the general metaphysical crisis being enacted in the narrative. As a simple warning to Pym, the note is little more than a convention of the popular romance. As another reflection on the question of "poetic" writing, the note demonstrates the difficulty of transcending the differential system of language to deliver a unified truth. The note is a palimpsest — *the* palimpsest of language itself, whose messages are always intertexts. Writing appears to defer the presence it desires by constituting a divided present that prefigures its own erasure. Meaning may be situated only within the functions produced by this play of differences. Augustus's message serves as a signifier whose signified is yet to be read by Pym. In this context, the blank side provides the "space" of such an interpretation. No such innocent reading is possible, however, since that supposedly blank sheet is already inscribed with a prior signification — a clumsy duplicate of a forgery. Such retention and protention characterize the temporality of writing, which replaces the less adequate measures of time in the text, such as Augustus's watch or the duration of Pym's "consciousness." [22]

Pym's experiences in the darkness of the hold with dreaming, reading, writing, and interpreting prefigure the world he enters on the deck. In the referential world of Edgarton, signs are employed as secondary mediations of reality. In the dynamics of deciphering Augustus's message, Pym gives the sign "blood" the status of an object in its own right. He is subsequently reborn into a poetic landscape where external phenomena have the characteristics of written signs. As Riddel has suggested in connection with the theory of animism in "The Fall of the House of Usher," "In Poe the images of nature are already metonymic substitutions for words — or substitutions for substitutions." [23] In this world, when one is cut off from such familiar bases for meaning as family, home, school, law, and society, the ordinary distinctions between appearance and reality no longer signify. Every "natural" phenomenon may be understood only according to what it may be said to "produce" within a semiotic system.

This is dramatically expressed by Pym's formal entrance into this world. Disguising himself as Hartman Rogers, a sailor poisoned by the brutal mate, Pym attempts to strike panic and confusion among the mutineers. He emphasizes the powerful reality constituted by his representation: "As I viewed myself in a fragment of looking-glass which hung up in the cabin, and by the dim light of a kind of battle-lantern, I was so impressed with a sense of vague awe at my appearance and at the recollection of the terrific reality which I was thus representing, that I was seized with a violent tremour, and could scarcely summon resolution to go on with my part" (769–770). Pym and Peters carefully design the context in which this phantasm will appear. "The isolated situation of the brig" makes Pym's presence especially unaccountable to the crew. The raging tempest is not only "awe-inspiring," but it also contributes to the "uncertain and wavering light" cast by "the cabin lantern, swinging violently to and fro" (772). This gloom is intensified by the huge quantities of rum the crew has consumed, as well as by Peters's conversations with them "upon the bloody deeds of the mutiny" and "the thousand superstitions which are so universally current among seamen" (771). This poetic composition has the power to strike the mate "stone dead" and cast the other mutineers into such confusion that they are easily overpowered. Pym's plot manipulates the sailors' assumption that perception constitutes a pure and direct awareness of the thing itself. Like Pym's earlier deception of his grandfather, this performance implies that perception is in fact the product of a system of heterogeneous psychic and social codes. [24]

Daniel Hoffman refers to the "regressive imagination" that seems to determine the imagery in this latter portion of *Pym*. [25] Davidson claims that a spiritual progress takes place "by the steady recession of any 'fact' world — the facts of ships and men, sequence of days, food and drink, society, law, justice, and honor — and the gradual domination of a chimera or the world as it really is behind the mask of ostensible reality." [26] Every experience and phenomenon contributes to an emerging psychic landscape. Rescued from the drifting wreck of the *Grampus* by the *Jane Guy,* Pym returns to a world of apparent order. The narrative devotes increased space to factual explanations, extracts from accounts of historical voyages, and scientific discourses on subjects as various as navigation and the drying of *biche de mer.* But the marked discrepancy between these realistic details and Pym's uncanny experiences emphasizes the ineffectiveness of any empirical account of this voyage. On the island of Tsalal, the psychic drama is enacted in the confrontation of "civilized" whites with "primitive" natives.

Regardless of how we view the natives in relation to Pym's inner voyage, their associations with darkness, burial, and deceit make them emblematic of a subterranean level of psychological reality. Their close ties with their surreal environment are suggested by their expressive language, which is "a loud jabbering . . . intermingled with occasional shouts" in apparent imitation of natural sounds. In fact, the word for the taboo of white is "Tekeli-li," which is the cry of the "gigantic and pallidly white birds" that fly from beyond the veil in the final episode. [27] The natives treat nature as though it were sentient, a conventional indication in Poe's writings that one has entered a "landscape of the soul." When the cook accidentally cuts into the deck with his axe, Too-wit "immediately ran up, and pushing the cook on one side rather roughly, commenced a half whine, half howl, strongly indicative of sympathy in what he considered the sufferings of the schooner, patting and smoothing the gash with his hand, and washing it from a bucket of seawater which stood by" (821). Unlike the whites, the natives apparently do not recognize their own reflections. Glimpsing his image in the cabin mirrors, Too-wit throws himself on the floor and buries his face in his hands. In order to identify a photograph or reflected image with one's own person, the viewer relies on a conception of iconic representation, in which the signifier and signified share an actual resemblance. The inability of the natives to view reflections as icons reinforces the notion that we have left the realm of signs and things to enter a textual space in which reference is only possible among differing signs. [28]

This outlook may help in synthesizing a number of the more extraordinary interpretations of the curious water on the island, which is both veined and limpid, varied purple in hue and unreflecting. Both Marie Bonaparte and Walter Bezanson emphasize the veined character of the water in order to equate it with blood. [29] Ricardou considers the water a metaphor for the text itself, ingeniously arguing: "If an imaginary perpendicular line is made to sever a given line of writing, the two severed fragments remain united in the idea by an intense syntactic cohesion. If, on the other hand, a horizontal separation is made between two lines, the broken link, essentially spatial in nature, provides a very inferior sort of adhesion. This double complicity of the liquid with written language — by contiguity and similitude — encourages us to believe that what we are faced with is a text." [30] Maurice Mourier also concentrates on the curious divisibility of the water — the separability of the veins along their boundary lines, the inseparability of the fluid across the veins — in order to draw an analogy between the stream and human musculature. [31] All of these interpretations suggest that the stream is a metonymy for another physical thing: body or text. And this confusion of body and writing/thing and word has been taking place from the very beginning of the narrative. We have entered a realm composed of objects that frustrate ordinary representation. As the episode in the chasms will illustrate, we have entered a world in which word and thing are no longer distinguishable, frustrating the illusion of self-presence that operates explicitly in iconic representations but is also implicit in other forms of mediating representation.

Burying the crew of the *Jane Guy* and driving Peters and Pym deep into the interior of the island, the natives help uncover what the writing of *Pym* has been performing: the interplay of the unconscious and the conscious. In the final episodes, this psychic relation is established both as the very scene of writing and as the generative source of human interpretation. Just as Tiger emerges from Pym's dream to deliver the message of blood, so the natives open a path for Peters and Pym to discover the writing on the chasm walls. The "alphabetical characters" carved in the marl, however, are already inscribed within an enveloping textuality. The relation between the irreducibly figurative landscape and the graphic nature of the narrative is made explicit in Pym's drawings of the shapes of the chasms themselves. These sketches (figures 1, 2, 3, and 5) indicate the scriptural characteristics of the world in which the message of figure 4 is inscribed. As the anonymous editor of the final Note explains: "Figure 1, then figure 2, figure 3, and figure 5, when conjoined with one another in the precise order which the chasms themselves presented, and when deprived of the small lateral branches or arches (which, it will be remembered, served only as a means of communication between the main chambers, and were of totally distinct character), constitute an Ethiopian verbal root — the root $\Lambda \cap \bigcirc\mathbf{:}$ 'To be shady,'— whence all the inflections of shadow or darkness" (853). Mr. Poe's narrative has thus reached a point at which his language and that of the world coincide. Concerned as it is with the inner voyage of Pym, the text reveals at this point the extent to which its re-presentation of the adventure must begin with that which is already a system of representation. The relation between the chasm shapes and the carvings on the walls ought to indicate how any account of Pym's voyage must inevitably expose the original metaphorics of such a journey.

What is in fact inscribed at the heart of the island is the doubleness of writing, which we have seen enacted as a major theme of the work. The chasms present themselves as signs of the darkness and ambiguity in which man finds himself imprisoned. Carved as they are in the black marl, the "alphabetical characters" identified by Peters seem to repeat this message. Yet, if we grant the validity of the translation of these figures offered in the Note, then we recognize that what is signified — "to be white" in "the region of the south" — denies both the black signifiers and the field of their inscription. Throughout the narrative, the apparent opposition of white and black is gradually transformed into a reciprocal relationship. Neither doubles of each other nor polar opposites, white and black constitute one of several binary pairs transformed by the narrative into metaphors for metaphysical and psychic difference. For Poe, language has the power to destroy the facticity of human experience and present that "other world" for which human beings instinctively yearn. Yet, the language of both poetry and the psyche frustrates its own desire for transcendent unity by producing a self-perpetuating system of signification. Every effort to confront the purity of cosmic absence *or* presence — a differential desire for both extinction and survival — involves a participation in the psychic writing that is the supplementation of an immediacy that can never been retrieved.[32]

In the foregoing interpretation I have argued that writing itself is the central subject of *Pym*, and have attempted to rethink the "educational" aim of that work in terms of its reflection on the function of language. Assuming a paradoxical materiality in the shapes of the chasms and the traces in the marl, this writing serves to constitute an illusion of psychic depth by means of a complex interplay of metaphors. Thus, Mr. Poe makes visible through inscription what could never be discovered by any empirical journey of exploration. The implicit poetics of such a theory of writing poses no problem for Georges Poulet: "To create a beauty that cannot exist in time, the poet is obliged to recompose the elements of that time and to invent with the help of their multiple combinations a new, imaginary duration, analogous to the divine eternity. This imaginary duration is that of dream."[33] Yet, the "duration" of the "dream" in *Pym* has been expressed in terms of fundamental differences contributing to the temporalizing function of psychic inscription. The wholeness of consciousness presented in the poetic "dream" is an illusion disguising the interplay of past and future traces. Poe may have longed for a writing that would imitate the lost presence of cosmic unity, but he has staged in this work a writing that constitutes the differential "throb" of a cosmic or psychic process. In *Eureka*, Poe demonstrates how "Thought" relies on such difference:

> *The amount of electricity developed on the approximation of two bodies, is proportional to the difference between the respective sums of the atoms of which the bodies are composed. That no* two bodies are absolutely alike, is a simple corollary from all that has been here

said. Electricity, therefore, existing always, is *developed* whenever *any* bodies, but manifested only when bodies of appreciable difference, are brought into approximation.

　　To electricity — so, for the present, continuing to call it — we *may* not be wrong in referring the various physical appearances of light, heat and magnetism; but far less shall we be liable to err in attributing to this strictly spiritual principle the more important phenomena of vitality, consciousness and *Thought.*[34]

This *élan vital* seems to be characteristic of Poe's poetic principle. The "energy" of thought and consciousness constitutes itself in the endless struggle of language both to transcend its spatio-temporal bounds and defer its ends. *The Narrative of A. Gordon Pym* prefigures Harry Levin's interpretation of the cosmic order in *Eureka:* "The perfection of indeterminacy."[35]

　　Thus, the final image in Pym's journey toward a metaphysical and psychological center betrays the duplicity of the sign we have witnessed throughout the voyage: "And now we rushed into the embraces of the cataract, where a chasm threw itself open to receive us. But there arose in our pathway a shrouded human figure, very larger in its proportions than any dweller among men. And the hue of the skin of the figure was of the perfect whiteness of snow" (852). The offered "embrace" of the opening "chasm" is checked by the exaggerated "human figure" that appears to block the path. This is the complex that has already been inscribed in the text, particularly in the relation of the chasm shapes to the carvings in the marl. Pym's vision of the end bears the traces of those prior representations, which had already offered in the pictograph of figure 4 "a human figure standing erect, with outstretched arm" (843). Death and deferral, revelation and repression all serve to compose the shifting center of this psychic voyage. I can find no fault with Marie Bonaparte's reading in this instance, because her Freudianism seems so appropriate for describing the originary difference of this creative principle:

> For now we behold the form to which all Pym's wanderings and adventures led; the great maternal divinity whose sex, though unmentioned, must be that of the "shrouded" figure, the "woman in white," who appeared to the raving Poe in Moyamensing Prison; . . . it is the mother reclaiming her son. . . . On the one hand, she is white as the South Pole and warm with milk and with life, so recalling that blessed time when he was suckled at his mother's breast but, on the other, now related not to milk but to snow, representing *coldness* and death and so recalling unconscious memories of his pale, dead mother. Given the indifference to time characteristic of the unconscious, we see condensed in this figure the two main attributes Poe successively attached to his mother: *milk* and *death.*[36]

This is an interpretation already prefigured by Poe, who would write in *Eureka:* "Their [atoms of fragmentation] source lies in the principle, *Unity.* *This* is their lost parent. *This* they seek always — immediately — in all directions — wherever it is even partially to be found; thus appeasing, in some measure, the ineradicable tendency, while on the way to its absolute satisfaction in the end."[37] Found only "partially," such "unity" is in fact displaced by a contrived facsimile or clumsy duplicate. To borrow from Bonaparte's lexicon, I might suggest that the center remains the mother without the father, a lack which is disclosed in the son's attempts to supplement it.

The end has already been deferred by those inscriptions which have prepared for this ultimate representation, this final forgery — all of which is displaced again by a postscript, an appended note subverting its customary function as a final word. The Note is offered as yet another reading, a supplementation of those inscriptions in the text that have constituted the play of the psychic structure. This editorial interpretation relies on philological roots, whose scholarly authenticity John Irwin has demonstrated, in order to translate the universal writing of the psychic journey.[38] The text itself has become a machine for the production of surplus signifiers. The figures in the marl and the chasms themselves may serve as signifiers of the final vision, but that image remains unread in the Note. Concentrating on the problem of translating the inscriptions, the anonymous editor emphasizes the impossibility of escaping the hermeneutical circle in which any "truth" must be figured. Thus, the signifiers graven in the hills are displaced by those of the Note, both sets of which emphasize the generative qualities of a text whose signified remains "shady." In this process of inscription and reinscription a kind of psychic palimpsest has been constructed, the illusory depth of which involves an inevitable encounter with the surface of writing itself.

In his reading of Freud's "Note Upon the Mystic Writing-Pad" and Freud's general use of a graphic figure to describe the functioning of the psychic apparatus, Jacques Derrida argues that the relation between psychic strata cannot be viewed as a simple "translation" or "transcription" duplicating in consciousness "an unconscious writing." Freud himself had demonstrated that the text of the dream is a system of signifiers lacking "a permanent code" that would allow "a substitution or transformation of signifiers while retaining the same signified."[39] The dream content, according to Freud, is "expressed in a pictographic script (*Bilderschrift*)," which for Derrida is "not an inscribed image but a figurative script, an image inviting not a simple, conscious, present perception of the thing itself — assuming it exists — but a reading." The content of the dream assumes meaning in the traces it carries and the series of events (always textual) it activates. Derrida's analysis has the effect of deconstructing the Freudian hierarchy extending from the conscious to the unconscious, and substituting instead a fundamental *différance* of which every written sign bears the mark:

Let us note that the *depth* of the Mystic Pad is at once a depth without bottom, an endless reverberation, and a perfectly superficial exteriority: a stratification of surfaces each of whose relation to self, whose inside, is but the implication of another similarly exposed surface. It joins the two empirical certainties by which we are constituted: infinite depth in the implication of meaning, in the unified envelopment of the present, and, simultaneously, the pellicular essence of being, the absolute absence of a grounding.[40]

We have seen in *Pym* how such distinctions as inner and outer, lower and higher, unconscious and conscious merely metaphorize two functions in the ordinary movement of signification. In this narrative and in *Eureka,* Poe's own desire for "Unity" operates as part of a generative system for dissemination and the production of differences. Doubtless, Poe would hesitate at such an unexpected swerve in his metaphysical project and blindly reassert the transcendent ground in a "divine volition." But the writing in *Pym* and *Eureka* continues to deny any such monism. As Hoffman argues: "A double motion, where what Poe sought, what he ached to discover and return to, was a *single* motion. . . . But the nature of existence betrayed that desire. At the deepest level of his being Poe felt, Poe *knew,* that there can be no such unitary stasis."[41]

In *The Narrative of A. Gordon Pym,* Poe lingers on the verge of establishing writing itself as the constitution and facilitation (*die Bahnung*) of psychic experience: "A writing advanced as conscious and acting in the world (the visible exterior of the graphic, of the literal, of the literal becoming literary, etc.) in terms of that exertion of writing which circulates like psychical energy between the unconscious and the conscious."[42] Derrida demonstrates how Freud moves through neurological and optical metaphors for the functioning of the psychic apparatus, only to establish tentatively the graphic metaphor of the "Mystic Writing-Pad" as an *inadequate* representation. Poe transforms the scriptural metaphor into a poetic "actuality" that facilitates the divided perception at the end of Pym's Antarctic voyage. Language may still appear to be a limitation for Poe that "veils" the signified behind and within the ambiguous drift of signifiers leading to the end of the journey. However, it is not a "veiled" but a "shrouded" figure baring the winding sheet of finitude, which is at once disclosed and repressed in the supplementary movement of psychic signification. Thus, deferral and supplementarity describe the *différance* of a writing activity carried out by a diverse cast of interpreters in *Pym:* Poe, Pym, Mr. Poe, the "editor" of the Note, as well as such lesser factorers of script as Augustus, Dirk Peters, even Tiger.

The writing itself has performed an unsettling of thought and intention we might never have expected from the ostensible author of *Eureka: An Essay on the Material and Spiritual Universe.* Poe's gnostic and idealist attitudes appear to have been questioned by the very theory of writing that ought to have confirmed their values for the artist. It should no longer be necessary to account for the "accidental" death of Pym or the reluctance of Mr. Poe to offer a final explanation. They have been written *into* the text and have thus "discovered" themselves in their facilitation of the movement of signification. They have situated themselves in both the time and space of writing by effacing both the metaphysical and psychic presence that would obliterate their text. Further readings and writings are always already inscribed in this narrative, which provides its own appendix as the sign of the necessary *Nachträglichkeit* of voyaging: a literal, a literary footnote.[43]

5.

Ecliptic Voyaging: Orbits of the Sign in Melville's "Bartleby the Scrivener"

But judgment was passed on the dead by the living themselves; and that not merely in the case of private persons, but even of kings. The tomb of a king has been discovered — very large and elaborate in its architecture — in whose hieroglyphs the name of the principal person is obliterated, while in the bas-reliefs and pictorial designs the chief figure is erased. This has been explained to import that the honor of being thus immortalized was refused this king by the sentence of the Court of the Dead.
— Hegel, *The Philosophy of History*

If he lays him down, he can not sleep; he has waked the infinite wakefulness in him; then how can he slumber? Still his book, like a vast lumbering planet, revolves in his aching head. He can not command the thing out of its orbit; fain would he behead himself, to gain one night's repose.
— Melville, *Pierre or The Ambiguities*

In the preceding chapters, I have investigated basic problems of poetic representation that are related to the authors' conceptions of language, social organization, and human psychology. Each work criticizes nineteenth-century American culture for its growing disregard of those poetic and imaginative faculties that ought to be fundamental to our acts of self-understanding. The American fall is consistently interpreted in terms of our increasing neglect of our spiritual nature. Yet, these authors are not just nostalgically recalling a lost metaphysical order that would relate such a nature to a classical concept of unity or divine presence. In each case, the effort to rethink basic metaphysical problems has led these authors to study human expression and behavior, thus resituating spirituality within the domain of either self-consciousness or a language that allows such consciousness to be thought. In these texts, philosophy, poetics, and psychology have mutually transgressed their traditional disciplinary boundaries, and each discourse has threatened to usurp the most powerful concepts and strategies of the others.

In each text, however, the possibilities of such knowledge are associated with a poetic discourse or imaginative mode of reflection that is distinguished from ordinary acts of communication and behavior. This "literary displacement" is reflected in the narrative structures of these works, which variously employ spatial metaphors to suggest a movement from the world into poetic textuality. In both *A Week* and *Pym*, a voyage is used to suggest a romantic withdrawal from the ways of the world to a reflective space in which language and consciousness become the proper objects of cognition. For both Thoreau and Poe, the transformation of the physical journey into a psychic exploration is itself a demonstration of the powers of the creative imagination. Coverdale's detachment in his woodland hermitage or in his boardinghouse room in the city are necessary correlatives of a psychic distance required by the imagination for its freedom.

These spatial metaphors suggest that despite the insistent critique in these works of such dualistic notions as inside and outside, action and reflection, experience and representation, there still remains a longing for an external perspective that escapes the corruptions of the world it oversees. Coverdale's composition of an imaginative space of narrative in which he might reflect upon himself and his relations with others exposes the secret longing for freedom that undermines every existential philosophy. Jacques Lacan concisely analyzes the ultimate impotence of such a consciousness: "Existentialism is judged by the justifications which it gives to the subjective impasses which in fact result from it: a liberty which never affirms itself so authentic as when within the walls of a prison, an exigency of *engagement* in which the impotence of pure consciousness to surmount any situation is expressed, a voyeur-sadistic idealization of sexual relationship, a personality which can only realize itself in suicide, a consciousness of the other which can only be satisfied by the Hegelian murder [that is, by a refusal of the master-slave dialectic in the mutual annihilation of both one and the other]."[1]

Thus, even in these marginal texts that radicalize certain romantic tenets, there remains a lingering desire for a purer script and a freer imagination. In *A Week*, Thoreau may acknowledge the divine as a principle of "identity-in-difference" that conceals itself within the very structure of his prose, but language remains governed by an idea of divinity that by virtue of its self-concealedness still directs human discourse. In Poe, poetry enacts its own dissolution in order to indicate the cosmic truth that it may never adequately represent. Indeed, it is the absence of that originary principle of divine unity that continues to prompt the psychic impulse toward reunification, and this play of absence and presence preserves the word in its differential mediation of day and night, time and eternity. Nevertheless, there is still an intentionality in language that ranges from the mere "journalism" of ordinary expression to the immediacy and nonreferentiality of those angelic colloquies the poem tries to simulate. The visionary poet might disrupt the ordinary circuits of communication, just as Dupin mocks the futile investigations of the Prefect, but, like Mallarmé, Poe still maintains a distinction between the "Book" and the "newspaper" that threatens to purify poetry of any contamination by the world.

Because they preserve poetry as a mode of reflection on consciousness or language that takes place in a textual space distinct from the world, these writers cannot carry their insights concerning the nature of language and the psyche into the realm of action. As a result, their social criticism remains negative: a catalog of what has been repressed by modern culture. This does not mean, of course, that these works are devoid of particular and focused social criticism. We have already seen how Thoreau's poetic reflection is related to his attacks on Christianity and American colonialism. Hawthorne satirizes not only utopian reform movements but all efforts to resolve the productive differences of human nature. The obsessive concentration in these works on their own poetic processes involves more than the world-denying aestheticism of the symbolist poet, but we still must question the nature and function of the poetic detachment that is made possible by these metaliterary works.

Some of these problems are illustrated by the preeminent poetic voyage in nineteenth-century American literature: *Moby-Dick*. Although this work establishes the theoretical foundation for Melville's *Pierre*, "Bartleby the Scrivener," and *The Confidence-Man*, it tends to preserve the poetic vantage that I have discussed above. Ishmael's voyage is not undertaken to escape contemporary society and history. The *Pequod* is an international microcosm that enables Ishmael to undergo a profound education in the natural, psychological, and social needs of man. Yet, as the observer and narrator of the story, Ishmael maintains a poetic vantage that enables him to survive the voyage with his own paradoxical identity intact. This identity is hardly the self-reliant Ego of Emersonian man; instead, it is distinguished by its contradictory capabilities. David Minter has related Ishmael's character to Keats's notion of "Negative Capability":

> His desire to make meaning of the puzzling and confounding action that he witnesses never displaces his ability to entertain "uncertainties, mysteries, doubts, without any irritable reaching after fact and reason." . . . His commodious consciousness buoys him up in the destructive sea, permitting him to survive and say. . . . The essential inscrutability of life, what Ahab chiefly hates, Ishmael accepts as the primary characteristic of specifically human vision. He survives because he is able to "be social" not only with horror and evil but with the final ambiguity of things: he can accept a "black bubble" as a life-giving force, a coffin as a life buoy.[2]

Indeed, this distinction between Ishmael's life-affirming wit and Ahab's life-denying rage has become something of a commonplace in studies of *Moby-Dick*. As Warwick Wadlington puts it: "Ishmael can 'take' the vast practical joke; Ahab refuses to." [3]

Perhaps for these reasons, Ishmael does not develop as a character; he merely realizes in the narrative action a double personality that is already given in his initial mode of address. Ishmael's character is evidence that when Melville wrote *Moby-Dick* he still imagined the possibility of an identity that might become the source of a narrative. Ishmael is the only character on board the *Pequod* who might tell the story, because he is the only one capable of sustaining those contradictions in human nature that are dramatized in the events of the voyage. Like an existential hero, Ishmael can remain "other" or "strange" to himself and yet still encompass such difference within a singular personality. Such psychological contradictions might well produce a narrator or author distinctly different from our traditional conception of the romantic poet, who tunes his soul to the organic unity of Nature, but it still suggests the possibility of compassing within a single narrative voice the conflicting forces of society, tradition, language, and myth. [4] Ishmael's capacity to accept the ambiguity of human meaning without surrendering his own will to truth is unquestionably part of his poetic identity, and yet it is because of this identity that he maintains his detached vantage. His primary vocation is to return to the world with *his* tale, in order to provide some mediation between Ahab's metaphysical alienation and the language of social man. Thus, Ishmael is an exemplary character for the reader, who struggles to imitate his cheerful nihilism. Wadlington suggests that Ishmael's "playfulness and irony do not merely celebrate his authorial freedom; they coach the reader to secure his own liberty." [5] Yet, it is both the exemplary status of Ishmael as narrator and the liberty of the individual that Melville questions in his subsequent works.

In *Moby-Dick*, Ishmael's ineptitude as a sailor is perhaps compensated for by his narrative and reflective powers, but his inability to act in the world is an indirect indictment of his art. Critics have often asked why Ishmael fails to rebel against Ahab, even though he understands so well the captain's monomaniacal madness. In part, Ishmael's "negative capability" tends to unfit him for social action, except through the indirection of his narration. However, in his subsequent works, Melville uses the language of the text to question, agitate, and subvert the illusions of social man in such a way that the language of the text is itself questioned as a part of its "social environment." Certainly, the deceptiveness of art — both its manipulation of appearances and its proclivity for sophistry — is repeatedly exposed in *The Confidence-Man*. Not only does this work provide satiric portraits of Melville's literary contemporaries and their "arts," but the very method of the work is exposed as a fundamental confidence-game that tricks the reader into accepting either a facile nihilism or a sort of religious echolalia. The multiple avatars of the confidence-man neither suggest a collective model for poetic knowledge nor offer isolated examples of proper vision. Instead, each trickster adapts his language to his interlocutor in order to force or prompt — to design — a response. Ishmael's narration still preserves the romantic conception of reading as a process of organic education that develops according to a dialectic of positive and negative examples. Wadlington argues that *Moby-Dick* is the last book that Melville wrote in this mode: "After *Moby-Dick*, there is no figure comparable to Ishmael in Melville's works to encourage and cajole the reader directly and to set the example by responding to the world and to the problem of artistic creation as he would have the reader respond to the act of reading — as forms of self-definition." [6]

The Confidence-Man replaces the idea of reading as self-definition or self-actualization with reading as a violation or subversion of the self. Melville's mixed narrative seems to question those phenomenological theories of reader response that inevitably end in the "improvement" of the reader's "awareness." [7] The confidence-man represents nothing more than the subversive power of art, which in its own right is nothing and thus can be made known only in its use or interpretation. More often than not, the challenge posed by the confidence-man to the cherished values of his victims is avoided, neglected, repressed, or angrily rejected. Yet, in these very gestures, his victims tell their own stories in spite of themselves, betraying their own bad faith or intellectual naiveté. Reading becomes an act of interpretation in which either we expose to ourselves or repress our deepest fears and narrowest prejudices. Hardly an activity of self-definition, reading becomes an act of questioning what we thought we had known to be "ourselves." Nothing could be more unsettling.

This method of artistic confidence is illustrated in *The Confidence-Man* by the story of "China Aster." Egbert borrows the tale from his master, Mark Winsome, and narrates it in the voice of Charlie Noble, whose identity he has assumed at the request of Frank Goodman for the sake of their "hypothetical" discussion of friendship. Egbert tells this transcendentalist parable in order to demonstrate the dangers of philanthropy or a "friendly loan," which Emerson and Thoreau criticized so often as a violation of the self-reliant nature of the borrower and as a disguised form of narcissism: "The moral of the story, which I am for commending to you, is this: the folly, on both sides, of a friend's helping a friend. For was not that loan of Orchis to China Aster the first step towards their estrangement?" [8] Egbert's mode of narration has already betrayed the absurdity of Emersonian self-reliance; the borrowed or stolen character of all writing is a constant reminder of our inextricable involvement in the discourses of society and history. Used as it is to avoid Frank's request for a "hypothetical loan," the story itself is employed to avoid the human charity or sympathy that is the aim of transcendentalist writing.

Within the story, China Aster's hope to illuminate the darkness of human existence with ever-purer light is pursued only by means of his dependence on the shoemaker Orchis, "whose calling it is to defend the understandings of men from naked contact with the substance of things." In fact, the spermaceti candles are suggested to China Aster by Orchis, who urges him to "drop this vile tallow and hold up pure spermaceti to the world" (*CM*, 178). Like Pierre, China Aster struggles to simulate divine illumination at the cost of his ability to meet the demands of the world. Read either as a parody of American Transcendentalism or as an expression of Melville's own bitterness concerning a writer's frustrated ideals, "China Aster" reveals how all ambitions for "purer light" make individuals incapable of coping with their temporal situations. Winsome-Egbert-Charlie-Goodman's "story" subverts its own ostensible aim of explaining and defending transcendentalist notions of self-reliance and philanthropy. Orchis himself is ruined by a still higher "confidence" that he places in a sect of Pennsylvania "Come-Outers." China Aster is as scrupulously honest as his father, "Old Honesty," who died in the Poorhouse. His "heavenly" honesty is matched by Orchis's inconsistent and unpredictable nature. Like Plinlimmon's distinction between chronometrical and horological measures, China Aster and Orchis represent the conflict between the ideal of unity and consistency and an inconsistent and contradictory existence.

The names China Aster and Orchis refer respectively to the stars toward which man aspires and the earth into which the genitallike root of the orchid burrows. These names seem to support the philosophical critique of romantic idealism that is the ostensible subject of the tale, but we are reminded by various puns that "Orchis" also refers to the testicles and that the China aster is a garden flower with large, perhaps inviting blooms. The tale certainly confirms this crude pun: Orchis does "screw" China Aster. In another sense, Orchis provides the semen/spermaceti that China Aster cannot make productive, suggesting in the crude banter of Mississippi rivermen a pun on philanthropy as a sort of buggery or otherwise infertile sexuality. Indeed, Orchis himself is ruined at the hands of the "Come-Outers," which may well argue for an allegory of onanism, or wasted, scattered seed. The sexual puns undermine the idealism of this discussion of transcendental friendship in the same way that the form of the story employs a multiple "authorship" to subvert the ostensible message of self-reliance.

The doubleness of human nature suggested by the story of China Aster is expressed in terms of sexual desire and idealism, dionysian ecstasy and apollonian self-consciousness, confidence and self-reliance. All of these terms might be gathered under the large heading of the doubling of the unconscious in our conscious images; however, such doubling is not mere replication but translation (of sexuality into idealism, of confidence into self-reliance). John Irwin argues that the "main problem in deciphering the human 'characters' inscribed by hieroglyphic doubling is precisely their doubleness — that doubleness which is at once the theme and method of *The Confidence-Man*." [9] The process of psychic "deciphering" is always an operation of interpretation, whereby the crossing of different codes produces an energy that might variously be termed psychic, literary, or critical. In a sense, all such interpretation is a wandering from its intended meaning, and thus is as much wasted as the seed/money of Orchis. Indeed, much of the story's irony depends upon the doubling of fertility and impotence, eros and thanatos. China Aster appears to supplement the infertility of his financial relation with Orchis by producing several children, who subsequently become such burdens to his indigent widow that she is hurried to her grave. The children are themselves condemned to the poorhouse. Although this relation between impotence and fertility merely repeats an old cliché ("the rich get richer; the poor get children"), it also suggests how every system of representation produces its meanings only by repressing its own dissipation: the straying of the letter that is the fear of every author.

In the story of China Aster, confidence and friendship are related to sexual violation (the postscript added to China Aster's tombstone reads: "The *root* of all was a friendly loan" [my italics]). In *Pierre,* such violation is thematized as incest, which Melville relates not only to the violation of the family but also of Nature itself. The earth-bound Titan, "the son of incestuous Heaven and Earth," struggling for the heavens, is Pierre's mythical double. Enceladus serves as an emblem for Pierre's incestuous writing in the same ways that Bartleby and the confidence-man represent the fundamental violation of man's will to truth, which motivates his representations. Nietzsche considers such a desire for knowledge to be the original myth of Nature's transgression by man:

> An ancient popular belief . . . holds that a wise *magus* must be incestuously begotten. If we examine Oedipus, the solver of riddles and liberator of his mother, in the light of this Parsee belief, we may conclude that whatever soothsaying and magical powers have broken the spell of present and future, the rigid law of individuation, the magic circle of nature, extreme unnaturalness — in this case incest — is the necessary antecedent; for how should man force nature to yield up her secrets but by successfully resisting her, that is to say, by unnatural acts? [10]

The doubleness of man's nature suggested by this "original transgression" can never be harmonized in a single psychic or verbal character in Melville's later works. Pierre is destroyed by his inability to reconcile his sexual passion for his half-sister, Isabel, and his "innocent" love for Lucy Tartan. When Frank Goodman charges Egbert with "inconsistency" in the story of "China Aster," Egbert can only mime the Emersonian cliché: "Inconsistency?

Bah!" Suggesting his own vastness of spirit as the warrant for encompassing contradiction, Egbert's self-assertiveness is undermined by the derivative nature of his story, his narrative pose, and even his conversation (an anthology of transcendentalist clichés). The very idea of "self" is undermined by the fundamental doubleness of man's nature; every effort of self-assertion requires a powerful act of repression, in which negation is itself the means by which the confidence-man exposes the inevitable contradictions of man's will to self-mastery. The confidence-man is a psychoanalytic trickster, who manipulates those significant negations of his patients. As Freud writes in "Negation": "The subject-matter of a repressed image or thought can make its way into consciousness on condition that it is *denied*. Negation is a way of taking account of what is repressed; indeed, it is actually a removal of the repression, though not, of course, an acceptance of what is repressed." [11] In a similar way, the negations of the confidence-man's victims force a reaction to what is repressed, thus involving them in a mode of storytelling that betrays their own secret, unmastered natures.

The art of the confidence-man operates within the rhetoric of culture, forcing that language to turn against itself to reveal its own limitations. The characters aboard the *Fidèle* lead themselves into the darkness; the confidence-man merely confronts them with their own willing self-blindness. The method of such "diabolical" subversion is not offered as a model or exemplum for more humane behavior; the lack of charity and trust among the passengers is not balanced by the sympathy or compassion of the Cosmopolitan. In all his various guises, he is a metaphor for the text itself, which agitates and troubles the complacency of its readers. In its own way, Melville's narrative participates in the selfishness and brutality to which it responds; in the confidence-man's masquerade, deception of others is celebrated as a self-deception, the very nature of which is inextricably involved in a basic will to authority and power. The psychology of the characters exposed in this "pilgrimage" is thus the foundation for a more general social genealogy, which must be carried out by means of a style like the confidence-man's: a critique that reveals itself to be yet another will to deception.

The various styles of *Pierre*, "Bartleby the Scrivener," and *The Confidence-Man* anticipate Twain's struggle in *Pudd'nhead Wilson* to expose within the rhetoric of a culture the power of its pretensions to "truth" and "value." In each work, Melville's effort to reflect upon his own activity of writing is related to a dominant set of metaphors for some area of human experience. In *Pierre*, the "family" — origins, patrilineal and filial relations, sexuality, marriage, genealogy, etc. — focuses the varied concerns with representation, meaning, and communication. In *The Confidence-Man*, interpersonal relations ("friendship") are used to explore social and religious codes. In "Bartleby," the law and state authority organize Melville's reflections on the nature and function of signification. This concern with the law is fundamental to Melville's explorations of familial and social modes of representation, because it remains the source of the very genealogical and ethical hierarchies that are questioned in *Pierre* and *The Confidence-Man*. In "Bartleby," the relation of truth to its representation is investigated as the problem that haunts both literary and legal texts. Unlike Thoreau, Hawthorne, and Poe, Melville does not set a poetic script against social rhetoric, but reveals within the discourse of the law that the poetic principle is in fact nothing other than the "being" of language. Nothing undermines the law in "Bartleby" other than the rhetoric of the law itself, which is ironically echoed in the technical legal sense of Bartleby's characteristic word: "prefer" (as in the legal phrase "prefer charges"). What the law represses in the Wall Street world of the narrative is its own incapacity to control the fundamental psychic forces that are in fact the true authors of any law.

Thus, there is no need for "Bartleby" to displace the social realm of Wall Street with a more poetic space in the same manner that the "voyages" in *A Week, Blithedale,* and *Pym* transport us into a freer realm of imaginative self-reflection. Of all Melville's characters, Bartleby the Scrivener is distinguished by his implacable resistance to movement and his avowed preference "to be stationary."[12] Entombed within the walls of the city, Bartleby is described as the "pallid," "cadaverous," "ghostly" scrivener, who "never spoke but to answer" and who prefers to "do no copying" (*B,* 34, 39). Walls, screens, stones, columns, temples, tombs, offices, cells, hermitages, retreats, locks, keys encrypt him like some Egyptian mummy in the labyrinthine depths of a modern pyramid. His death and interment seem ultimately superfluous, because he has always been buried in life by the social restrictions that have driven him into his corner. Gradually reduced to both immobility and silence, Bartleby is petrified by a society that either excludes or appropriates differences in order to preserve its illusion of order and truth. Divine fool or hopeless victim, Bartleby has generally been considered a distorted example of Melville's *isolato;* Bartleby seems to turn Ishmael's saving detachment from others into a destructive obsession to retreat entirely from the world of men. Apparently making the free choice to give up copying entirely, Bartleby seems to reflect Melville's own skepticism about the significance or originality of any writing.

For these reasons, Bartleby is frequently considered a kind of complementary opposite of the artful, metamorphic confidence-man. If the various avatars of the trickster seem to represent "a further working-out of the implications of Ishmael's art," then Bartleby epitomizes the artless refusal to play the game that distinguishes the man of despair or transcendent knowledge.[13] Thus, existentialist critics have considered him an urban martyr, whose passive resistance asserts the absurdity of existence and the vanity of man's creations.[14] For similar reasons, myth critics have related him to a host of religious ascetics ranging from Christ to Buddhist and Hindu figures of self-denial and transcendence. Most of these comparisons have emphasized Melville's ironic use of mythic archetypes. Here, for example, is a passage from H. Bruce Franklin: "It is also in part the story of this strange being, who replays much of the role of Christ while behaving like a Hindu ascetic, and who ends by extinguishing himself and making dead letters of the scripture which describe his prototype." [15] Psychobiographers have employed some of the same themes of nihilism to argue that the story "reflects Melville's doubts about his recent work"; [16] or that by functioning as a form of creative daydreaming, "Bartleby" enables Melville to deal indirectly with his own "submerged death wish." [17] In contrast, certain formalists acknowledge the hopelessness of the Wall Street world, only to insist upon the redemptive values of the literary narrative that has been prompted by the scrivener's spiritual desolation. As Marvin Fisher argues, the narrator demonstrates in his story that "he has grasped the general lesson that Bartleby never fully articulated" in order to communicate Melville's conviction that "art, which could reverse the conventional view of the world and invert the more typical judgments of society, is our feeble means of redemption." [18]

Yet, for all the critical attention that "Bartleby" has received, the primary questions raised by the narrative about writing and the law, copying and authority seem to be minimized or forgotten. A great deal has been written about the law offices and the narrator's legal function as a Master in Chancery: one of those official "referees of disputes" in "matters of equity for which the narrowness of the law courts provided no relief." [19] In addition, few critics fail to mention that Bartleby's hopeless condition is the direct result of the drudgery of copying, which seems to be opposed to Melville's own creative efforts. [20] But this simple distinction between the endless repetition of copying and the originality of the literary text is precisely what Melville renders problematic in his writings, particularly in the period from *Pierre* (1852) to *The Confidence-Man* (1857). Mistaken by the prison grub-man for "a gentleman forger," Bartleby closely resembles that divine fool of truth and originality, Pierre, whose great unfinished work is condemned by his publishers as a vile plagiarism, "filched from the vile Atheists, Lucian and Voltaire." [21] *Pierre* subverts the idea of literary originality and the possibility of an innocent self-expression; "Bartleby" undercuts the concept of writing as the representation or "copy" of an original object or idea that escapes the constraints of language. Both texts may be considered extended reflections on the nature of writing, especially as it is related to the presumed depth of psychic experience.

The office of a Master in Chancery is directly concerned with the origins of ownership and the legal authority for property. Bartleby appears in a library or archive of such origins; he is contracted to produce those copies that will confirm the unbroken genealogy of the law. The narrator is especially qualified for such an office because he has spent his legal career as "a conveyancer and title-hunter, and drawer-up of recondite documents of all sorts" as well as having done "a snug business among rich men's bonds, and mortgages, and title-deeds" (*B,* 23, 16). In his offices, the testimony taken in his "High Court of Chancery" is carefully copied for records and those occasions of reference when particular disputes are settled by legal committees. Since a Master adjudicates those cases not adequately covered by statute law, he must interpret the available evidence pertinent to ambiguous claims of equity in relation to his understanding of common law (or "common usage"). The nature of his legal work is indirectly suggested in his initial description of the problems confronting him in the narration of Bartleby's career:

> While, of other law-copyists, I might write the complete life, of Bartleby nothing of that sort can be done. I believe that no materials exist, for a full and satisfactory biography of this man. It is an irreparable loss to literature. Bartleby was one of those beings of whom nothing is ascertainable, except from the original sources, and, in his case, those are very small. What my own astonished eyes saw of Bartleby, *that* is all I know of him, except, indeed, one vague report, which will appear in the sequel. [16]

Although a Master is concerned primarily with "original sources," most of his cases involve either small or questionable sources. In the case of clear title, reference to this court would be inappropriate. In the case of Bartleby, the narrator must rely on eyewitness testimony and "one vague report," subsequently minimized as "one little item of rumor." Viewed in this way, Bartleby presents a legal problem that challenges the most skilled faculties of a Master in Chancery. From the beginning, the legal determination of original authority and proper ownership is related to philosophic concepts of identity and meaning.

Even though all legal decisions depend upon reasoned interpretations, the judgments of a Master in Chancery seem especially subject to the interpretative ambiguities that lurk behind every legal authority, and particularly those hermeneutic problems raised by written texts and records. Such an official ultimately would have to confront the relation of legal writing to some philosophic understanding of truth. Although Plato insists upon the importance of written documents to facilitate the system of justice described in the *Laws,* Socrates suggests the limitations of writing in the *Phaedrus*: "[Our earlier conclusions] have shown that any work, in the past or in the future, . . . whether composed in a private capacity or in the role of a public man who by proposing a law becomes the author of a political composition, is a matter of reproach to its author (whether or no the reproach is actually voiced) if he regards it as containing important truth of permanent validity." [22] Plato's insistence that the only "important truth of permanent validity" is "veritably written in the soul" emphasizes the need to examine legal questions in light of philosophic ideals of justice that are intimately bound up with human nature. The narrator's unique experiences with Bartleby seem to confirm the subordination of legality to ontology; no mere legal record or document may serve as an adequate substitute for true justice. The origins of any sort of ownership must depend upon a philosophical analysis of what is proper to a man, which relies in turn on what is proper to man.

Although the narrator hears testimony and takes depositions, he is primarily charged with recording and evaluating written documents. He himself claims that he is "one of those unambitious lawyers who never addresses a jury, or in any way draws down public applause" (*B*, 16). He appears to have contempt for the deceptions of persuasive rhetoric and to favor a more "prudent" and "snug" consideration of truth and justice. For him there can be only one original text — or proper name — for the truth that governs the meaning of the various legal signifiers. All the copies produced in his offices may be reduced to a single purpose that does not change: the determination of justice and equity. Every legal document is part of an ideal representational system that promises to prefer the true to the false, the just to the unjust, good to evil. In this way we may understand the narrator's dogged insistence upon the accuracy of copy; absolute justice depends upon the infinite repetition of its sameness, of its unchanging essence in the multifarious works that make up the archives of the law. Justice is that identity which governs the differences of life, reducing all distinctions to aspects of a unified order or a centered structure. Justice is the truth that makes the architecture of the law possible, a foundation that assigns to each text its proper place in the edifice. Justice may be read in every text (in terms of either its presence or absence) only because its proper site is located outside or beyond any text, engraved enduringly in the souls of men. It is thus no coincidence that a Master in *Chancery* derives his title from signifiers of guardianship: chancery, chancellor, chancel, *cancellarius, cancellus, cancelli*. A *cancelli* is a lattice, railing, or grating behind which the *cancellarius* worked, so named as "the keeper of the barrier," the "secretary." And "secretary" itself retains the traces of such gate-keeping and the determination of proper limits or bounds. A *secretarius* is one entrusted with secrets, a noun formed from the past participle of *secernere*, "to set apart" or "separate." Thus, the narrator guards the secret truth that is enshrined/entombed in the tower of texts that accumulates as the law.

This system of law substitutes a writing of pure repetition in order to control the subversive movement of signification that relies on the absence of a signified and thus denies any pure mastery or original authority. Such copying preserves the hierarchical structure of this society by demonstrating the insufficiency of writing as an independent mode of knowledge. Writing may only "note" or "rememorate" what is already known, but may have been "forgotten" or "repressed" by the undisciplined. As Jacques Derrida argues in "La Pharmacie de Platon," Plato struggled to subordinate writing to the presence of truth contained in the "living word" of the Socratic dialectic. In the *Phaedrus,* Socrates illustrates the problem in the parable of Theuth (Thoth), the Egyptian god named in myth as the inventor of writing. When Theuth presents his invention to King Thamus (Ammon Rā, the sun-god), the King rejects the invention as a dangerous simulacrum of the actual truth "veritably written" in the soul: "If men learn this, it will implant forgetfulness in their souls; they will cease to exercise memory because they rely on that which is written, calling things to remembrance no longer from within themselves, but by means of external marks; what you have discovered is a recipe not for memory, but for reminder. And it is no true wisdom that you offer your disciples, but only its semblance." [23]

Derrida emphasizes the distinction Plato makes between two forms of repetition: the "good" repetition that actively presents the truth of the soul and the mechanical representation of the living repetition in the physical marks of writing. Like the narrator of "Bartleby," Plato strips writing of any self-generating powers in order to preserve the metaphysical ideal of a truth that governs but escapes the constraints of human language:

> The hypomnesis ["reminder"], from which writing is announced and lets itself be thought, not only does not coincide with memory but is construed as dependent upon memory, and as a consequence of the presentation of the truth. At the moment it is called upon to appear [*comparaître,* as in a legal appearance] before the paternal hearing [*instance,* legal proceedings], writing is determined within a problematic of knowledge-memory; it is thus deprived of all its attributes and all its fraying powers. Its power of fraying is not cut off by repetition but by the evil of repetition, by that which in repetition divides itself, redoubles itself, repeats the repetition and in so doing, separated from the "good" repetition (that which presents and unites being in a living memory) is always capable, abandoned to itself, of not repeating itself. Writing would be a pure repetition, thus a dead repetition that can always fail to repeat anything or is incapable of *spontaneously* repeating itself: that is to say as well, to repeat nothing but itself, the hollow and abandoned repetition. [24]

The teacher/master/king/god preserves his authority over the rememorated repetition of writing by insisting upon the living presence of justice and truth to which he has access, which his "voice" authorizes. The "hollow and abandoned repetition" must always appeal to those authors (legislators, judges, philosophers) who already control the signifiers that "writing only consigns." On this basis, writing is subject to correction according to the proprieties of the truth, which in the Western tradition have always limited free play and constrained the sign within logical or rational bounds.

In "Bartleby," the scriveners endlessly copy documents whose significance is determined by the Master. The narrator authorizes which works will be included in the record in order to repress the arbitrariness of ownership that the law — and his office in particular — has been instituted to control. The construction of a legal archive simulates a hidden meaning, a buried concept of justice that governs the order and relation of the documents. Like the walls of the city, these signs are stones, petrifactions that symbolize the elemental truth that sustains them: a church/law built upon a rock.[25] Yet, like the mute stones scattered in *Pierre,* these legal copies merely mime the external form of the Petrine rock, which is infused with the presence of the divine spirit. Like Hegel's pyramids, the architecture of the city is an empty shell or form, whose geometric construction suggests an artistry other than Nature, but whose informing spirit is symbolized only by virtue of its absence. The pyramids are appropriate monuments to the dead, because they symbolize the spirit that remains at a distance, to which the souls of the dead fly.

Hegel clarifies this conception of Egyptian art as symbolical in his consideration of Memnon stones — those sculptures that were reputed to moan and groan with the rising of the sun: "The work done, therefore, even when quite purified of the animal aspect, and bearing the form and shape of self-consciousness alone, is still the silent soundless shape, which needs the rays of the rising sun in order to have a sound which, when produced by light, is even then merely noise and not speech, shows merely an outer self, not the inner self."[26] For Hegel, artistic representation in the symbolic mode has not yet realized spirit within its own form; the work itself betrays only its inner absence, and thus the form is the mere desire for spiritual realization. In a similar sense, the architecture of the Wall Street world is a metaphor for the writing of the copyists, which must take its authority from a source beyond its own form. The contingent and secondary character of writing becomes a necessary component in this system of representing justice. The master-slave relationship between the narrator and his scriveners determines the nature and possibility of individual authority and ownership.

As Derrida recognizes, Plato employs writing as a metaphor for the truth at the very moment that he attacks writing as unnecessary and even dangerous in the quest for knowledge. Yet, what is "veritably written" in the souls of men is a complex of psychic functions that is never present or unified but always differential in its presumed appearance. The notion seems especially compatible with Melville's own efforts to rethink the relationship between writing and truth. In *Pierre,* he suggests that writing never represents a simple object or primary signified, but shares a symbiotic relationship with the system of psychic inscription:

> Two books are being writ; of which the world shall only see one, and that the
> bungled one. The larger book, and the infinitely better, is for Pierre's own

private shelf. That it is, whose unfathomable cravings drink his blood; the other only demands his ink. But circumstances have so decreed, that the one can not be composed on the paper, but only as the other is writ down in his soul. And the one of the soul is elephantinely sluggish, and will not budge at a breath. Thus Pierre is fastened on by two leeches; — how can the life of Pierre last? Lo! he is fitting himself for the highest life, by thinning his blood and collapsing his heart. He is learning how to live, by rehearsing the part of death. [*P,* 304–5]

The physical writing may be inferior to the "larger book" written in the soul, but the text in ink is the actualization of its other: not a mechanical representation of the psyche, but that which facilitates the system itself.[27] Pierre is deeply involved with "the primitive elementalizing of the strange stuff, which in the act of attempting that book, has upheaved and upgushed in his soul" (304). In the effort to discover the deep truth of his origins (paternity and family relations), Pierre frays the boundaries presumed to separate the conscious and the unconscious. "Meaning" is generated by this intertextual violence, which involves the unsettling of Pierre's stable identity and the coming to consciousness of that system of differences whereby he is constituted.

Pierre's anguished struggle to write in "infernally black ink" while imprisoned by "four leprously dingy white walls" makes psychic experience possible and preserves life in the face of death: the psychic immobility of the "hollow and abandoned repetition." Identified only with writing that circulates without destination between two mutually constituting strata, Pierre denies his name and learns "how to live, by rehearsing the part of death." *Pierre or The Ambiguities:* the rock is the elemental Word that remains unlettered, the source of being that condemns all significance as inadequate to its meaning; "The Ambiguities" displace the rock with the absence that they both hide and reveal:

The old mummy lies buried in cloth on cloth; it takes time to unwrap this Egyptian king. Yet now, forsooth, because Pierre began to see through the first superficiality of the world, he fondly weens he has come to the unlayered substance. But, far as any geologist has yet gone down into the world, it is found to consist of nothing but surface stratified on surface. To its axis, the world being nothing but superinduced superficies. By vast pains we mine into the pyramid; by horrible gropings we come to the central room; with joy we espy the sarcophagus; but we lift the lid — and no body is there! — appallingly vacant as vast is the soul of a man! [*P,* 284–85]

Two texts are being written that double each other, confusing the "inner" and "outer," "blood" and "ink." As Derrida notes: "Writing is unthinkable without repression. Its condition is that there be neither a permanent contact nor an absolute break between strata: the vigilance and failure of censorship."[28] The effort to unravel the verbal wrappings of things adds only another cloth, patched from the old and already unraveling. Writing carries within itself the force of deferral and repression that makes differentiation possible; the multiple strata in "the soul of a man" are simply metaphors for the economy of signification.

As an agent of the law obligated to deal with legal ambiguities, the narrator of "Bartleby" achieves order only by substituting copying for writing and maintaining a hierarchy of "originals" and "duplicates." The narrator's offices are "but a three minutes' walk" from the post office, but Bartleby resolutely prefers not to pick up or post messages. The law and the post both rely on the illusion of origins and ends — author-audience, sender-receiver, legislator-society — that grounds the movement of signification by simulating direction and intention. The narrator himself imagines that charity involves this sort of communication, twice informing Bartleby that "if, after reaching home, he found himself at any time in want of aid, a letter from him would be sure of a reply" (*B*, 35).[29] Bartleby's "prefer not to," however, is not simply a refusal to complete an appointed task, but an interruption of habitual circuits of communication. Bartleby is the figure of frustrated destinations that stands between sender and receiver, an author and his reader. Every message carries the possibility of its failure to achieve its end or deliver its meaning. Bartleby raises the possibility that the "original" text may be led astray, that the "copy" may take the place of its model. In his critique of Lacan's "Poe Seminar," Derrida analyzes a similar situation in terms of the supposed presence of the signifier in the unconscious: "The divisibility of the letter . . . is what puts in jeopardy and leads astray, with no guarantee of return, the remnant of anything whatever: a letter does *not always* arrive at its destination, and since this belongs to its structure, it can be said that it never really arrives there, that when it arrives, its possibly-not-arriving [*son pouvoir-ne-pas arriver*], torments it with an internal divergence."[30]

In his reading of *Moby-Dick,* Rodolphe Gasché stresses the importance of Ishmael's description of his "draught of a systematization of cetology" as "a ponderous task; no ordinary letter-sorter in the Post-office is equal to it":

> The letter-sorter hinted at by Ishmael here reminds us of course of Bartleby, who had to deal with those letters which "on errands of life . . . speed to death." Bartleby undoubtedly is an ordinary letter-sorter who is not equal to his task, for he is overcome by the letters which pull him to death. Bartleby as an ordinary letter-sorter is no exegete of the letters, he does not take hold of the letters bodily, in their entire volume, in order to sort them boldly that way.[31]

Bartleby is certainly no "ordinary letter-sorter," but "a subordinate clerk in the Dead Letter Office in Washington," politically at least the "central" post office and proximate to the legislative and judicial bodies that govern the law.

"Suddenly removed by a change in the administration," like the narrator who subsequently loses his position as Master in Chancery, Bartleby may be assumed to have an intimate knowledge of both the arbitrariness of authority and the potential failure of a message to reach its destination. As a homeless wanderer who makes his unhomely site in the offices of an attorney, Bartleby figures the difference of writing itself as the presence-absence of its own inscription. Like the writing ceaselessly produced by the scriveners, Bartleby is *always there*, and yet his presence is always determined by signs of negation: "prefer not to," "ghostly," "cadaverous," "pathetic," "dead-wall reveries."

Bartleby gathers the sublimated rebellion of the other scriveners that erupts in a variety of trivial incidents, and he prefers it to the Master as an insurmountable obstacle to the workings of an absolute justice. The two other scriveners are frenetically active by turns, as if impatient with the relentless immobility of copying. They are certainly dehumanized by their work, emptied of any psychic complexity by that inner law of justice that reduces all differences to an endless repetition of the same. Although Pierre suffers greatly in his effort to write, he prefigures Bartleby's implacable immobility, buried in "his own solitary closet," "so muffled" against the cold that "he can hardly move of himself" (*P,* 415, 419). Pierre's "movement" or signs of life must be expressed on the twin pages of paper and soul; he himself becomes a letter, consigned for an alien destination: "But is Pierre packed in the mail for St. Petersburg this morning?" (419). Nippers and Turkey, however, alternate between diligent, attentive copying and periods of "florid" and "nervous" distraction. Their respective outbursts constitute the "time" of the offices, removed as they are from any direct view of the sun. Rebelling against this timeless copying, these two characters provide their own horologicals:

> It was fortunate to me that, owing to its peculiar cause — indigestion — the irritability and consequent nervousness of Nippers were mainly observable in the morning, while in the afternoon he was comparatively mild. So that, Turkey's paroxysms only coming on about twelve o'clock, I never had to do with their eccentricities at one time. Their fits relieved each other, like guards. When Nippers's was on, Turkey's was off; and *vice versa.* This was a good natural arrangement, under the circumstances. [*B,* 22]

It is tempting to imagine that Bartleby's dead-wall reveries and consistent refusals suggest some "chronometrical" alternative to the "horologicals" of the other scriveners in the office, in accord with Plotinus Plinlimmon's distinction between "celestial" and "terrestrial" time in *Pierre.* Yet, Bartleby's view from his window is a constant reminder of his distance from the sun, which is alien from man as a result of the city's architecture. Bartleby's situation in the offices indicates how man's self-generated alienation from the sun prompts him to simulate "forgeries" of the "sun's" authority.

The behavior of the scriveners has some direct, albeit superficial, effects on the copy work itself. In the afternoon, Turkey is not only "disposed, upon provocation, to be slightly rash with his tongue," but he is also so "inflamed" and "flurried" as to be "incautious in dipping his pen into his ink-stands" (*B*, 18). The narrator is tempted to "abridge his labors" on account of "all his blots upon my documents." Turkey's blots are trivial signs of rebellion against the insistence upon perfect copy, but Nippers's inability to adjust his desk properly betrays a deeper dislike of copying. In fact, the narrator accuses Nippers of more substantial gestures toward the "usurpation of strictly professional affairs, such as the original drawing up of legal documents." Nippers is clearly an ambitious man, who works as "a ward-politician" and does "a little business at the Justices' courts" and "on the steps of the Tombs" (20). Politics, economics, and the law seem interchangeable in this Wall Street world; the narrator suspects Nippers of passing off a "dun" as a "client" and "a bill" as an "alleged title-deed." The narrator himself confesses to have been "not insensible" to the "good opinion" of his former client, John Jacob Astor: "a name which, I admit, I love to repeat; for it hath a rounded and orbicular sound to it, and rings like unto bullion" (17). Nippers merely imitates the authority of his master and thus assures his imprisonment by supporting the hierarchical structure of the law.[32]

Bartleby, in contrast, remains the sign of immobility. Yet, this very immobility is interpreted by the narrator as an indication of Bartleby's vagrant condition. The narrator refers to Bartleby's "I would prefer not to" as "that mulish vagary," an oxymoron that seems basic to the scrivener's function in the narrative. Ultimately, Bartleby is arrested and charged with vagrancy, an application of the law that threatens to unsettle the very definition of the term. Considering desperate measures to rid himself of this ghost, the narrator reflects on this paradox: "A vagrant, is he? What! he a vagrant, a wanderer, who refuses to budge? It is because he will *not* be a vagrant, then, that you seek to count him *as* a vagrant. That is too absurd" (*B*, 46). "Vagrancy" is a wandering from what is proper, a threat to propriety and decorum as well as to the abstract concept of justice that equates propriety with property. As the narrator acknowledges, the legal definition of vagrancy contains nothing but tautologies, prompted by the essential fear this society feels toward the alien and unaccountable, toward that which cannot be appropriated: "No visible means of support: there I have him. Wrong again: for indubitably he *does* support himself, and that is the only unanswerable proof that any man can show of his possessing the means so to do" (46). Bartleby causes every legal question to be evaluated in philosophic terms; the narrator translates "support" (wages and purchasing power) into the ontological category of Bartleby's "being-there." Legal vagrancy, however, also applies to those who "loiter" without a "proper abode," which is certainly applicable to Bartleby's spiritual homelessness. Yet, what prevents the narrator from immediately thrusting Bartleby into the street is precisely this "homeless" or "unhomely" quality. Bartleby seems to figure as what Freud would subsequently describe as the "uncanny" in psychic experience: *das Unheimliche* itself.

Freud begins "The Uncanny" (1919) by offering various equivalents for *das Unheimliche* in several languages, as well as exploring some similarities between *heimlich* and *unheimlich* in different German lexicons. Freud is especially interested "to find that among its different shades of meaning the word *heimlich* exhibits one which is identical with its opposite, *unheimlich*. . . . In general we are reminded that the word *heimlich* is not unambiguous, but belongs to two sets of ideas, which without being contradictory are yet very different: on the one hand, it means that which is familiar and congenial, and on the other, that which is concealed and kept out of sight. The word *unheimlich* is used customarily, we are told, as the contrary of the first signification, and not of the second." In particular, Freud singles out a reference to Schelling in Daniel Sanders's *Wörterbuch der deutschen Sprache:* "'"Unheimlich" is the name for everything that ought to have remained . . . hidden and secret and has become visible,' Schelling." [33] From this point on, Freud will gradually develop the "uncanny" as the surfacing of a familiar event or sign that has been made unfamiliar through repression.

Elaborating Otto Rank's interpretation of the *Doppelgänger,* Freud argues that the "double" is always divided between the "primary narcissism" that projects a double "as a preservation against extinction" and the later stages in the development of the ego in which the double "becomes the ghastly harbinger of death." [34] Verbally and psychically, the uncanny involves a doubling or play of oppositions in the same term, *heimlich:* familiar/alien, life/death, protection/fear. In his earlier review of Karl Abel's *Über den Gegensinn der Urworte,* Freud draws the analogy between a dream's "special tendency to reduce two opposites to a unity or to represent them as one thing" and Abel's thesis that in ancient Egyptian "we find a fair number of words with two meanings, one of which says the opposite of the other." [35] Freud requotes Abel's quotation from Alexander Bain's *Logic* to demonstrate how such a linguistic phenomenon is possible "on purely theoretical grounds as a logical necessity": "'The essential relativity of all knowledge, thought, or consciousness cannot but show itself in language. If everything that we can know is viewed as a transition from something else, every experience must have two sides; and either every name must have a double meaning, or else for every meaning there must be two names.'" [36] Just as Derrida suggests that the *différance* of writing (language) is both a differing and deferring, so the differences within the signifier, *heimlich,* depend for Freud upon a psychic process of repression:

> If psycho-analytic theory is correct in maintaining that every emotional affect, whatever its quality, is transformed by repression into morbid anxiety, then among such cases of anxiety there must be a class in which the anxiety can be shown to come from something repressed which *recurs*. This class of morbid anxiety would then be no other than what is uncanny, irrespective of whether it originally aroused dread or some other affect. In the second place, if this is indeed the secret nature of the uncanny, we can understand why the usage of speech has extended *das Heimliche* into its opposite *das Unheimliche;* for this uncanny is in reality nothing new or foreign, but something familiar and old-established in the mind that has been estranged only by the process of repression.[37]

Repression thus functions in the displacements of language ("the usage of speech") to alter what language would represent. Representation participates in and helps activate this psychic system of inscription by generating those differences and deferrals that we spatially represent as higher and lower strata: the conscious and the unconscious. Language is not merely a means of re-presenting an object or concept, but is also a system for keeping hidden what is fearful or threatening; language is a system of intercourse and defense. These two functions are never divisible: the presumed object of a verbal representation is always an economy of prior representations variously uncovered and erased, expressed and repressed in the supplementary movement of signification.[38]

In his essay, "Remarks on the Function of Language in Freudian Theory" (1956), Emile Benveniste attempts to refute Freud's suggestion that there is any " 'actual' correlation between oneiric logic and the logic of a real language."[39] Benveniste carefully dismantles Karl Abel's philological argument for the antithetical sense of primal words, and he accuses Freud of confusing certain nuclear or archetypal psychic constituents with historical origins. The thrust of Benveniste's critique, however, primarily depends on his rigorously structuralist distinction between *langue* and *parole*. Benveniste's argument is little more than an effort to preserve the structuralists' distinction between the objectivity of *langue* as a regulating system and the performative subjectivity of *parole*.[40] Yet, the distinction between *langue* and *parole* — as well as the distinction between synchronic and diachronic linguistics — reveals the more general effort to distinguish the literal from the literary. Indeed, the very concept of *langue* depends upon a normative system determined by its literalness and the eccentric stylization that it permits. I might put the issue more economically by proposing that structural linguistics preserves the distinction between realism and style in the very method of its analysis.

For Benveniste, the proper linguistic analogy with the script of dreams is not "language" as the term is generally used by Freud, but *parole* as that distinct performance in which the "laws" of *langue* are stylized: "For it is style rather than language that we would take as term of comparison with the properties that Freud has disclosed as indicative of oneiric 'language.' One is struck by the analogies which suggest themselves here. The unconscious uses a veritable 'rhetoric' which, like style, has its 'figures,' and the old catalogue of tropes would supply an inventory appropriate to the two types of expression." [41] It is precisely this tropological aspect of language that Benveniste associates with myth rather than history. [42] As soon as one refuses this distinction between *langue* and *parole,* between systematic regularity and stylized performance, then the contrast Benveniste establishes between the symbolism of dreams and that of language vanishes. The synchronic language-state is nothing but an illusory economy of diachronic particulars; its apparent literality is only a repression of an originating metaphorics or rhetoric that is the language of both the psyche and the alphabet. Freud finds in Abel's philology a historical evolution that is simply a convenient analogy for an originary characteristic of psychic writing, which the linguist Benveniste must relegate to the eccentric regions of dream or poetry: "Freud could have found in surrealist poetry (which, according to Breton, he did not understand) something of what he was seeking, wrongly, in organized language." [43] However, the writing of dreams and poems always exceeds and undoes linguistics by virtue of its irreducibly differential process. Neither Freud nor Melville could subscribe to Benveniste's sharp distinction between *langue* and *parole* or between linguistic synchrony and performative diachrony. As Fred See writes of Melville: "The nature of the sign itself changes for Melville. Its synchronic aspect, that which enables the sign to bracket noumena, is petrified; it falls into silence. And the diachronic aspect of the sign — the burden of history which all signs must bear, the capacity for combinations and sequences — becomes dominant." [44]

Thus, Bartleby's role as a psychological double must be considered in relation to his presentation of the uncanny, the surfacing of what in the narrator's view "ought to have remained hidden and secret." In *Pierre,* Melville offers an interpretation of how repression functions to alter the familiar into the unfamiliar. In a digression prompted by Pierre's unexpected discovery of Plotinus Plinlimmon's pamphlet, "Chronometricals and Horologicals," which Pierre finds buried in the lining of his coat, Melville reflects:

> Possibly this curious circumstance may in some sort illustrate his self-supposed non-understanding of the pamphlet, as first read by him in the stage. Could he likewise have carried about with him in his mind the thorough understanding of the book, and yet not be aware that he so understood it? I think that — regarded in one light — the final career of Pierre will seem to show, that he *did* understand it. And here it may be randomly suggested, by way of bagatelle, whether some things that men think they do not know, are not for all that thoroughly comprehended by them; and yet, so to speak, though contained in themselves, are kept a secret from themselves? The idea of Death seems such a thing. [*P,* 294]

The narrator characterizes Bartleby's condition by means of various images of blindness, madness, religious asceticism, ruin, privation, immobility, and death. Existentialist critics have emphasized these images in their interpretations of Bartleby as the harbinger of nothingness and death, the blankness behind the "pasteboard masks." Yet, Bartleby's association with death touches only one part of his figuration, one aspect of the language that he opposes to the copying of the scriveners and the authority of their master. Bartleby dramatizes the repression of death that operates in language as both its desire and its dread, its resource and its fear. Abstractly, he signifies the erasure of any conception of "original" justice and its replacement by the only true equalizer, the just leveler in the Book of Job (3:11, 13-14):

> "Eh! — He's asleep, ain't he?"
> "With kings and counselors," murmured I. [*B,* 46]

Death is not simply negation but is the motive for psychic mobilization, the encrypted hollow that sustains the form of man's expression. Bartleby's uncanny presence is not only a declaration of the unmasked truth of mortality, but is a dramatization of the way man keeps secret what is most familiar to him.

Is it any wonder, then, that the narrator should feel that "Bartleby was billeted upon me for some mysterious purpose of an allwise Providence, which it was not for a mere mortal like me to fathom" (*B,* 44)? Most critics consider this passage to be one more attempt by the narrator to defer action and avoid personal responsibility for the scrivener. Predestination would seem to subvert the possibility of human charity, leaving grace entirely to "an all-wise Providence." Yet, what the narrator considers metaphysical predestination might also be viewed as a psychological compulsion that transcends the conscious subject. Bartleby's uncanny presence is characterized by his maddening repetition, "I would prefer not to," which seems to be an ironic substitute for the hollow repetition of the other scriveners. As we have already seen, Freud associates the uncanny with a "repetition-compulsion":

> It must be explained that we are able to postulate the principle of a *repetition-compulsion* in the unconscious mind, based upon instinctual activity and probably inherent in the very nature of the instincts — a principle powerful enough to overrule the pleasure-principle, lending to certain aspects of the mind their daemonic character, and still very clearly expressed in the tendencies of small children. . . . Taken in all, the foregoing prepares us for the discovery that whatever reminds us of this inner *repetition-compulsion* is perceived as uncanny.[45]

Thus, Freud interprets "involuntary repetition" as a means of turning "something fearful into an uncanny thing." The narrator variously identifies with and is repelled or frightened by Bartleby, who is situated in the inner office but isolated from the lawyer by a green folding screen. As the secret sharer who asserts himself by means of a repetitive formula, Bartleby epitomizes the character of the uncanny as a doubling that is always other and alien.[46] Certainly, Bartleby may be said to provide the narrator with an excellent reminder of that "inner *repetition-compulsion*" which he attempts to master by directing an office of copyists. Bartleby forces the narrator to confront what he cannot control, that process of psychic inscription which is always informed by prior traces, former frayings.

As I have suggested, this entire system of psychic motivation relies on the fundamental Freudian difference: fear/desire of death. Death is the only true "justice" or "law" that language both memorializes and defers. In his role as the uncanny element in the language of the psyche that undercuts every determinate meaning, Bartleby subverts the narrator's presumed mastery of social law and questions his capability as an interpreter. Not only does Bartleby remain an undecidable figure that has motivated a narrative that cannot be adequately concluded, but the narrator reveals far more of his own psychological nature than may reasonably be assumed to have been intended by him.[47] Writing as record-keeping (*hypomnesis*) that is timeless in its repetition of an original truth has been replaced by a complex system of psychic facilitation in which the differences produced constitute the time and space of what we would have naively thought to be experience and memory.

Thus, Bartleby substitutes a different kind of monument for the archival pyramid and stony letters that sustain Wall Street and its law. Dorothee Finklestein and John Irwin have explored Melville's obsessions with hieroglyphs, pyramids, obelisks, and ancient monuments as either symbols of the "structure and form . . . in which the sacred mysteries of existence are encased and enwrapped" or as tokens of that act of hieroglyphic doubling that originates the language of the self.[48] In developing this essentially Hegelian metaphor, however, Melville creates two distinct kinds of monuments. On the one hand, there is the mute, stony tomb itself, which Melville describes in the *Journal* of his visit to Egypt in the following terms "(*Color of pyramids same as desert.*) . . . *No vestige of moss upon them. Not the least. Other ruins ivied. Dry as tinder. No speck of green.* . . . Line of desert & verdure, plain as line between good & evil. An instant collision of alien elements. . . . Grass near the pyramids, but will not touch them, — as if in fear or awe of them."[49] In his poem "The Great Pyramid," Melville echoes another entry in the *Journal* ("It was in these pyramids that was conceived the idea of Jehovah. Terrible mixture of the cunning and the aweful"):

> Craftsmen, in dateless quarries dim,
> Stones formless into form did trim,
> Usurped on Nature's self with Art,
> And bade this dumb I AM to start
> Imposing him.[50]

The idea symbolized by these "vast, undefiled, incomprehensible, and aweful" monuments dominates the Wall Street world as well, where the illusion of enduring walls and permanent structures sustains the "idea of Jehovah" and his divine Cogito.

Yet, when the narrator visits Bartleby in the Tombs, he discovers a somewhat different monument: "The Egyptian character of the masonry weighed upon me with its gloom. But a soft imprisoned turf grew under foot. The heart of the eternal pyramids, it seemed, wherein, by some strange magic, through the clefts, grass-seed, dropped by birds, had sprung" (*B*, 53). In Hegelian terms, the image that crosses the abstract symbolism of the pyramid with the organicism of grass would suggest that self-consciousness has achieved a dialectical relation with Nature.[51] In Heideggerian terms, such a crossing would express the differential complex of *physis* and *logos*. For Freud, the image brings together eros and thanatos, whose coincidence or doubling I have described as the uncanny. In different ways, Hegel, Heidegger, and Freud conceptualize these "crossings" in linguistic terms, suggesting a general analogy with the activity of metaphor itself. Melville uses Egyptian architecture in "Bartleby" to emphasize the alienation from Nature that results from our longing for the ideal, but he suggests that such negation is a violation that also produces language and representation, as Hegel defines it: "The hieroglyphic symbol of another meaning, the hieroglyph of a thought."[52]

The association of Bartleby with ancient Egypt encourages me to read him as an avatar of Thoth: Rā's secretary, inventor of writing, prototype of the messenger/thief/boundary keeper Hermes, judge of the gods' disputes, and reputed author of the Book of the Dead. Thoth's association with the setting sun in the Pyramid Texts symbolizes his role as the scribe who usurps the power of his master, Rā, in Derrida's words, "replacing him in his absence and essential disappearance."[53] Thus, an Egyptologist like Budge describes Thoth's usurpation in terms of his power over words: "Without his words the gods, whose existence depended upon them, could not have their place among the followers of Rā."[54] And it is precisely this association with language that gives Thoth the distinction of being his own father: "'Lord of Khemennu, self-created, to whom none hath given birth, god One.'"[55] As the originator of himself, of language, he lays proper claim to the title "master of law," because the judgment of the soul is determined by the words that *are* that soul: "Thoth as the great god of words was rightly regarded as the judge of words, and the testing of the soul in the Balance in the Hall of Osiris is not described as the judging or 'weighing of actions,' but as the 'weighing of words.'" Thoth as language itself is properly the usurper and thief by virtue of his "personification of the mind of God."[56] He is the "spirit" who appears in the form of Bartleby, whose "dead-wall reveries" reflect upon the displacement of the sun. Representation itself is the "thief," who robs the divine of its identity and thus, as Derrida explains, "is never present. He appears nowhere in person. No being-there *properly* belongs to him."[57]

"He" is the god whose difference is cast out by Socrates in the *Phaedrus* only to be recuperated as the psychic signature, "veritably written in the soul of the listener." "He" is the style of language's unending play that is hidden by the law or truth that would control such wandering, but is exposed at last in the act of narration. "He" is that language of representation in which the metaphors ordinarily associated with art replace the figurative authority and law of Scripture: the double name in the anagram of Bartleby (Art/Byble). Bartleby/Thoth must preserve this difference of the profane and the divine, the artificial and the spiritual. "This god-messenger is a god of the absolute passage between opposites. If he had an identity — but he is precisely the god of nonidentity — he would be [a] *coincidentia oppositorum*."[58] In a sense, Bartleby redeems Pierre, whose primary mythic identification is with Phaeton, who remains secondary to Helios by virtue of his mortal birth (out of Clymene) that signifies his weakness. Phaeton is the unsuccessful usurper of the father/sun/god's place; Thoth succeeds as the fatherless figure who displaces the god.[59]

Hegel's Egyptian pyramid and the Wall Street world entomb only the negation of unrealized Spirit; Bartleby transforms the Tombs into a dwelling where death and life are conjoined, an abode for the spirit itself. When Redburn visits Liverpool, he regrets that the docks have not been named after "those naval heroes, who by their valor did so much to protect the commerce of Britain." This observation prompts him to reflect on the nature of monuments:

> And how much better would such stirring monuments be; full of life and commotion; than hermit obelisks of Luxor, and idle towers of stone; which, useless to the world in themselves, vainly hope to eternize a name, by having it carved, solitary and alone, in their granite. Such monuments are cenotaphs indeed; founded far away from the true body of the fame of the hero; who, if he be truly a hero, must still be linked with the living interests of his race; for the true fame is something free, easy, social, and companionable. They are but tombstones that commemorate his death, but celebrate not his life.[60]

The true monument celebrates the "commerce" that is made possible by the real hero, a commerce defined as "the living interests of his race." In terms of Bartleby, I would translate this to mean the living commerce of human justice, sustained by the active interpretation that struggles to preserve the freedom of human intercourse. Redburn makes it clear in the subsequent passage that the "naval hero" and the "commerce" of Britain are metaphors for the writer himself and the trade he conducts: "But to build such a pompous vanity over the remains of a hero, is a slur upon his fame, and an insult to his ghost. And more enduring monuments are built in the closet with the letters of the alphabet, than even Cheops himself could have founded, with all Egypt and Nubia for his quarry."[61] The alphabetic monument is not simply a physical cenotaph, but a celebration: the dance of life and death. A book must always be displacing its site or denying its proper meaning, always building an inner crypt that is "erected by its very ruin, held up by what never stops eating away at its foundation," as Derrida describes the "artificial unconscious" produced in language.[62] The monument of the psyche, of being-in-the-world, is always composed of simulating letters, of copies that refer to other copies but to no original.

What is proper to man is language, whose differential system is by its very movement a wandering from the proper name, the hidden truth. "Ownership" is an illusion that depends upon the possibility of a meaning, a signified that would remain unaffected by the endless straying of signifiers. Three times the narrator compares Bartleby to yet another simulated stone: a plaster-of-paris bust of Cicero that decorates the inner office. At the very heart of Cicero's definition of justice in the *Offices,* we find the following principle: "Whatever belongs either to all in common, or particular persons as their own property, should not be altered, but made use of accordingly." This basic tenet of justice, however, causes Cicero to question the nature of ownership itself: "Now no man can say that he has anything his own by a right of nature; but either by an ancient immemorial seizure, as those who first planted uninhabited countries; or, secondly, by conquest, as those who have got things by the right of the sword; or else by some law, compact, agreement, or lot."[63] "Property" is the result of an original transgression of man's nature, an arbitrary determination of right that is rationalized by social law. The mode of signification that Bartleby's uncanny presence opposes to mere copying subverts the system of representation on which the narrator's law is based and recalls the homeless wandering that is veritably written in the souls of men. Bartleby shares the indeterminacy of Derrida's Thoth: "His property is impropriety, the floating indetermination that permits substitution and play."[64] Verbal commerce replaces property, the goods themselves defined by their transport and exchange. In language, the signifier economizes those prior traces that have motivated it and makes possible the supplement that will appropriate it in turn. We have already observed this movement as the circulation of a writing that constitutes the psychic system and gives the illusion of depth to the process of signification, which is represented by such metaphors as the "conscious" and the "unconscious."

Thus, Bartleby figures as the agent of a renewed intercourse, which begins to invade the city and transgress its customary boundaries. From his retreat in the inner office, Bartleby wanders into the hall, the stairway, and the entryway, until the narrator is informed: "Everybody is concerned; clients are leaving the offices; some fears are entertained of a mob; something you must do, and that without delay" (*B,* 48). Bartleby has been moved from his hermitage, which has been always associated with the textual tissue in which he figures: "Throughout, the scrivener remained standing behind the screen, which I directed to be removed the last thing. It was withdrawn; and, being folded up like a huge folio, left him the motionless occupant of a naked room" (46). Just as Bartleby causes his master to dismantle the offices of the law, so he escapes the confines of a book and its formal meaning to stray into that larger text of the Wall Street world. Yet, if he causes the narrator to move his offices and become a temporary vagrant himself, wandering "about the upper part of town and through the suburbs, in my rockaway," Bartleby prompts a defensive reaction on the part of the narrator and the authorities of this society (50). The narrator tells him: "I find these chambers too far from the City Hall; the air is unwholesome" (46). Seeking a closer proximity to the central order that reinforces his own concept of order, the narrator fails to recognize that City Hall, like the Tombs, is already threatened by the rebellion of Bartleby:

> "I'll take odds he doesn't," said a voice as I passed.
> "Doesn't go? — done!" said I, "put up your money."
> I was instinctively putting my hand in my pocket to produce my own, when I remembered that this was an election day. The words I overheard bore no reference to Bartleby, but to the success or non-success of some candidate for the mayoralty. [*B,* 41]

A "slip" confirms Bartleby's figuration of the straying of the letter, of the failure of a message to reach its destination. A significant error betrays the anxiety of the narrator concerning this threat to his ability to control the vagrancy of texts.

Finally, Bartleby is conducted to the Tombs — "or, to speak more properly, the Halls of Justice" (*B,* 51) — where the little revolution he has initiated is apparently quelled. He is put to sleep, his eyes closed by the narrator, and thus socially exorcised and psychically repressed in order to restore order and reason. A "luny," "deranged," "moon-struck" figure whose vagrancy has unsettled lawyers and landlords is consigned to that enclosed space where other threatening elements are constrained. Yet, his physical imprisonment is displaced by his narrative circulation; he has achieved his ghostly destiny in activating the narrator's psyche, a narrator who is no longer a Master in Chancery and writes without hope of commanding his text. No longer a scrivener in a legal office, no longer a singular character in a fiction, "wasted Bartleby" fulfills his own definition of himself: "I am not particular" (*B,* 49). Transforming the physical Tombs into the psychical monument, Bartleby continues to circulate as the principle of *différance:* the uncanny and vagrant property in language that motivates expression. The avowed purpose of this tale has been "to awaken curiosity," which the narrator is "wholly unable to gratify." We are left only with a "vague report" of "a certain suggestive interest," in which "dead letters" and "dead men" are equated. These letters clearly suggest the human destiny: "On errands of life, these letters speed to death" (*B*, 54). Yet, it is only within this circuit that one "learns how to live, by rehearsing the part of death." Bartleby dramatizes what Gasché terms "the dispersing movement of the letters which circulate only to leave behind them the traces of death."[65] And thus he prepares for his own supplementary movement in the narrator's appended note and the awakened curiosity in the reader, which is already directed toward the alphabetical monument that has appropriated the stony pyramids of the Wall Street world. As Melville writes in *Pierre:* "The profounder emanations of the human mind" are always ruined towers that "never unravel their own intricacies, and have no proper endings; but in imperfect, unanticipated, and disappointing sequels (as mutilated stumps), hurry to abrupt intermergings with the eternal tides of time and fate" (*P*, 141).

6.

Trumping the Trick
of the Truth:
The Extra-Moral Sense
of Twain's *Pudd'nhead Wilson*

If the morality of "thou shalt not lie" is rejected, the "sense for truth" will
have to legitimize itself before another tribunal: — as a means of the
preservation of man, as *will to power*.
 — Nietzsche, *The Will to Power*

Often the surest way to convey misinformation is to tell the truth.
 — Mark Twain, *Notebook 32*

Man has not a single right which is the product of anything but might.
 — *Mark Twain's Notebook*

Virtually any work by Mark Twain might be studied in terms of its
marginal relation to the American literary tradition; the majority of Twain's
writings continue to be judged either as flawed masterpieces or as the abortive efforts of a misdirected or distracted genius. Each work in turn seems
eccentric to whatever composite "Mark Twain" we might patch together
according to our various conceptions of literature, history, and the personality of the artist. Canonized by the public as the American saint of practicality
and common sense, Twain commands an elaborate mythology of folk values.
Yet, his contempt for arbitrary authorities of all sorts and his general
"republicanism" frequently seem at odds with his tirades against the masses:
"The majority is always in the wrong. Whenever you find that you are on the
side of the majority, it is time to reform — (or pause and reflect)." [1] This
apparent contradiction generally has been explained as a version of Emersonian self-reliance; Twain himself symbolizes the radical individual, whose
autonomy and rebellion against shams of all sorts ought to be the ideals of a
true republicanism: a community of individuals sustained by their mutual
respect and independence.

Such views are usually supported by interpretations of the moral integrity of Huck Finn, whose complicity in social lies is never so deep that he loses the instinctive goodness of his "heart." [2] Huck's desire to preserve youthful spontaneity and moral purity functions centrally in the Twain mythology; Huck's eternal impulse toward the Territory has been conventionalized as the characteristic American rebellion against the determining forces of society. Yet, a number of critics have argued that Twain's ambiguity concerning the origin and nature of Huck's "heart" is the basic problem in that work. Huck's self-reliance certainly does not originate solely from the natural world that is presented in *Huckleberry Finn;* the "strong brown god" of the river is a powerful force without moral reference. And the "natural goodness" of the child is neither pure nor original. As Albert Stone suggests, Twain's children betray from their earliest years the unresolved human duality that characterizes the adult. They are "kind-hearted and yet given to cruel practical jokes, anarchic yet conditioned to their moral decisions by social experience, free from the trammels of adult life but never really able to light out for the Territory, victors perhaps in all the small skirmishes with grown-ups but defeated in the larger battle, surrendering the moment of moral insight so painfully achieved." [3]

Huckleberry Finn dramatizes the frustration of the human desire for autonomous and self-reliant identity at the same time that it seems to deny the possibility of any viable development of the individual within society. The contradictions in this novel are frequently used to characterize Twain's own equivocal ethical position in his major writings — contradictions so profound that they would ultimately result in the outraged nihilism of Twain's later writings. For genetic critics, Twain's inability to account for Huck's freedom and honesty drove him into a skepticism that would end with the seeming mechanistic determinism of such works as *What Is Man?* [4] At the same time, Twain continued to produce sentimental romances in the manner of *The Prince and the Pauper* (1882). Twain's ability to write such a withering indictment of American culture as *Pudd'nhead Wilson* (1894) and then turn without interruption to the composition of such popular indulgences as *Personal Recollections of Joan of Arc* (1896) and *Tom Sawyer: Detective* (1896) remains one of the most marked eccentricities in the nineteenth-century American literary tradition.

Substantial biographical explanations for Twain's ambivalent attitudes have been offered, especially for his writings after 1892. Twain's mounting problems with the Paige typesetter, the failure of his publishing house in the panic of 1893, his round-the-world lecture tour in 1895–1896 to pay creditors, the surrender of his financial affairs to Henry Huttleston Rogers and Livy, and the death of Susy in 1896 are only a few of the biographical events that have been used to explain the marked discrepancies in his thought. These literary idiosyncrasies have also been attributed to the general fin de siècle atmosphere in America in the last quarter of the century; Twain's personal difficulties, like those of Henry Adams, certainly intensified his own sense of the apparently irreconcilable cultural conflicts that defined post-Civil War America.[5] Such biographical and historical explanations are frequently complemented by interpretations of Twain's roots in the folk tradition and his reliance on vernacular prose and humor. Personally distracted and culturally disoriented, Twain seemed to retreat into a backwoods skepticism directed against any sort of rigorous or systematic thinking.

The tone of such critical assessments remains largely pejorative, even in those studies that celebrate the Americanness of Twain's vernacular genius. Critics often conclude that Twain was unable to control his diverse energies sufficiently to pursue the philosophical implications of *Huckleberry Finn*. Bernard DeVoto's mandarin judgment that Mark Twain "had no conscious aesthetic" and thus "stood at the opposite pole from Henry James" continues to support the main tradition of Twain criticism.[6] Yet, the idea that Twain should be taken at his word as a "jackleg" novelist who could hardly be expected to provide a coherent philosophy is no less misleading than the impulse to minimize the contradictions in his thought according to a genetic analysis.[7] Granting the difficulty of drawing a coherent portrait of Mark Twain, Louis Budd still views his life and works as far more intellectually ordered than most critics would allow: "Perhaps the central, essentially consistent Twain cannot be drawn with sharp lines. . . . Still, politically at least, the contradictions in Twain's ideas are not as serious as they may look; they often clear up if he is taken on his own terms instead of being used to prove a sweeping theory about the American mind or psyche, if he is put in his milieu and allowed to change his stand from year to year or from decade to decade as fresh problems emerge."[8] Budd comments that "the faculty of humor . . . usually seems to be correlated with inner tensions," but like other critics of various theoretical persuasions he does not consider Twain's eccentricity to be related to any necessary literary strategy.

These differing critical approaches to a major American author raise some interesting questions about order, coherence, consistency, and unity as criteria for both literature and philosophy. Twain's humor, for example, certainly depends upon "inner tensions," contradictions, and double meanings, but such contrariety is considered particularly antiintellectual and unphilosophic. Critics are fond of singling out particularly discordant farcical or humorous episodes in Twain's works to demonstrate his apparent inability to subordinate his wit to the higher demands of thematic and intellectual coherence. The evasion plot at the end of *Huckleberry Finn* has, of course, frequently drawn this kind of critical reproach; the radical indictment of slavery in *Pudd'nhead Wilson* is often considered flawed by Twain's apparently gratuitous humor concerning the superstitions and pretensions of black slaves. Several critics have traced the central problems in *A Connecticut Yankee* to the discrepancy between its intellectual themes and its apparent inception in Twain's farcical sense of himself transposed to the court of Arthur: "Dream of being a knight errant in armor in the Middle Ages. Have notions and habits of thought of the present day mixed with the necessities of that. No pockets in the armor. Can't scratch. Cold in the head — can't blow — can't get a handkerchief, can't use iron sleeve. . . . Always getting struck by lightning. Fall down and can't get up" (*MTN*, 171).

Yet, Twain recognized both the philosophical and psychological powers of his comic mode, which is more accurately described as "wit" than "humor": "Somebody has said 'Wit is the sudden marriage of ideas which before their union were not perceived to have any relation'" (*MTN*, 185). Although this passage might be understood to say that the audience recognizes a new relation resulting from the careful design of ordinarily contrary elements, it might also be interpreted as a statement of the author's deliberate strategy to discover new relations even beyond the limits of his own conscious intention. William Spengemann traces Twain's use of the "ironic voice of the 'inspired idiot'" back to his early journalistic writings, and the persona figures centrally in such major works as *Huckleberry Finn, Connecticut Yankee*, and *Pudd'nhead Wilson*.[9]

Twain was not always willing to make sharp distinctions between the fictive mask of the "puddingheaded clown" and the coldly ironic author. If Twain's most self-conscious characters are unable to escape all the effects of social conditioning, then the author must thoroughly question his own claim to lucid detachment. The problem is complicated by Twain's insistence that social corruptions are perpetuated by language itself, the subtlest force constraining one's struggle to transcend a particular history. Forced to employ the language of his white masters, Jim can only express his new-found freedom in the language of slavery: "I owns myself, en I's wuth eight hund'd dollars. I wisht I had de money, I wouldn' want no mo'."[10] Twain's struggle to develop a strategic method that would allow him to criticize culture without denying his inevitable entanglement in its language seems consonant with the prevalent tendency in modern philosophy from Nietzsche to Derrida to deconstruct the autotelic closure of philosophic systems and the presumption of value-free judgments.

Like Nietzsche, Twain was increasingly attracted to the expressive possibilities of aphorisms and maxims: those apothegmatic sayings that Twain tagged "affyisms." The more than three hundred aphorisms Twain wrote hardly compare with the volume of Nietzsche's production; Twain's aphorisms contribute to the formal organization of only *Pudd'nhead Wilson* and *Following the Equator*, whereas the majority of Nietzsche's works derive their organization from the internal structure of the aphorism. Most of Twain's aphorisms were notebook jottings occasionally incorporated into "Pudd'nhead Wilson's Calendar" or buried in the narrative style of his works.

William Gibson points out that Twain composed aphorisms throughout his career, but "most of them originated during the 1890s"; he considers them part of Twain's "determination to achieve a pure, vigorous style and to find the right word." [11] Gibson's view agrees with Richard Bridgman's general judgment of Twain's antitheoretical attitude toward language: "For Mark Twain the relationship between word and thing, symbol and referent, was unusually direct. He ignored metaphysical dispute and assumed a right word could be found, not mechanically, but artistically: almost musically." [12] Yet, the idea that Twain's aphorisms were attempts to "reduce life to its lowest terms" or "put it all into one paragraph if you could get it right" seems an especially inappropriate explanation of such internally divided statements as: " 'Two souls with but a single thought' ‹ is a quite common thing.› not a bad average, for it is a half a thought apiece. This village has approached it sometimes, but not often enough to attract attention." [13]

With the exception of Gibson's analysis of "The Pudd'nhead Wilson Maxims" in *The Art of Mark Twain,* there has been little consideration of the structural significance of Twain's aphorisms for his prose style and his general aesthetic outlook. Recent studies of Nietzsche, however, have placed great importance on the aphorism as a crucial form for his thought. Like Twain, Nietzsche was preeminently concerned with the subversive power of language and the ability of unrecognized conventions to mislead even the wariest rebel against metaphysical traditions: " 'Reason' in language: oh what a deceitful old woman! I fear we are not getting rid of God because we still believe in grammar." [14] In this context, one may recall the incident in *Huckleberry Finn* during the Peter Wilks affair when Huck, posing as the king's valet, finds his extemporized stories about England challenged by Joanna Wilks:

> "Honest injun, now, hain't you been telling me a lot of lies?" . . .
> "None of it at all. Not a lie in it," says I.
> "Lay your hand on this book and say it."
> I see it warn't nothing but a dictionary, so I laid my hand on it and said it. [*HF,* 138]

Language is nothing but lies for both Nietzsche and Twain, but neither writer could ever transcend the systematic deception of words that poses as metaphysical truth. At best, one might hope to expose the problem of the word's fundamental metaphoricity and its existence in irreducibly figural relations to other words. Nietzsche reacted violently to a Western philosophic tradition that treated verbal signs as merely instrumental referents for concepts that remained untouched by the divisive diachrony of representation. As a system of appearances that functioned to symbolize an inaccessible reality, language could be employed in the service of the most arbitrary authorities and thus help further that priestly denial of life for the sake of fetishes — *Ding an sich,* Being, God, truth — which Nietzsche viewed as a decadent "nihilism." Yet, Nietzsche himself seems hopelessly ensnared by the grammar of such decadence; he sought in the aphoristic mode a strategy that might liberate him from the disguised teleology that governed the formal rules for expression.

David Allison argues that the aphorism repudiates the static categories of metaphysical thought in favor of the metamorphic power Nietzsche associated with *Übermensch* and his affirmative will to power. The Nietzschean aphorism exposes the essentially metaphorical quality of language and knowledge because it demands interpretation at the same time that it asserts the power that has constituted it *as* interpretation: "The aphorism demands that an operation be performed upon itself for its very intelligibility: that it be inserted into ever new contexts, that it be related to ever new referential sets. The aphorism, then, is essentially metaphorical: it gathers, culls, collects, compares, and assembles — however briefly — this movement of thought." [15]

The conception of language as irreducibly metaphorical relies on the rejection of the presumed authority of the subject over its own expression. Twain's attacks on the "ego" have generally been considered part of his late theory of determinism, which has been described as a forerunner of "the psychological theory of extreme behaviorism." [16] Although Twain often seems to share the views of contemporary Social Darwinists, he was openly critical of such naive conceptions of social evolution and historical progress in works like *Life on the Mississippi.* Twain's and Nietzsche's attacks on the freedom of the subject have been misunderstood as arguments for deterministic schemes; their respective critiques of the free individual are based on a conception of language that is equally at odds with the behaviorist's claim that one can control the social and historical forces governing personality. Although determinism deprives the subject of its assertive power, it still rests on the unity of the subject as a factor to be affected, trained, or conditioned. Nietzsche and Twain would also question the assumption that the behaviorial scientist can achieve a sufficient self-consciousness and objective detachment to be able to manipulate these same forces by which the scientist is constituted. Nietzsche is quite clear about the illusion of the subject's unity: "The subject: this is the term for our belief in a unity underlying all the different impulses of the highest feeling of reality: we understand this belief as the *effect* of one cause — we believe so firmly in our belief that for its sake we imagine 'truth,' 'reality,' 'substantiality' in general. — 'The subject' is the fiction that many similar states in us are the effect of one substratum: but it is we who first created the 'similarity' of these states." [17]

In Twain's later writings, the themes of twins, doubles, and exchanged identities that pervade all his works coalesced in a philosophic attitude concerning the inevitable duality of the human being. By the time he came to write *Pudd'nhead Wilson,* Twain could no longer save what Hank Morgan had hoped to salvage from the almost untraceable genealogy of individual training: "that one microscopic atom in me that is truly *me.*" [18] Twain manipulated literary devices of doubles, matching halves, and exchanged or mistaken identities in order to question ever more rigorously the presumed presence of the self to itself, that "self-knowledge" on which nineteenth-century theories of identity and meaning had generally depended. Like Nietzsche, Twain understood the subject as a grammatical fiction, employed to perpetuate obedience to authorities with the most palpable reality: church, aristocracy, law, school, family. Twain's aphorisms reveal a general rebellion in his later writings against the illusions of uninterpreted truth and individual autonomy.

Pudd'nhead Wilson (1894) is Twain's most sustained effort to trace the genealogy of moral values in a slave-holding society in which he himself was raised. Twain's struggle to represent the covert system of slavery that pervades all forms of behavior is complicated by his knowledge of the inevitable entanglement of slavery as a social institution with the subtler metaphysics of slavery inherent in Western modes of thought. Twain was especially interested in the ease with which the corrupt values of slave-holding societies controlled the behavior of those characters who maintained the humane values of justice, equality, and truth. The genius of *Huckleberry Finn* is Twain's ability to render ambiguous the initial distinctions drawn between citizen and criminal. Such figures as the slave hunters are quickly drawn caricatures of popular stereotypes; their cruelty and greed receive minimal attention in the narrative. Twain is far more concerned with such characters as Judge Thatcher, Widow Douglas, Miss Watson, Judith Loftus, and Silas Phelps. When the judge kindly offers to help Huck out of his straits with Pap by drawing up a contract that permits Huck to sell $6,000 to the judge for the "consideration" of $1, we recognize the arbitrary economic and legal fictions of this culture at the same time that we acknowledge the judge's good intentions. The Widow Douglas's maternal desire to educate Huck to the ways of society is undercut by our awareness that Huck's "fortune" compels this society to acknowledge his potential power. Like Silas Phelps, who preaches in a backwoods church and buys up runaway slaves, Judith Loftus holds double moral standards that are more obviously hypocritical than the confused values of the judge and the widow. The sharp line she draws between a "runaway apprentice" and a "runaway slave" emphasizes the moral and legal discriminations that are so ruthlessly satirized in *Pudd'nhead Wilson.* Yet, Mrs. Loftus's frontier practicality and her prompt sympathy for Huck's fabricated sufferings provide a brief sketch of what subsequently appears to be the essence of Huck's own humanity.

In *Huckleberry Finn,* Twain preserved his own detachment from such characters to the same degree that he was able to retain unsullied the extra-social "goodness" of Huck's "heart." However, in *Pudd'nhead Wilson,* every character is so constrained by unconscious cultural determinants that no objective point of reference or analysis seems possible. Although in works like "The Man That Corrupted Hadleyburg" and *The Mysterious Stranger* Twain did employ "ironic strangers" to reveal the contradictions in human values, such figures are mere technical devices — *diaboli ex machina* — designed to establish the logic of these parables. In *Pudd'nhead Wilson,* the very possibility of an outside or estranged view is rigorously questioned; the problems of authorial detachment and intention become the main subject of the narrative, but in ways that are intimately related to the more explicit issues of slavery, freedom, and justice.

The repeated critical complaint that *Pudd'nhead Wilson* suffers from undeveloped or contradictory characters seems absurdly at odds with the themes of the work itself; certainly, every member of a slave-holding society is affected by those contradictions and hypocrisies that constitute the infrastructure of the culture. The idea of a well-rounded or unified character in a work devoted to the study of social disunity and fragmentation seems to be a blatant attempt to force the work to fit a formalist paradigm for literary value.[19] The contradictions between critical judgment and literary performance seem especially striking given Twain's insistent critique of the autonomous subject in *Pudd'nhead Wilson.* Not only are well-rounded characters ruled out by the social and political issues in the work, but such characters must be considered at odds with Twain's conception of the ontological division of the individual into an internal dialectic of master and servant. Unlike Hegel, Twain could not imagine a sublation of the conflicting forces in man that might lead to a more harmonious or synthetic personality; he had to confront Wilson's pudd'nheaded character as a fundamental contradictoriness in humanity that must be the primary subject in any critique of social values.

Twain used the folk term *pudd'nhead* frequently in his writings, and the colloquial epithet assumes a marvelous ironic power when considered as a philosophical concept. In *A Connecticut Yankee,* Hank Morgan offers the fullest analysis of this notion. Pursued as runaway slaves by an angry mob, Hank and the King climb up the branch of a tree that hangs low over a stream and hide themselves in the foliage. Hank fears that their pursuers will suspect such a trick, so they carefully climb into an adjacent tree. When the mob arrives, the master commands a servant to search the tree with the overhanging branch for precisely the reasons Hank had predicted:

> I was obliged to admire my cuteness in foreseeing this very thing and swapping trees to beat it. But don't you know, there are some things that can beat smartness and foresight? Awkwardness and stupidity can. The best swordsman in the world doesn't need to fear the second best swordsman in the world; no, the per-

son for him to be afraid of is some ignorant antagonist who has never had a sword in his hand before; he doesn't do the thing he ought to do, and so the expert isn't prepared for him; he does the thing he ought not to do: and often it catches the expert out and ends him on the spot. Well, how could I, with all my gifts, make any valuable preparation against a near-sighted, cross-eyed, puddingheaded clown who would aim himself at the wrong tree and hit the right one? And that is what he did. He went for the wrong tree, which was of course the right one by mistake, and up he started. [*CY,* 247]

Although this "puddingheaded clown" seems to be little more than a clumsy fool, whose unpredictability is a threat to a man of "science" such as Hank, Twain recognized that every apparently rational intention has something "pudd'nheaded" about it. Twain's "ironic stranger" is often considered an idiot by the culture he invades precisely because he is a stranger, but many of Twain's most powerful characters are prone to unpredictable errors in judgment or knowledge. In fact, Morgan's failure in *A Connecticut Yankee* might well be attributed to his inability to recognize his own liability to errors in judgment and lapses in knowledge; his scientific pretensions blind him to his own contradictory nature.

Although Twain often pokes fun at his own ignorance, he considers artistic expression to be as dependent upon the unconscious as on the conscious. He makes this explicit in his introductory note to "Those Extraordinary Twins," in which he recounts the curious genesis of *Pudd'nhead Wilson:*

And I have noticed another thing: that as the short tale grows into the long tale, the original intention (or motif) is apt to get abolished and find itself superseded by a quite different one. . . . I had a sufficiently hard time with [*Pudd'nhead Wilson*], because it changed itself from a farce to a tragedy while I was going along with it — a most embarrassing circumstance. But what was a great deal worse was, that it was not one story, but two stories tangled together; and they obstructed and interrupted each other at every turn and created no end of confusion and annoyance.[20]

Critics have studied *Those Extraordinary Twins* in order to account for the apparently undeveloped characters of Luigi and Angelo or the mechanical functions of Aunt Patsy Cooper and Rowena in *Pudd'nhead Wilson.*[21] Yet, what is most remarkable about *Those Extraordinary Twins* is the form in which it was published. Twain's introductory note and running comments transform the unfinished narrative into a critical account of the ways an author's process of composition subverts his original intentions and swerves into unexpected, even long repressed, areas of concern. What Twain characterizes as the method of the "jackleg novelist" agrees with the misdirection of the pudd'nhead. If Twain hoped to write about those unconscious fears and desires that secretly govern our history and behavior, then he had to find some method of violating his conscious intentions in order to expose his own thought to the tangled forces of social training that had generated it. As Twain wrote in his notebooks: "A man's brain (intellect) is stored powder; it cannot touch itself off; the fire must come from the outside" (*MTN,* 365). Taken together, *Pudd'nhead Wilson and Those Extraordinary Twins* is a literary monstrosity, whose grotesque form and conflicting intentions provide a metacommentary on the problems facing a white man struggling to represent the repressed genealogy of slave-holding societies.[22]

Thus, for both formal and polemical purposes, *Pudd'nhead Wilson* relies on a necessarily contradictory structure. The themes of the novel involve myriad doublings, mutual exchanges, and matching and unmatching halves; the form of the novel is equally dependent on oppositional relations that struggle with each other for dominance. The narrative is internally divided between the conventional detective plot and the philosophical issues partially announced in the "Calendar" entries. One way to conceptualize this conflict is to consider the two different kinds of temporality at work in the popular narrative and the "Calendar." Twain is at some pains to give the period 1830–1853 the illusion of narrative coherence and continuity. The attention he pays to family genealogies, such intervening events as Roxy's "freedom" as a chambermaid on *The Grand Mogul,* and the biographies of Luigi and Angelo contributes to Twain's indictment of slavery, but it also betrays the technical need to fill in apparent historical blanks and provide the cause-and-effect chronology so essential to any detective plot. And yet, such causal relations constantly break down or reveal their artificiality. The normal course of events is often interrupted by improbable visitors; actions are motivated by coincidental meetings, unwitting confessions, and unanticipated conflicts. The sequence of events that begins with Luigi's and Angelo's history of the knife and reaches a climax with Tom's insulting reference to the Twins as "this human philopena" is crucial to the unfolding of the plot. These unlikely events are unmistakably the "motives" for subsequent actions: Judge Driscoll's duel of honor with Luigi, the judge's slander of Luigi as an "assassin" during the political campaign, Tom's murder of the judge with the Indian knife, and the general suspicion of Luigi as the avenging murderer. Often the dramatic presence of the major characters and narrative contiguity are the only factors that bring together such disparate events as palm readings and political meetings. In fact, Wilson shares our inability to understand these events solely on the basis of their temporal succession. Empirical evidence such as Wilson gathers is of little help in untangling the psychological motives that transform mere actions into significant events.

The chronology of the plot may be measured against the time of "Pudd'nhead Wilson's Calendar," which seems to rely on the time of writing itself and the notion that events are constituted as such by the consequences of their interpretations. Twain wants to know what cultural attitudes make possible certain representative events in the narrative and how it is possible for us to interpret those interpretations. In one of his maxims, Twain remarks: "No occurrence is an Event until our feelings promote it to that dignity. The birth of Christ was not an Event; in nineteen centuries it has risen to a summit where it overshadows all other events." [23] The detective plot relies on conventions that require a coherent conclusion; Twain's "other narrative" violates this impulse toward order and coherence in order to reveal the murky struggle for power and domination that is rationalized by the romance. Twain gives us a hint of this divided narrative structure in his introductory note to *Those Extraordinary Twins.* In his farcical account of how he struggled to rid the story of Rowena, Twain suggests at least one explanation for the relation of the Calendar entries to the narrative:

> I didn't know what to do with her. . . . I finally saw plainly that there was really no way but one — I must simply give her the grand bounce. It grieved me to do it, for after associating with her so much I had come to kind of like her after a fashion, notwithstanding she was such an ass and said such stupid, irritating things and was so nauseatingly sentimental. Still it had to be done. So at the top of Chapter XVII, I put a "Calendar" remark concerning July Fourth, and began the chapter with this statistic:
> "Rowena went out in the back yard after supper to see the fireworks and fell down the well and got drowned." [*ET,* 210–11]

The sentimental character, Rowena, is performatively "drowned" by the Calendar's irony; the "other narrative" of ironic wisdom serves to subvert and disrupt the illusion of order and continuity in the popular plot structure. Thus, the reader is prompted to reject the denouement of the detective story and search for the significance of the narrative in relation to what the romance seeks to repress and rationalize. This narrative tension is reflected both in the divided personality of David Wilson, the ostensible author of the Calendar and the detective in the romance, and the divided personality of the author himself, who vacillates between the desire to tell an entertaining story and the need to attack social corruptions.

The thematic development of the problem suggested by the dissonant narrative structure begins with Pudd'nhead Wilson's "fatal remark" on the day that he arrives in Dawson's Landing. In an apparent effort to ingratiate himself "with a group of citizens," Wilson idly comments on the "yelp and snarl and howl" of "an invisible dog":

> "I wish I owned half of that dog."
> "Why?" somebody asked.
> "Because I would kill my half."
> The group searched his face with curiosity, with anxiety even, but found no light there, no expression they could read. They fell away from him as from something uncanny, and went into privacy to discuss him. [*PW,* 6]

This "parable of the dog" has received much critical attention, most of which has been devoted to judgments of Wilson's subtle wisdom or his greenhorn ignorance of southwestern humor. As Cox points out, however, the joke is "an old chestnut in the provinces"; the local citizens may be quite literal in certain respects, but Missouri folk humor is notoriously double-edged.[24]

Read in terms of Twain's indictment of slave-holding society, Wilson's remark strikes at the heart of southern hypocrisy. Like the dog, the community is an organic whole that cannot be divided into such halves as black and white or slave and master without destroying the entire organism.[25] Such an interpretation seems appropriate when we consider how subtly Twain shows that the apparent unity of this community is in fact secretly divided on every level; the essential opposition of black and white is multiplied by the political divisions between the temperance and rum parties, the various divisions of the social hierarchy, the familial distinctions between parent and child, even the sexual divisions between man and woman. The organicist argument, however, assumes the possibility of a unified community, in which particulars might be related to an ideal whole that would reconcile differences and provide a form for order. By the time he came to write *Pudd'nhead Wilson,* Twain no longer believed in the possibility of any utopian society in which equality and brotherhood might flourish. Like the invisible dog, each individual is fundamentally divided, composed of differences that could never be synthesized in a unified character.

Critics who enthusiastically embrace Twain's social criticism often hastily generalize that Twain opposed the free individual to the dehumanized slave produced by southern culture. Yet, it is precisely this myth of the free individual that sustains the system of slavery and the aristocratic pretensions of this society. "Identity" is the property of those titled aristocrats who assert their own power only by reducing blacks to chattel with specific economic values. "Identity" is an elaborate game of words and proper names: slaves have no surnames and thus lack social individuality. The aristocrats claiming descent from the First Families of Virginia appropriate a gaudy panoply of noble names: Cecil Burleigh Essex, Percy Northumberland Driscoll, Pembroke Howard, York Leicester Driscoll. These Old World borrowings are maintained only by virtue of the existence of their opposites: those dehumanized others who make even the concept of ownership possible. To claim title either to a name or a parcel of property, one must sustain the reality of impoverishment for others; the slaves and even the unlanded townspeople exist for the sake of aristocratic identity. Individual identity as unified and self-present defines the character of those in authority; Twain suggests more than mere fidelity to regional customs by giving the aristocrats the primary powers of the law in this town. The dependence of the identity of the aristocrat on the legal inhumanity of the slave is made explicit when young Chambers saves his apparent master Tom from drowning. Tom's enemies take advantage of this moment of weakness to taunt him: "They laughed at him, and called him coward, liar, sneak, and other sorts of pet names, and told him they meant to call Chambers by a new name after this, and make it common in town — 'Tom Driscoll's niggerpappy' — to signify that he had had a second birth into this life, and that Chambers was the author of his new being" (*PW,* 32). The very being of Tom as master depends upon the paternity of the slave, whose nonexistence under the law makes "mastery" possible as a concept.[26]

Twain's frequent references in the novel to Tom Driscoll as a "dog" or "hound" and the general treatment of blacks as animals complement our understanding of Wilson's "invisible dog." Although southerners regularly termed blacks "dogs," Twain manipulates this epithet to suggest a more general servitude. A brief comment in Twain's notebooks expresses his sense of how dogs and cats are related to human behavior: "Cat is freeman, the dog a slave."[27] The human being is by nature a divided creature, defined in part by temperament and in part by training. Wilson's remark recalls Huck Finn's disgust with his own socially determined conscience: "If I had a yaller dog that didn't know no more than a person's conscience does, I would pison him" (*HF,* 181). Considered separately, neither one's conscience nor temperament (Huck's "heart") provides a proper moral standard for actions. Temperament turns all too quickly into selfishness; conscience alone results in blind obedience to the most arbitrary social authorities. And yet, the necessary relationship between one's own desire and social duty is never organic, but is a continuing struggle of conflicting forces for dominance. One's "being" is defined by this heterogeneous relation, in which the very difference of forces generates life as a dynamic process of assertion and submission. Slaveholding societies polarize these internal differences and project them as distinct social roles: master and servant. The differences whereby the individual is constituted provide a system of checks against excesses of social conditioning or the expression of one's own unfettered desires. By subordinating one force to the other, the aristocrat turns the black into an element controlled by the overriding category of white identity. Slavery is a suppression of human differences that strips the other of any ontological status; the black is merely a commodity owned by white identity. In his secret rage against the ambiguous differences of life itself, the white man develops an elaborate scheme that excludes the black from existence itself in order to assert the unity of his own identity. To "have" or "own" one's self, one must kill that other — the social, natural, and psychic order — that threatens the mastery of the self by itself. In the parable of the dog, the killing of one half destroys the whole not because the parts are organically related but because their differential relation is what constitutes life as such.

The ownership of slaves not only contributes to the economic and ontological determination of the white man's "responsibility" in society, but it assures his dominance by excluding the black from participation in social relations except as an item of exchange. The most elemental form of owner-ship is one's own labor, which provides the promise of future production and the possibility of both credit and identity. Yet, the system of slavery legally transfers the ownership of the black slave's labor to the master, thus stripping the black of identity, responsibility, and economic power.[28] The problem is reflected in the conversation of the townspeople about Wilson's remark:

> "Said he wished he owned *half* of the dog, the idiot," said a third. "What did he reckon would become of the other half if he killed his half? Do you reckon he thought it would live?
>
> "Why, he must have thought it, unless he *is* the downrightest fool in the world; because if he hadn't thought it, he would have wanted to own the whole dog, knowing that if he killed his half and the other half died, he would be responsible for that half just the same as if he had killed that half instead of his own." [*PW*, 6]

In slave-holding societies, the two halves of the individual are transformed into the social concepts of ownership and impoverishment, which means that the half that owns takes responsibility for the other half and thus effectively owns the whole. Differences are replaced by binary oppositions — + / − or 1/0, which subtly authorize the power of one pole of the dialectic. It is thus not surprising that the elemental opposition of black and white is further legitimized by the evolution of such moral associations as black with evil or chaos and white with goodness or purity.

A closer examination of Twain's halves, twins, or doubles reveals that the parts constitute each other by mutual invasions and violations rather than by complementary coordination. The antithetical personalities of Luigi and Angelo repeatedly conflict in both *Those Extraordinary Twins* and *Pudd'nhead Wilson,* but Twain gets a good deal more farcical mileage out of these dif-ferences in the former work. Pure resemblances, like pure oppositions, are merely abstract illusions for Twain; the identical twins are respectively teetotaler/imbiber, religious/freethinking, peaceful/aggressive, nonsmoker/ smoker, traditional in dress/fashionable, prone to indigestion/prone to spicy foods, etc. And the indulgences of one generally affect the other: Angelo gets drunk when Luigi drinks; Angelo is wounded when Luigi duels; Luigi catches cold when Angelo is baptized. Although in *Pudd'nhead Wilson* the twins have moments in which their differences produce a kind of harmony, such as when they play a marvelous piano duet at Aunt Patsy's house, Twain emphasizes the conflict between their apparent identity as twins and a hidden war of psychological differences. The legal farce in *Those Extraordinary Twins* depends upon the court's inability to distinguish between the innocent Angelo and the guilty Luigi for the purposes of punishment. In this case,

Wilson's defense relies on the divided personalities inhabiting a single body, which enable him to render ambiguous the clear and distinct moral categories on which the law is based. Robert Regan considers Wilson's argument to be a "showy display of sophistry," but the confusion that Wilson produces seems commensurate with the disruptive aims of Twain himself in *Pudd'nhead Wilson*. [29]

A small anthology could be composed exclusively of Twain's maxims that deal with this paradoxical relationship of halves, doubles, and twins. Twain writes in his notebooks: "Gives me a cold horror to see a person eating one of those odious things, an English walnut — he seems to be ‹ digging › lifting the brains out of a shell on his nutpick." [30] The halves of the walnut recall Tom Driscoll's insulting reference to the twins as "this human philopena" during the Sons of Liberty meeting. *Philopena* is a slang term for "sweetheart," because it was the popular name for joined kernels of nuts used in a game of the same name. The word itself — *philos poena*, "love of punishment" — derives from the game in which "two kernels of a nut are shared by two people, one of whom, if failing to fulfill a given condition, must pay a forfeit to the other." [31] This game of exchanges in which your friend is in fact your antagonist certainly has a more brutal counterpart in the game of social relations in Dawson's Landing. In addition, Twain's association of the twin kernels of the nut with the two lobes of the brain suggests that the twin motif in the novel refers to the fundamental duality of the human being, in which the two lobes might be termed respectively unconscious and conscious, slave and freeman, temperament and training, conscience and heart. Like Twain's twins or the two lobes of the brain, the unconscious and the conscious are constituted by their mutual violation of each other, a differential relationship that recalls Freud's *facilitation* or "fraying" (*die Bahnung*) whereby neural impulses move violently from one psychic level to the other. [32]

In *Pudd'nhead Wilson,* the deliberate confusion of apparently distinct forces is dramatized both within the individual and in interpersonal relations. Twain's treatment of miscegenation, still a taboo subject at the end of the nineteenth century, suggests how the social projection of white master and black slave is related to the psychic hierarchy in which consciousness controls unconscious impulses and social forms are designed to mask private behavior. Roxy's act of switching the babies in their cradles initiates an inmixing that will cause the private to surge into the public, the repressed power of life as the endless interchange of differences to violate social proprieties. Social repression inevitably weakens the aristocrats' power, which is abstracted further and further from the dynamic energy of the differences within man and among men. White women in *Pudd'nhead Wilson* are unsexed by the logic of the slave system, which substitutes the purity of the southern belle for the sexual potency that threatens the white master's ideal authority. Transferring the duties of motherhood to the mammy, the white master drives sex into that repressed — nonexistent, inhuman, uncivilized — under-world of primal passions.[33]

Thus, any effort to understand Twain's representation of slavery in terms of strict oppositions between freedom and slavery merely replicates the ideology of this culture, which invents the concept of slavery in order to preserve the illusion of individual identity and noble autonomy. Like the symbolic struggle between the twins, a constant battle is waged in human nature and is itself the best sign of life and vitality. Yet, such an internal conflict is equally the source of anxiety, because individuals long for a resolution of this psychic war and a clear sense of their ability to control their existence. Literary artists are never free of this psychic paradox, regardless of the claims their works make for human self-consciousness and understanding. Irwin has observed that Melville's discovery that bipolar opposites are in fact mutually constitutive tempted Melville to embrace that nihilism in which all epistemological relations are equally illusory.[34] Both Melville's and Twain's nihilistic inclinations repeat the secret fear that all meanings are arbitrary — the same fear that prompts social man to develop determinate laws, classes, and authorities. The desire to master the human situation and transcend an intrinsically divided human nature is a life-denying impulse that, for both Melville and Twain, represents "original sin."

Twain's analysis of the aristocrat's strict adherence to abstract codes of honor exposes a fundamental dread of sensuous complexity. This sterility resembles the rancor that Nietzsche's "base" man (*das Man*) directs against life itself, despite the fact that Twain and Nietzsche appear to be concerned with two socially distinct groups. Nietzsche's concept of *ressentiment*, however, has often been misunderstood as the envy of those who have been deprived of power. The concept has been misappropriated by such social theorists as Max Scheler to account for working-class rebellions and to reaffirm the priority of aristocratic values.[35] But Nietzsche's "noble" and "base" souls are not to be equated with contemporary social classes; the noble man for Nietzsche rejects the impulse toward "self-sovereignty" that is the motive for social authority and power. As Alphonso Lingis explains this, "The power of the noble life should not be confused with social, political, or military power, where power does not lie in life in itself, but in the role occupied by an individual in an institutional apparatus."[36] The aristocrats of Dawson's Landing betray precisely the *ressentiment* against life that might mistakenly be associated with the slaves alone. Twain's aristocrats are as much enslaved by their own system as those human commodities they have defined in order to preserve their illusion of autonomy and control. Nietzsche writes in *The Genealogy of Morals:* "The slave revolt in morals begins by rancor turning creative and giving birth to values — the rancor of beings who, deprived of the direct outlet to action, compensate by an imaginary vengeance. All truly noble morality grows out of triumphant self-affirmation. Slave ethics, on the other hand, begins by saying *no* to an 'outside,' an 'other,' a non-self, and that *no* is its creative act. This reversal of direction of the evaluating look, this invariable looking outward instead of inward, is a fundamental feature of rancor."[37]

This "no" to what is imagined to be "outside," to what is invented as "other" (the "non-self") is characteristic of the aristocratic impulse in Twain's South. It is little wonder that the parody of aristocratic values by black slaves should be employed by Twain to suggest how such values are themselves intimately involved in a "slave morality." Nietzsche maintains that the "noble person will respect his enemy, and respect is already a bridge to love. . . . Indeed he requires his enemy for himself, as his mark of distinction, nor could he tolerate any other enemy than one in which he finds nothing to despise and much to esteem."[38] In Twain's slave-holding communities, every outside influence is viewed as a threat to the internal order of the society, and it must be absorbed as quickly as possible or else categorized as inhuman, criminal, or mad. The townspeople's attitudes toward Luigi and Angelo as well as toward the "stranger" David Wilson reveal a good deal about the primary motives that give rise to the moral values of slave-holding societies. By the 1890s, Twain knew quite well how America would come to substitute the "knife-wielding" Italian immigrant for the "chicken-stealing" black slave of the pre-Civil War period.

Ressentiment is prompted by a fundamental aversion to the transience and difference of life that the *Übermensch* repeatedly affirms. Many critics have noticed the subtle entanglement of aristocratic, economic, and religious values in such works as *Huckleberry Finn*. In general, the "romance" of the Old South and the God who would condemn Huck to eternal damnation for his human sympathy are considered rationalizations of the primary drives for economic and social power in this culture. Repeatedly in *Huckleberry Finn* and *Pudd'nhead Wilson*, human concerns are subordinated to economic demands. Yet, behind even the drives for money and power, there is a more powerful desire to escape time, mortality, and difference. Heidegger's analysis of Nietzschean *ressentiment* seems especially relevant to this aristocratic teleology in Twain's writings: "Revenge is the will's aversion to time, and that means the ceasing to be, its transience. . . . For Nietzsche, the most profound revenge consists of that reflection which posits eternal Ideals as the absolute, compared with which the temporal must degrade itself to actual non-being."[39] We have already seen how the slave is defined as "non-being" for the sake of the aristocrat's "being." But this "being" is associated with "eternal Ideals," values authorized by unchanging laws. The aristocrat's propriety and honor are based on myths of blood and birth that suppress the idiosyncrasies of individuals in such lineages. Offered two different accounts by Wilson and Tom of why Tom took Luigi to court rather than fighting him on the field of honor, Judge Driscoll promptly accepts Tom's story despite all evidence to the contrary. Personal scandals are suppressed in order to preserve the family's noble ideals; the judge tacitly approves of Tom's gambling trips to St. Louis, because Tom's absence from Dawson's Landing helps the family avoid embarrassing incidents. Colonel Cecil Burleigh Essex's biography is omitted from the narrative itself because his sexual relations with Roxy pose a threat to the purity of the family line. The sexuality of both white women and men is repressed; violence is tolerated among the aristocrats only to the extent that it is ritualized in dueling or as part of an ideal martial code.

Roxy's exchange of the babies helps dramatize the arbitrary origins of all claims to nobility, and in particular it exposes the decadence of southern aristocratic values. Some critics have complained that by stressing the corruption of a black in a white role, Twain makes an indirect judgment about black temperament. Twain makes it clear, however, that "'Tom' was a bad baby *from the very beginning of his usurpation*" (*PW*, 26; my italics). Tom's dissolute habits are less attributable to his black origins than to the historical deterioration of aristocratic authority, which was well under way before Tom was born. Tom's nominal father, Percy Driscoll, squandered much of his fortune in land speculations, which seems an appropriate prelude to Tom's gambling in St. Louis, a habit he picked up from friends at Yale. As aristocratic power is weakened by its own internal contradictions, the arbitrariness of its original rights becomes increasingly evident. Property rights are validated by laws designed to suppress the original theft that makes the concept of personal property possible. The Duke's and Dauphin's sham titles in *Huckleberry Finn* suggest that all aristocratic pretensions are simply masks for the most ruthless robbery and deceit. Tom's gambling and burglaries are only apparently at odds with the aristocratic values of the judge; in a deeper sense they are perfectly consonant with the historical development of aristocratic rights.

Roxy's justification for switching the babies helps reveal the metaphysical implications of such aristocratic values. Her understanding of "free grace" emphasizes the arbitrariness of all metaphysical systems that depend on an inaccessible authority: "It was dat ole nigger preacher . . . said dey ain't nobody kin save his own self — can't do it by faith, can't do it by works, can't do it no way at all. Free grace is de *on'y* way, en dat don't come fum nobody but jis' de Lord; en *He* kin give it to anybody He please, saint or sinner — *He* don't kyer. He do jis' as He's a mineter" (*PW*, 22). Where such a God of Chance rules, there can be only the most illusory freedom; where the ways of God are absolutely indecipherable, then all is permitted and any moral system must be suspect. When Roxy exchanges the babies, she assumes the power of an arbitrary providence. She has not misinterpreted the concept of God as unaccountable judge, but instead has acted quite properly on the assumption that one is left only with action as the means to test such judgment. Confused as she is by the motley moral lessons she has received

from her masters and fellow slaves, Roxy inadvertently manages to step outside the moral system of this society. Like Twain's narrative and Wilson's
detective work, Roxy's decision shares all the signs of the pudd'nhead's
misdirected stab at the truth. In her desire to save her child and herself, she
initiates a sequence of events that will bring into question the life she has
known as a slave and the moral system on which such a life is based.

As soon as she has made the switch, however, Roxy begins to relapse
into the familiar world of masters and servants. Yet, the plot device of the
changelings causes the reader to consider every action taken by Tom to have
the double agency of master and slave. We begin to experience directly how
titles and roles affect the behavior of social man, and we realize how social fictions assume the power of unshakable realities governing our psychological
behavior:

> By the fiction created by herself, he was become her master; the necessity of
> recognizing this relation outwardly and of perfecting herself in the forms
> required to express the recognition, had moved her to such diligence and
> faithfulness in practicing these forms that this exercise soon concreted itself into
> habit; it became automatic and unconscious; then a natural result followed:
> deceptions intended solely for others gradually grew practically into self-
> deceptions as well; the mock reverence became real reverence, the mock obse-
> quiousness real obsequiousness, the mock homage real homage; the little
> counterfeit rift of separation between imitation-slave and imitation-master
> widened and widened, and became an abyss, and a very real one — and on one
> side of it stood Roxy, the dupe of her own deceptions, and on the other stood
> her child, no longer a usurper to her, but her accepted and recognized master.
> [*PW,* 28–29]

This forgetting of origins is, of course, one of Twain's main targets in much
of his social criticism. We are no longer able to distinguish black from white
in the character of Tom, even though the roles of master and servant are
perfectly evident to the townspeople. Confusing conventional distinctions,
Twain forces his reader to play the dangerous game of looking for those
behavioral clues that might enable one to separate the black from the white,
the slave from the master, in Tom's divided person.

Tom's doubleness is a potential power that might enable him to operate
outside the confines of the social system. As long as he remains unaware of
his own duplicitous origins, however, Tom is little more than an imitation
white or imitation black. Only when he learns the truth of his birth from
Roxy does Tom begin to step outside the dialectic of this world and approximate the vision of his author: "Why were niggers *and* whites made? What
crime did the uncreated first nigger commit that the curse of birth was
decreed for him? And why is this awful difference made between white and
black? . . . How hard the nigger's fate seems this morning! — yet until last

night such a thought never entered my head" (*PW*, 76). The truth of Tom's origins, however, is already governed by the fictions of this culture. Even granting the distinctions between blacks and whites, who is to say that the son of a black mother and white father is black or white? We know already that this society preserves its authority — and its sense of radical oppositions — by suppressing the facts of miscegenation and declaring any person with a fraction of negro blood to be de facto a slave. Roxy's one-sixteenth part negro blood and Tom's one thirty-second portion are sufficient to subject them to the fate of being sold down the river and to property laws. Tom's reflection on the question of black identity may seem quite self-evident to the contemporary reader, but it is precisely the difficulty of approximating such knowledge in slave-holding communities that is Twain's main subject in *Pudd'nhead Wilson*. For a brief moment, Tom experiences an enormous transformation of his habitual values:

> A gigantic eruption, like that of Krakatoa a few years ago, with the accompanying earthquakes, tidal waves, and clouds of volcanic dust, changes the face of the surrounding landscape beyond recognition. . . . The tremendous catastrophe which had befallen Tom had changed his moral landscape in much the same way. Some of his low places he found lifted to ideals, some of his ideals had sunk to valleys, and lay there with the sackcloth and ashes of pumice stone and sulphur on their ruined heads. [*PW*, 77]

It seems especially appropriate that the two metaphors Twain chooses for Tom's revelation and the author's own swerve from farce to tragedy — volcanic eruption and caesarean birth — are both associated with violent creations. Although powerfully affected by such knowledge, Tom never fully recognizes that the human being is by nature both master and slave, whose divided personality is the condition of being. In his notes for *Pudd'nhead Wilson*, Twain clearly intended Tom to consider the baseness of slavery as the result of social values based on economic and ontological property: "The high is either color, when undegraded by slavery — the base is *slave*-owning *effects* not slave *blood* — it is the white blood in me but brutalized by slave-owning heredity."[40]

In the final narrative, Tom only momentarily achieves an external perspective on the moral values of Dawson's Landing, but Roxy attempts a more extensive subversion of the society that has condemned her both in slavery and "freedom." As Twain himself admits, Roxy is the most interesting character in this work; her will to power suggests a method for both the artist and the criminal. Tom is frightened and awed by the youthful power his mother exhibits when she returns to the town. For the most part, Tom becomes merely the instrument of Roxy's will; even his rage against his origins and fate derives from Roxy's indignation. Yet, Roxy's extra-moral rage against her masters is strangely perverted by her blind faith in most of the abstract values that support this culture. At various times, she defends the ideals of birth, family, honor, law, and property that define the social hierarchies. The conflict between her rebelliousness and obedience helps dramatize the analogous contradiction in the character of the author himself.

The power that enables Roxy to switch the babies is renewed when she is forced to return to Dawson's Landing to beg from her old master, Tom. Her "freedom" on board *The Grand Mogul* has been simply another deceptive romance; crippled by arthritis at the age of thirty-five from the constant labors of washing and scrubbing, Roxy retires only to find that her meager savings have been lost in a bank failure. Scorned and rejected by Tom, Roxy assumes an unexpected power over him that technically derives from her secret knowledge of his origins. Yet, Roxy's will to power emerges at the moment she recognizes the discrepancy between her own illusions of freedom and the reality of her servitude. Roxy has experienced the legal freedom granted to former slaves and thus knows the extent of social lies. The slave may always parody or mime the values of the master, but a person who knows that both slavery and freedom end in the same despair is driven by an almost transcendental rage.

Roxy's thirst for revenge shares the unconscious *ressentiment* against life itself that governs the aristocrat's idealism, and it is for this reason that Roxy can do little but invert the moral values of Dawson's Landing. Yet, most critics overlook the fact that her covert masterminding of Tom's burglaries has important social ramifications. Her primary intention is to help Tom protect his inheritance, presumably so that she will continue to receive the monthly allowance he grudgingly pays her. Roxy's concern for Judge Driscoll's will, however, involves more than the twenty-five dollars that Tom pays her. Were Tom to inherit the estate, Roxy would be in a position of power, albeit still covert, that would subvert the ordinary distinctions between master and slave. For an imitation white to inherit the fortune, titles, and privileges of the most prominent citizen in town would be the beginning of respectability for the offspring of miscegenation, a way of redeeming that secret history even the narrative tends to suppress. The narrator may claim that Colonel Cecil Burleigh Essex was "another F.F.V. of formidable caliber," but "with him we have no concern" (*PW,* 4). This apparently casual remark has certain similarities to Twain's reluctance to deal with Chambers's troubled future at the end of the novel. Trapped by legal fictions between the equally unacceptable worlds of the slave and the master, Chambers would seem to be an important figure in Twain's treatment of miscegenation. However, Twain abruptly concludes his hasty summary of Chambers's problems: "But we cannot follow his curious fate further — that would be a long story" (202). The suppressed biography of Colonel Essex is precisely what might achieve respectability, should Roxy's son inherit the kind of economic power that makes even Huckleberry Finn a social figure to be acknowledged. The extent to which Roxy plans this covert invasion of white respectability is certainly questionable, but her intentions are less important than the possible effects of her actions. And it is clear that Twain gives Roxy the power to command and the ability to punish that seem far in excess of what we might expect from a disappointed ex-slave seeking merely the means to live out her days in modest poverty.

David Wilson may be an ironic stranger who is not what he seems, but Roxy is another version of the stranger who visits society to question its values. She shares the metamorphic power of Nietzsche's *Übermensch* by achieving an extra-moral sense that comes from her recognition of humanity's will to self-delusion. Roxy and Tom together combine the myriad dualities that are manifest in this society: age and youth, master and slave, man and woman, aristocrat and criminal (tramp, gambler, burglar, murderer), white and black. Escaping the confines of a moral system in which identity or nonidentity is determined by conventional stereotypes, Roxy and Tom assume that plurality of identity so necessary to those who would transcend such training. To go "beyond good and evil," one must partake in the Dionysian power that invigorates Nietzsche's noble man: "The essential thing remains the facility of the metamorphosis, the incapacity *not* to react. . . . he possesses to the highest degree the instinct for understanding and divining. . . . He enters into every skin, into every emotion; he is continually transforming himself." [41] Early in the narrative, Roxy recognizes Wilson's dangerous powers and imagines that "he's a witch." In her own intoxication with power, Roxy is also a witch who haunts the margins of society with a power that threatens to exploit every social weakness. Roxy quickly sees through David Wilson's ruse of advertising a public reward for the stolen knife and offering a private reward to pawnbrokers; in numerous ways, she proves a match for Wilson's uncanny intellect.

Roxy's ultimate failure, however, has nothing to do with her "immorality" or "evil nature." Too many critics have sentimentalized her by imagining that Twain intends her to provide a little moral lesson. For example, Clark Griffith advises that "nothing good can come of her undertaking, for it involves a violation, emphatic and terrible, of the very humanity it was meant to assert." [42] Roxy's exchange of the children has little to do with generalized human values but is prompted by her rage against a master and God who would condemn her to impotent bondage. In fact, Roxy fails because she succumbs to an excess of misdirected humanism and an irrational maternal affection for Tom. When Roxy agrees to be sold back into slavery to save Tom, she justifies her sacrifice in terms of a maternal instinct comparable to the blind devotion of white mothers: "Ain't you my chile? En does you know anything a mother won't do for her chile? Dey ain't nothin' a white mother won't do for her chile. Who made 'em so? De Lord done it. En who made de niggers? De Lord made 'em. In de inside, mothers is all de same. De good Lord he made 'em so" (*PW,* 143). In this moment, Roxy's maternal instinct sounds all too much like Huck's admiration of Jim expressed in language of the white culture: "I knowed he was white inside" (*HF,* 213). Roxy's feeling for Tom is governed by the morality of the class system; her emulation of "white mothers" is just the sort of vanity to override her knowledge and experience of his cowardice, deceit, and laziness. Roxy is not defeated by her own "immoral" will to power, but by the lapsing of her power when she succumbs to an "instinct" that plays an important part in the white mythology of self, family, birth, and law.

Twain ruthlessly attacks the illusion of such family instincts in a number of his writings, but no work makes the discrepancy between parent and child more explicit than *Huckleberry Finn.* The majority of Huck's fabricated stories have a similar structure: Huck is an orphan or waif whose parents or surrogate parents have failed in their natural duties due to illness, accident, or neglect. Like slaves, children are exploited in Twain's societies and familial love is made over in the image of the surrounding culture: the struggle by the self (father, master, authority) to appropriate the other (slave, child, stranger). It has often been noticed that *Tom Sawyer* and *Huckleberry Finn* are full of surrogate parents — aunts, uncles, judges, and teachers who would replace the free and easy love of Huck and Jim with the training implied by social forms. Roxy imagines that she knows Tom as her own flesh and blood, but she knows him only insofar as she recognizes the behavior of one who is forced to submit, the cowardice of the slave. Raised in the household of the judge and his widowed sister, Mrs. Rachel Pratt, Tom can no longer be considered his mother's child.

Roxy is incapable of sustaining the discipline of what Nietzsche terms the noble individual's "will to self-responsibility":

> That one is ready to sacrifice men to one's cause, oneself not excepted. Freedom means that the manly instincts that delight in war and victory have gained mastery over the other instincts — for example, over the instinct for "happiness." The man *who has become free* . . . spurns the contemptible sort of well-being dreamed of by shopkeepers, Christians, cows, women, Englishmen, and other democrats. The free man is a *warrior.* — How is freedom measured, in individuals as in nations? By the resistance which has to be overcome, by the effort it costs to stay *aloft.* One would have to seek the highest type of free man where the greatest resistance is constantly being overcome: five steps from tyranny, near the threshold of the danger of servitude.[43]

Roxy may approximate this extra-moral sense of freedom when she rebels against the social order, but she succumbs in the end to the sentimental delusion of maternal instincts. Twain is not coldly attacking a mother's love for her child, but questioning the way Roxy's "instincts" have been perverted by a society that has turned her son into a stranger. Nietzsche joyously asserts the noble individual's extra-moral freedom; Twain recognizes the difficulty facing anyone who would step outside the influences of training. For Twain, the possibility of any thoroughly extra-moral perspective remains a useful but unrealizable fiction.

Tom's murder of Judge Driscoll is thus the botched, accidental act of a base burglar. The revolutionary fervor Twain had originally planned would inspire Tom is defused — not merely because Twain believed it impossible for Tom to step outside his training, but also because Roxy's more powerful will is doomed to succumb to the confusion of one's feelings and training. Pudd'nhead Wilson's own misdirected revelation of the truth makes sense only in the context of Roxy's frustrated will to power. In *Those Extraordinary Twins,* Wilson triumphantly vindicates Luigi and Angelo before the law by subtly confusing the twins' divided identity. In that work, Wilson reinforces Twain's point that the illusions of free choice and individual autonomy have been created primarily for the purposes of punishment and to support the law that legitimizes aristocratic power. In *Pudd'nhead Wilson,* every character eventually succumbs to this illusion of individual identity; even Roxy assumes that Tom is at heart her son and that she herself is above all a mother. Wilson becomes the agent for reapportioning those forces that have erupted to confuse identities and blur social boundaries; Luigi is defended on the basis of Tom's identity as a black slave, whose motives for both theft and murder are rationalized according to the character of the slave.

With both his palmistry and fingerprinting, Wilson ends up justifying the traditional oppositions of being and not being, master and slave. His interests in palmistry and fingerprinting parallel Twain's own fascination both with technology and psychic phenomena of all sorts. Twain had already introduced the science of fingerprinting in *Life on the Mississippi,* and it is well known how fascinated he was by the uncanny predictions of the palmist Cheiro, who predicted in 1895 that the bankrupt Twain "should become very wealthy" in eight years.[44] Yet, Twain was equally prone to poke fun at such supernatural legerdemain; Jim's reading of the "hair-ball oracle" in *Huckleberry Finn* is an unparalleled parody of the prophet's effort to hedge his bets. During Wilson's reading of Luigi's palm in chapter 11 of *Pudd'nhead Wilson,* there are a number of tantalizing hints that the demonstration is a ruse planned by the twins and Wilson to have some fun at Tom's expense. Once Wilson has "mapped out Luigi's character and disposition," the twins "declared that the chart was *artistically drawn* and was correct" (*PW,* 90; my italics). The complicated exchange of slips of paper on which Luigi's "secret" is variously written suggests something of the magician's diversion. Luigi writes down the prophecy that came true at Tom's urging, but he does so "privately"; Wilson claims that the secret is "too delicate a matter" to reveal openly, so he "wrote something on a slip of paper and handed it to Luigi." The possibility remains that Luigi could have prepared two notes in advance and subsequently substituted his covert note for what Wilson writes down. Whatever Twain's intentions in this episode, the reader remains unconvinced that Wilson's palmistry is to be taken at face value. At best, it seems to be merely a convention of the popular romance, which the rest of Twain's narrative so carefully disrupts and subverts. Certainly, Wilson's brilliance in reading a character and history in this episode seems radically at odds with his inability to read Tom's personality with any consistency in the remainder of the narrative, to say nothing of his difficulty in seeing through the various disguises employed by Roxy and Tom.

Yet, Wilson's interests in both palmistry and fingerprinting may serve to render ambiguous the "hard" scientific truth of the evidence he introduces in his triumphant defense of Luigi. Fingerprinting must be viewed as a more sophisticated form of palmistry, in view of the use to which Wilson puts it in the conclusion. The romance moves relentlessly toward the disclosure of the criminal's identity and the solution of the mystery; Twain's ironic narrative works with almost antithetical rigor to transform every identity into a complex of forces. Viewed from the perspective of Roxy's will to power and the covert efforts of aristocratic culture to preserve its authority, Tom's behavior appears to be merely one extemporized center for such conflicting forces. Tom does, of course, gamble in St. Louis, burglarize Dawson's Landing, insult Luigi and Angelo, and murder his uncle. All his actions, however, seem already determined by cultural or revolutionary forces beyond his control or understanding. "Tom" is a machine except for that one uncanny moment in which he experiences his own divided identity as imitation black/imitation white.

Wilson argues during the trial that: "Every human being carries with him from his cradle to his grave certain physical marks which do not change their character, and by which he can always be identified — and that without shade of doubt or question. These marks are his signature, his physiological autograph, so to speak, and this autograph can not be counterfeited, nor can he disguise it or hide it away, nor can it become illegible by the wear and mutations of time" (*PW,* 192). Fingerprints identify only a physical body, not a psychological personality. Like inherited privileges and ancestral titles, fingerprints are extrinsic characteristics of a human being. In order to untangle the deception Roxy has played, Wilson must revert to a myth of origins and blood lines that the covert narrative has already questioned. Wilson's glass slides are carefully dated and named; a man's fingerprints and his identity are unchangeable for Wilson — and this society — from birth to death. Yet, Tom's own history suggests how his aristocratic upbringing has made him a stranger to his own mother. Chambers's training as a slave seems to make Twain's point with even greater force. Restored to his "rightful" identity, Chambers hardly experiences the conventional hero's sense of reintegration.

Wilson's "science" of fingerprinting thus betrays a sleight of hand as suspect as his palmistry. He reads the psychological complexities of the individual in terms of fixed concepts and empirical evidence; it is little wonder that he should choose an economic figure to characterize his reading of human personality: "I have studied some of these signatures so much that I know them as well as the bank cashier knows the autograph of his oldest customer" (*PW*, 195). For the bank cashier, a customer's signature is little more than a reference to credit, a measure of personal identity in terms of economic exchanges. For Twain, an individual's signature occurs only in those moments of pure becoming when one transcends the unity of social identity to achieve that self-assertion that marshals one's multiple energies into an expressive gesture, an economy of forces that makes concerted action possible. To define the individual's ontological being in terms of physical prints is as absurd as to identify a man or woman according to skin color or sex.

Tom repeatedly chaffs Wilson about his collection of fingerprints by drawing a curious analogy between his glass slides and palace windows: "Wilson's got a scheme for driving plain window glass out of the market by decorating it with greasy finger marks, and getting rich by selling it at famine prices to the crowned heads over in Europe to outfit their palaces with" (*PW*, 85). Tom will ultimately make the marks that will hang him upon the "windowpane" of the courtroom. The association of the courtroom windows with the palace windows of European monarchs suggests Wilson's secret complicity in the aristocratic power structure of Dawson's Landing. His scientific reading of individual identity is merely a modernization of the aristocratic manipulation of fixed identity and its opposite, the nonidentity of the slave, in order to preserve its own authority and law.

Am I proposing that Tom is not actually responsible for the thefts and murder? Is Twain's romance subtly pervaded by a spiteful immorality and an inhuman affirmation of violent natures? The society of Dawson's Landing has established the immorality of the game; Roxy's frustrated will to power is no more immoral than the violent struggle for dominance that covertly haunts the proprieties of aristocratic life. The amoral energy of the river in Twain's writings is the constant clash of forces, the struggle of overcoming and outstripping. For Nietzsche, the extra-moral power of *Übermensch* comes from the recognition of vital and sensuous natural energies in conflict and the complementary knowledge that "he" is constituted only by a similar, internal struggle. The man of disguises and continual metamorphoses is the true Huckleberry Finn, who sustains himself only as long as he preserves this innocence of becoming, this refusal to "be himself." Only when he returns to society at the very end, appropriately trapped in the mask of Tom Sawyer (*the mask of masks*), does he risk domination by the fixed concepts of "sivilization." Nietzsche writes:

> No subject "atoms." The sphere of a subject constantly growing or decreasing, the center of the system constantly shifting; in cases where it cannot organize the appropriate mass, it breaks into two parts. On the other hand, it can transform a weaker subject into its functionary without destroying it, and to a certain degree form a new unity with it. No "substance," rather something that in itself strives after greater strength, and that wants to "preserve" itself only indirectly (it wants to *surpass* itself —).[45]

The immorality of Dawson's Landing originates in the effort to suppress the dynamic interchange of human and natural forces, to substitute moral and ontological categories for the sensuous experience of life as endless will to power. The noble man does not despise his enemies; he comes even to love them. He finds his personality, his force, in the sense of resistance that comes only from a world in which differences are joyously affirmed.

The outcast whose uncanny remark has threatened to unsettle the habitual modes of thought in Dawson's Landing eventually finds his social place. We should not forget that Dawson's Landing is undergoing the mild shocks of modernization: the sleepy riverport is becoming a modest urban center. In both *Those Extraordinary Twins* and *Pudd'nhead Wilson,* Wilson is elected the first mayor of the town. In *Pudd'nhead Wilson,* he is elected before the trial, and thus acts in his double capacity as defense attorney and social authority to reaffirm the status quo. Twain uses both Roxy and Wilson to suggest how illusory any detachment from society proves to be under scrutiny. Both characters may use different techniques in the effort to maintain their estrangement, but both are reappropriated by a society and history whose relentless training is finally inescapable.

There is, of course, another writing and another will to power that activate the narrative of *Pudd'nhead Wilson.* The crucial murder weapon, the Indian knife of the Gaikowar of Baroda, is inscribed with the names of its owners. The weapon of romance may serve Tom in the murder of the judge and serve Wilson in the solution of the mystery, but the true weapon is the dissonant narrative structure itself. Like the Indian knife and its inscribed history of violent appropriations, Twain's text provides a genealogy of the continuing struggles for power that hide behind even the most placid social setting. The history of the romance records the unexpected accidents of Wilson's arrival, the twins' foreign presence, Tom's crimes, and Roxy's revenge only to restore the order of continuous succession and the rights of birth and origin. Twain offers these "accidents" as the historical determinants of dominance and submission, tokens of the conflicting forces that produce ever-renewed frenzies of assertion and suppression. John Irwin makes explicit the reader's uneasy sense that the romance's use of palmistry, finger-printing, secret notes, and forged bills of sale suggests some ironic play on the author's own writing: "For an author, a man who is always using his hand to write, it can only seem of the deepest significance that a man's palm bears the history of his life in a hidden writing that is signed with the latent autograph of his fingerprint."[46] Yet, what is written in/by the palm is always already divided by the internal psychic struggle between master and slave, temperament and training. Constituted only by this heterogeneous system of differences that masquerade in social forms as self and other, white master and black slave, each individual "reads" himself only as the result of a supplementary writing.

The genealogist himself must become a puddingheaded clown, whose best efforts to capture the truth will inevitably swerve in unpredictable directions — perhaps only to reaffirm what he had hoped to escape, possibly to initiate novel, liberating appropriations. Both Nietzsche and Twain claimed to have written primarily for the future, for generations to come that might understand more fully or sympathetically their varied truths. In our jaded age, we have assumed that Nietzsche meant only the pseudodaring of the claim that God is dead, or that Twain's prophetic wisdom might be reduced to his mockery of Christian faith. In another sense, both Nietzsche and Twain employ literary strategies that depend upon the appropriation of their meanings by subsequent readings, those acts of will to power that would find truth in the assertion of their errors:

> Ought we not to stand on the threshold of a period which should be called, negatively at first, the *extra-moral:* today, when among us immoralists at least the suspicion has arisen that the decisive value of an action resides in precisely that which is *not intentional* in it, and that all that in it which is intentional, all of it that can be seen, known, "conscious," still belongs to its surface and skin — which, like every skin, betrays something but *conceals* still more? In brief, we believe that the intention is only a sign and symptom that needs interpreting, and a sign, moreover, that signifies too many things and which thus taken by itself signifies practically nothing.[47]

Like Nietzsche's deconstruction, Twain's dissonant irony teaches one "how to philosophize with a hammer." Questioning the possibility of any pure origins and thus subverting the *telos* of ideal ends, Twain's text historicizes the religious and philosophic ideals that one supposed were the very supports of history as a system. Twain's pessimism derives largely from his insistence on analyzing abstractions (self, God, justice, freedom) in relation to natural forces and conflicting human needs that produce such concepts; Twain refuses the "mastery" of knowledge for the sake of experiencing how one knows. Foucault reads Nietzsche in terms of a similarly historical impulse:

The historical sense can evade metaphysics and become a privileged instrument of genealogy if it refuses the certainty of absolutes. Given this, it corresponds to the acuity of a glance that distinguishes, separates, and disperses, that is capable of liberating divergence and marginal elements — the kind of dissociating view that is capable of decomposing itself, capable of shattering the unity of man's being through which it was thought that he could extend his sovereignty to the events of the past.[48]

Twain may identify with Wilson's double nature at the outset and with the rage that inspires Roxy, but he fears as well the stranger's or rebel's claims to any new mastery or reformed authority. He knew too well that the scientific progress of the post-Civil War period would only deepen the lies and divisions on which a younger America had based its moral values. His narrative aim is finally neither to achieve the social reconciliation of Mayor Wilson nor to complete Roxy's abortive inversion of values, but to preserve that sense of naiveté and willing self-blindness that opens every claim of truth to question. What Derrida says of Nietzsche's "styles" seems appropriate for our understanding of Twain's irony:

Somewhere parody always supposes a naivety withdrawing into an unconscious, a vertiginous non-mastery. Parody supposes a loss of consciousness, for were it to be absolutely calculated, it would become a confession or a law table. This inability to assimilate — even among themselves — the aphorisms and the rest — perhaps it must simply be admitted that Nietzsche himself did not see his way too clearly there. Nor could he, in the instantaneous blink of an eye. Rather a regular, rhythmic blindness takes place in the text. One will never have done with it. Nietzsche too is a little lost there. . . . lost as much as a spider who finds he is unequal to the web he has spun.[49]

Huckleberry Finn is the great nineteenth-century attack on slavery because it surpasses the moral simplicity of the abolitionist's tract; *Pudd'nhead Wilson* achieves its greatness by virtue of its strategic dissonance, its refusal to resolve its issues. The tension between the sentimental romance and the irony of the aphorisms prevents the characters and situations from achieving the dimensions that would give them the illusion of life. And it is the failure of vitality, the murder of life itself, that is represented in slave-holding communities like Dawson's Landing. Twain wrote in his notebooks: "The first thing I want to teach is *disloyalty,* till they get used to disusing that word *loyalty* as representing a virtue. This will beget independence — which is loyalty to one's best self and principles, and this is often disloyalty to the general idols and fetishes" (*MTN,* 199). Such disloyalty can hardly be taught; it must be prompted, awakened to action by that uncanny wit through which our deepest fears and desires are compelled to surface.

7.

The Authority
of the Sign in James's
The Sacred Fount

Not to be a man, to be the projection of another man's dream, what a
feeling of humiliation, of vertigo! All fathers are interested in the children
they have procreated (they have permitted to exist) in mere confusion or
pleasure; it was natural that the magician should fear for the future of that
son, created in thought, limb by limb and feature by feature, in a
thousand and one secret nights.
    — Borges, "The Circular Ruins"

The birth of the reader must be at the cost of the death of the Author.
    — Barthes, "The Death of the Author"

    Like Borges's magician, the narrator of James's *Sacred Fount* (1901) is
obsessed with preserving his artistic authority. He too wants to procreate in
such a fashion that he might escape the "mere confusion or pleasure" that
motivates most intercourse. Both artists nostalgically yearn for an authentic
voice free from the linguistic and natural determinants of experience. The
magician devotes his life to an idea of ontological purity, which he struggles
to achieve in the autotelic form of his dream. Thus, the magician is overcome
by humiliation and terror when he discovers at the very last that "he too was a
mere appearance, dreamt by another," only a character in the text of a story
controlled by the authority of language. James's narrator, however,
undergoes a disillusionment that enables him to survive the knowledge that
consumes the magician. The narrator sustains his voice only by acknowledging his submission to a language that permits him to exist. By undermining
his own authority, he discovers himself through a critical reflection on the
nature of signification.
    The Sacred Fount has been viewed as a transitional work in James's
career that establishes the theoretical program for the works of the Major

Phase. For some of the same reasons, it might also be considered a fitting introduction to the central problems of literary modernism in its traditional historical formulation. More than merely foreshadowing the themes of modernism, *The Sacred Fount* works through many of the concerns that would become intellectual and artistic impasses in subsequent works by such writers as Pound, Joyce, Eliot, Stevens, Mann, and Proust. On the one hand, this work enables me to bring my consideration of nineteenth-century modernity into relation with the main themes of twentieth-century modernism. On the other hand, *The Sacred Fount* undermines a number of the basic poetic, linguistic, and critical values of the modernist period. And the self-critical method of James's narrative functions secretly within the very rhetoric of modernism. In its most aestheticist pronouncements, literary modernism is already questioning its own claims to distinction and authority, and the New Criticism that grew out of modernism is erasing its own confidence in the integrity of the literary text.

Written before the Prefaces to the New York Edition, *The Sacred Fount* is a dramatic summary of James's critical revision of his *oeuvre*. In a qualified sense, the work has been well described as "a critical Preface in action."[1] Perhaps for this very reason, the novel has been celebrated as an anomaly in James's canon. In particular, critics call attention to James's omission of the novel from the New York Edition and to his neglect of it in the Prefaces. At worst, it has been labeled a "technical exercise" in Joseph Warren Beach's early study of James.[2] Beach's judgment survives in various forms in more contemporary criticism, which often refers to James's own comments on the work as a mere "*jeu d'esprit*" or the novel's "tenuity of idea."[3] In a number of cases, *The Sacred Fount* has been used by critics to provide an example of how art suffers when it disregards the criteria of "felt life" and "realized" drama. Thus, Ora Segal explains James's omission of the work from his collected edition: "Is it possible, one cannot help wondering, that in describing the idea of *The Sacred Fount* as 'tenuous' James was, after all, referring to the epistemological theme and not the initial *Notebooks* theme of spiritual vampirism; and that what he meant was that the pure epistemological theme, when not embedded in a richly human fable . . . was too abstract, too thin an affair, to justify the elaborate, ingenious treatment he accorded it?"[4] As a consequence, James's narrator has come to typify the artist as voyeur, pedant, inhuman anatomist — in short, as a caricature of Nietzsche's "theoretical man."

Like John Marcher, James's narrator does seem to stage a systematic withdrawal from an unsatisfactory reality into the "sacred space" of his own consciousness. In both of these characters, James seems indirectly to indict symbolist aestheticism or the "pure poetry" of early modernism. According to such a view, Pound's enthusiastic response to *The Sacred Fount* might be considered a characteristic misreading that identifies his own modernist formalism with the decadence of James's narrator: "In *The Sacred Fount* he attains form, perfect form, his form. It is almost the only novel about which he says not a word in his prefaces. Whether or no this was intentional, it seems to be one work that he could afford to sit back, look at, and find completed. I don't in the least imply that he did so."[5] Pound's comments have special significance when we recall his claim to have condensed "the James novel" in *Hugh Selwyn Mauberley*.[6] The narrator's "palace of thought" and Axël's Castle seem to share the same symbolist architecture. Literary form in its perfection achieves the condensed purity that transcends any need for commentary or interpretation, substituting its sheer artistic being for any "kinetic" meaning.

Yet, the familiar charges of aestheticism brought against the modernists rely on a naive understanding of their obsessive concern with poetic form. One reason that Pound might consider *The Sacred Fount* to attain the completion of "perfect form" is that the work deals so explicitly with its own literary possibility. What Beach sees as the "technical exercise" of the novel and Segal considers an excessive concern with the "epistemological theme" might be related to the work's critical self-consciousness. The drama and the method of *The Sacred Fount* are united so firmly that every action or event is simultaneously used as part of James's continuing reflection on the nature of literary expression. This concern might well explain James's reasons for trivializing the dramatic situation in such an extreme fashion. The insignificance of this weekend party at a country house reminds us all the more forcefully that none of James's artistic *données* involves any inherently tragic possibilities. As far as James's existential situations are concerned, he is a confirmed literary naturalist. His realism begins when he attempts to represent and analyze the ways in which the bare facts of human existence are embellished. Those acts of consciousness by means of which a world is seen constitute the only true actions in James's novels: "We want it clear, goodness knows, but we also want it thick, and we get the thickness in the human consciousness that entertains and records, that amplifies and interprets it."[7]

This marked discrepancy in James's works between the sheer poverty or triviality of objects and the rich complexity of their interpretation accounts in part for his characteristic irony. James's later works have been considered fundamental to the development of twentieth-century modernism because they can be used so effectively to illustrate the triumph of art over the vicissitudes of life. What the New Critics codified as the distinctive poetic features of irony, paradox, and ambiguity seem perfectly appropriate to James's transformation of life's confusions into the pattern and form of the artistic consciousness. Cleanth Brooks's formulation of this fundamentally paradoxical mode of literature can be directly applied to this modernist James:

If the poet, then, must perforce dramatize the oneness of the experience, even though paying tribute to its diversity, then his use of paradox and ambiguity is seen as necessary. He is not simply trying to spice up, with a superficially exciting or mystifying rhetoric, the old stale stockpot. . . . He is rather giving us an insight which preserves the unity of experience and which, at its higher and more serious levels, triumphs over the apparently contradictory and conflicting elements of experience by unifying them into a new pattern.[8]

For the New Critics, of course, the poet's ironic mode ultimately intends its transcendence in the resolved stresses of a poetic architecture whose "invulnerability to irony is the stability of a context in which the internal pressures balance and mutually support each other."[9] Despite John Crowe Ransom's objections to the limitations of the Imagists' "physical poetry," the poetic complex of forces presented in the image seems to suggest just such a balanced form achieved by means of an irony that is nothing other than style. Indeed, the New Critical marriage of modernist irony and Coleridgean organicism seems to define precisely the aestheticist tendencies of high modernist literature.

There is, however, another sort of ironic intention in modernism that works against the goal of resolved stress in poetic form and that recalls the older meaning of irony as verbal dissemblance. Pound's use of diverse poetic personae reflects the modernist's anxiety concerning the multiple voices not only of the poet but also of twentieth-century humanity. As the various personae of *Hugh Selwyn Mauberly* indicate, the poetic voice in such an age is always ironic by virtue of its apparent freedom from and latent bondage to the dominant cultural rhetoric. If Mauberley speaks of his contemporaries, London society, and the sources of the modern waste land, he is also always speaking of himself in the very poetic style whereby these particulars are given form and meaning. The dark truth of the phantasmagoric "London" that he struggles to uncover is a function of his own reflection on his conscious activity. It is no surprise that Mauberley should perish of his own subjective excesses; the world that he has represented is what he himself becomes, either in the midst of it (like a "Mr. Nixon") or in his own futile effort to escape it (like Ford Madox Ford). The irony or dissemblance of James's first-person narrator, Pound's Mauberley, or Joyce's Stephen Dedalus derives to a large extent from this doubleness of the narrative. The modern protagonist is often a critic of existing social reality who pretends to have achieved a necessary artistic distance, only to discover in the course of his narrative that this same society continues to function in his own process of representation.

In modernist literature, self-consciousness still preserves its romantic status as a liberation from social confinement and historical determinism.

Thus, the metaliterary qualities of much twentieth-century literature often indicate for author or narrator a possible road to freedom, self-expression, and redeemed identity. Yet, the intensely self-conscious characters in modern literature most frequently bring to consciousness the very confinements of the culture that constrain them. Indeed, the notable incompletion of the modern novel might be related to this tendency of self-consciousness to undermine its own claims to freedom and independence. For the embattled poet or novelist, ironic characterization is itself a device to preserve such romantic integrity. The profoundly autobiographical nature of *Remembrance of Things Past, Hugh Selwyn Mauberley,* and *Portrait of the Artist as a Young Man* might well be understood as cathartic or mithridatic: the author's desperate purgation of those excesses and impotencies that are represented by his characters.

In Brooks's New Critical view, the successful work resolves its ironic tensions in order to reaffirm the authority of an artistic consciousness that distinguishes itself by means of its poetic style. Modernist literature, however, might well be considered an illustration of how such an ironic mode fails to transcend itself and achieve "invulnerability." Given these conflicts within the very idea of consciousness, it should not surprise us that the modernists began to question the priority of thought to language contemporaneously with the development of structural linguistics. The student of Bergson, T. E. Hulme, insists that "thought is prior to language and consists in the simultaneous presentation to the mind of two different images." [10] Even in his early imagist phase, however, Pound implicitly questions this rather mechanical model. Hulme emphasizes the visual characteristics of the poetic image: "Each *word* must be an image *seen,* not a counter." [11] Pound rejects this visualization of the poetic image as well as the implication that the image is thereby made present by means of the perceptual consciousness. Instead, Pound emphasizes the presentation in the poem of a "verbal complex": "An 'Image' is that which presents an intellectual and emotional complex in an instant of time." [12] The directness and spontaneity of this "radiant node or cluster" is achieved only in language, even if Pound still insists upon the highly stylized language of poetry. Only such a mode of expression effectively uses the differential energy that is produced by the interplay of the cognitive and the affective, thus relying on the simultaneity of the conceptual and sensory in verbal signs.

Considered in relation to the development of literary modernism, structural linguistics might be considered a counterpart to the literary shift from the priority of consciousness to the authority of language. [13] Historically contemporary with the formulation of imagist theory in London, Saussure's lectures in Geneva (1906–1911) on the differential structure of the sign have certain affinities with Pound's "poetic complex." The message-sending process relies on the interrelation of an acoustic-image (signifier) and conceptual-image (signified) that seems to deny the simple linear relation of thought to word. Saussure's conception of the sign, of course, depends upon language as a system of regularities that always precedes any act of consciousness, which is itself effectively defined by grammatical, lexical, and phonic structures: "Without language, thought is a vague, uncharted nebula. There are no pre-existing ideas, and nothing is distinct before the appearance of language." [14] Saussure's effort to establish synchronic linguistics as the formal study of the regularity of a stable language state suggests a more comprehensive semiology that would redefine mental constructs in terms of linguistic categories. It is certainly this implication in structural linguistics that has caused critics to recoil before the spectre of linguistic determinism, which would transform the romantic artist-hero into a mere grammatical shifter or pronominal function.

The scientific claims of structural linguistics thus seem to strike a death blow to the modernist's desperate effort to preserve the integrity of an authorial consciousness. Benveniste describes two equally untenable attitudes concerning the relation of language and thought that might be used to characterize this modernist problematic:

> It is the nature of language to give rise to two illusions of opposite meaning: being learnable, consisting of an always limited number of elements, language gives the impression of being only one of the interpreters possible for thought, while thought, being free, autarchical, and individual, uses language as its instrument. As a matter of fact, whoever tries to grasp the proper framework of thought encounters only the categories of language. The other illusion is the opposite. The fact that language is an ordered totality and that it reveals a plan, prompts one to look in the formal system of language for the reflection of a "logic" presumably inherent in the mind and hence exterior to language. By doing this, however, one only constructs naïvetés or tautologies. [15]

Saussure's conception of the relation of signifier and signified as essentially unmotivated replaces the simple linear relation between the sign and its referent; the sign as such denies the temporal succession of thought and expression. Saussure's sign is constitutive of thought and serves as a node, cluster, or complex in which the potential of mind is realized. As Benveniste writes: "It is more productive to conceive of the mind as a virtuality than as a framework, as a dynamism than as a structure. It is a fact that, to satisfy the requirements of scientific methods, thought everywhere adopts the same procedures in whatever language it chooses to describe experience. In this sense, it becomes independent, not of language, but of particular linguistic structures." [16]

Benveniste's work is representative of the general aim of structural linguistics to replace the categories of thought with categories of language. Yet, in its insistent postulation of a deep-structure for language that might be termed the individual's capacity for signifying, structural linguistics recuperates the same problems of object and representation, concept and sign, presence and absence that are fundamental to modernist irony. Like Jakobson, Benveniste repeatedly argues that "the possibility of thought is linked to the faculty of speech, for language is a structure informed with signification." [17] At the same time, Benveniste preserves a concept of mind as a signifying capacity that shares the universality and reality of Kantian Categories. In general, the structural linguist restores some element or function that is a priori to language by establishing clear distinctions between the literal and the figurative, a linguistic capacity and particular languages, synchronic regularities and diachronic contingencies. Benveniste writes in "Categories of Thought and Language": "Chinese thought may well have invented categories as specific as the *tao,* the *yin,* and the *yang;* it is nonetheless able to assimilate the concepts of dialectical materialism or quantum mechanics without the Chinese language proving a hindrance. No type of language can by itself foster or hamper the activity of the mind." [18] Benveniste suggests that the specificity of the *tao,* the *yin,* and the *yang* depends upon the particularity of the Chinese language; the lexical value of these terms would be violated by translation into another language. Yet, such concepts as dialectical materialism and quantum mechanics seem to remain unaffected by the particular languages used to represent them.

In an earlier discussion of Benveniste's critique of language in Freudian theory, I argued that Benveniste relies on a strict distinction between the literal and metaphoric, between historical language and myth or poetry. For Benveniste, the poetic function of language (including oneiric symbolism) involves a suspension of meaning or rhetorical stylization that must be distinguished from the symbolism of the dominant cultural code, which is learned and "is coextensive with man's acquisition of the world and of intelligence, with both of which he finally becomes unified." [19] Poetic and oneiric symbols are subjective variations of the categories of a particular language; their analysis thus takes style and its affective components for its object. In contrast, the symbolism of a particular language (*langue*) is analyzed by the linguist to determine regularities that must be referable to the general faculties of language (*langage*). Although Benveniste rejects the assumption that synchronic analysis reflects some cybernetic logic in the mind itself, he does suggest that the symbols of *langue* provide clues to the nature of *homo significans.* Poetry and dreams depend upon a style that facilitates individual expression and verbal intention, but for this very reason these discourses are doubly removed from the individual's essential linguistic nature. Substituting Benveniste's structuralist terms for Emerson's transcendentalist formulation of a hierarchy of symbols in *Nature,* we can recognize structural linguistics as the best substitute for the romantic religion of consciousness:

1. Poems are symbols of linguistic facts.
2. Particular linguistic facts are symbols of general linguistic capabilities.
3. The human capacity for language is our "nature."

The structuralist's approach to the study of particular languages often results in what Fredric Jameson terms "a hypostasis of Language," which implies an order of thought that transcends the figurative or metaphoric.[20] Derrida demonstrates in *Of Grammatology* how Saussure restores the metaphysics of presence traditionally associated with consciousness by privileging the "sensible plenitude" of speech over the mere phonetic or graphic representation of speech. Despite Saussure's and Benveniste's efforts to demonstrate the ways in which linguistic functions simulate those categories hitherto recognized as cognitive, both theorists rely on a hierarchical conception of language (*langage, langue, parole*) that simply recapitulates the familiar epistemological order of Kantian philosophy.[21] Although working in a different discipline and with distinctly different goals, the structural linguist seems to replicate the characteristic tendencies of literary modernism. Both the poet and linguist assert the fundamental difference of the verbal sign only to repress such knowledge and reinstate a distinction between "literal" and "figurative" signification that defines such difference as the shadow of a deeper unity (the concept, the sensible plenitude of speech, the transcendental signified).

Like the modernist poet, the structural linguist provided a foundation for the distinction between poetic and scientific discourse that would continue to haunt critical thinking in the New Criticism. In order to realize his own fundamental principle that "in language there are only differences *without positive terms*," Saussure would have been forced to give up his claims to science in the very moment of establishing modern linguistics. Such an understanding of language would compel the linguist to redefine the synchronic study of language as a poetic activity, which performs its own verbal supplementarity. As Derrida writes:

Thus the name, especially the so-called proper name, is always caught in a chain or a system of differences. Metaphor shapes and undermines the proper name. The literal [*propre*] meaning does not exist, its "appearance" is a necessary function — and must be analyzed as such — in the system of differences and metaphors. The absolute *parousia* of the literal meaning, as the presence to the self of the logos within its voice, in the absolute hearing-itself-speak, should be *situated* as a function responding to an indestructible but relative necessity, within a system that encompasses it. That amounts to *situating* the metaphysics or the ontotheology of the logos.[22]

The task of situating the appearance of the "proper" meaning within a given cultural rhetoric can no longer be conceived of as a scientific procedure.[23] It would thus seem that the linguist must become a poet, who would follow the logic of Heidegger's poetic thinking. And yet, the very concept of the poet is hopelessly entangled in a modernist rhetoric that preserves the opposition between literal and metaphoric that also governs modern linguistics. Abandoning the possibility of a scientific investigation of language forces us also to surrender the idea of the poet. The task of situating the sorts of repressions that permit the inevitably figurative to pass for the literal must become the work of critics who acknowledge the derivative nature of their discourse, the limits of their analytic powers, and the necessary artifice of their methods.

The Sacred Fount offers us an excellent opportunity to explore these problems in modernist thought, because its narrator takes up in turn scientific analysis, artistic expression, and critical interpretation in his effort to understand the contrived social world in which he finds himself. The narrator does construct a symbolist "palace of thought" as an alternative to the forms, rituals, and general codes of the society in which he is inextricably involved. Yet, he ultimately dismantles the architecture of this imaginative dwelling for the sake of a critical discourse that reveals an inevitable dependence on its social pretexts and the determining system of language. The narrator's critical activity suggests a model for all aesthetic expression, once it has been stripped of the illusion of originality or authority. Such a critical outlook also questions the presumed reality of social conventions and habitual modes of behavior or expression. Writing constantly reminds us that we approach the world only through the preinterpreted signs that motivate and invade our own interpretations. Literature is always a metalanguage that discovers its own possibility in its anatomy of the normative functions of social usage. The failure of so many of James's characters is that they lack the imaginative powers to recognize the conventionality of their lives. For James, the literary imagination invents a space for its own play by determining the horizons of social and linguistic conventions. The form of the Jamesian novel is constituted by this tensive relationship between the desire for originality and the reflection on those social and linguistic constraints that frustrate such a desire.

James's obsessive concern with his own aesthetic processes is generally considered a measure of his modernity. Yet, the self-reflexive character of James's novels does not imply the aestheticism of the autonomous work of art. All of James's social dramas depend upon basic aesthetic questions raised by both the form of the novel and the situational ethics employed by the characters. The Prefaces to the New York Edition make the homology between social conscience and creative mind eminently clear, as does this representative passage from the Preface to *The Portrait of a Lady:* "Without her sense of them, her sense *for* them, as one may say, they are next to nothing at all; but isn't the beauty and the difficulty just in showing their mystic conversion into the stuff of drama or, even more delightful word still, of 'story'?"[24] James may be writing expressly about his recollection of how he developed his subordinate characters, but his reference to Isabel's "sense of them, sense *for* them" accurately reflects the basic problem of interpersonal relations in the novel. James's mastery in the Prefaces is his ability to marry questions of social relation and artistic technique so seamlessly. His characters frequently view their problems in aesthetic terms, debating what "role" to play in the social "drama," or choosing which "oils" to apply to the social "canvas." As most critics recognize, these are not merely playful moments in which the author tips his hand, but indications of how intimately creative expression and social reality are bound together. James's realism requires a self-conscious narrative that reveals its own fictive moves as basic to any understanding of the text. In a similar sense, James's readers are compelled to reflect upon the method — the poetic — that governs the rhetoric of society.

This literary reflection on social convention is not, however, a passive act of observation made possible by the text's distance from the world. The normative is determined by the active poetic effort to disrupt it, to violate its illusion of reality or fixed meaning. Such a dynamic reflection on the system of language locates conventions by employing them as signifiers for innovative expression. The literary text makes us conscious of conventions in the process of deconstructing their determinate meanings. The critic is intimately involved in this process, repeating in different form the exposition of language dramatized by the artist. We frequently assume that the critic wants to translate the expression of the artist into terms that are more readily understandable; the interpreter is always tempted to appropriate and conventionalize the text. The critic is besieged daily by students and readers who insist upon a clarity and understanding that would reduce the text to a commodity characterized by intentional meanings and demonstrable truths. Yet, the poetic reflection on language depends upon a conception of signification in which the signified is constituted only to the extent that it may be employed as a supplementary signifier. Poetry manipulates the arbitrariness of the sign in order to preserve the vitality of human language. The critic responds to the imperatives of the work by imitating this deconstructive mode. As Eugenio Donato writes in "The Two Languages of Criticism":

> There is never an *interpretandum* which is not already an *interpretans,* so that a relationship of both violence and elucidation establishes itself with interpretation. Interpretation does not shed light on a matter that asks to be interpreted, that offers itself passively to interpretation, but it can only seize violently an interpretation that is already there, one which it must overturn, overthrow, shatter with the blows of a hammer. . . . Interpretation then is nothing but sedimenting one layer of language upon another to produce an illusory depth which gives us the temporary spectacle of things beyond words.[25]

This violence of interpretation characterizes the poetic expression that enables us to measure — to experience — the dimensions of convention and innovation that characterize the movement of signification.[26] Interpretation may tend "to produce an illusory depth," but the deconstructive mode I have described rejects even this illusion of depth in order to function as a productive analysis.

The artist's struggle for self-expression necessarily involves a directed reflection on the history of language. Every literary act clarifies the sedimentation of cultural values that threaten originality, thus making poetic expression proportionately more difficult. This very struggle, however, is what constitutes literature and the access it gives us to the differential production of meaning. The true anxiety of the poet is the sense of how every effort to speak always calls up other voices that threaten possession and domination. And yet, without this resistance, which paradoxically facilitates expression, there can be only the most illusory voices. Benveniste is only partially correct when he claims that the subject is the invention of language: "It is in and through language that man constitutes himself as a *subject,* because language alone establishes the concept of 'ego' in reality, in *its* reality which is that of the being." [27] It seems more useful to define the subject as the invention or economy of signifying forces (psychic, verbal, institutional, etc.), which remain latent or become manifest according to the arrangement or vortex they assume in their particular implementation and use. Who or what uses these forces determines their relative motivation within a sociohistorical situation. Thus, our task is not to determine "who is speaking," but how forces of signification are economized into some function of authority: an author, a disciplinary discourse, a social institution, a rhetorical system, a linguistic code.

The ontology of writing does not depend upon the ability of the text to escape the determinants of social usage. Authors find their characters by means of a will to power that enables them to reflect on the structure of the cultural code that motivates their expression. James's novels demonstrate that individuals are free only to the extent that they recognize their bondage to a language that is never their own. The imperative that the central character in a Jamesian novel acknowledge the conventional basis for subjectivity is as strong as the insistence that to be possessed by social forms is a kind of death. Both the artificial closure of high society and the detachment of the romantic imagination are fundamental violations of the signifying process. For James, definitive authority becomes impossible within the social, literary, or critical text, and what is substituted is a mythology of authority that involves its own subversion. Jamesian society is fundamentally unauthored, as his novels so clearly demonstrate, even though it is sustained by various centers or points of view struggling to assert their dominance. James's protagonists from Daisy

Miller to Maggie Verver serve to question these false authorities as part of the writer's effort to restore the vitality of signification.

In their critical acts, however, these characters often substitute their own authority for that which they question. Thus, Maggie Verver's efforts to revitalize social and marital relations in *The Golden Bowl* end by affirming the conventional forms that had originally caused the dramatic problems in the novel. As I have already suggested, the character's dilemma generally seems to reflect the author's own struggle to define his creative enterprise. James himself begins with a carefully wrought social structure in which conventional values predominate. His own artistic method threatens to substitute a narrative voice for the object of its critique. James's characters, however, are inventions that permit the writer to expose the grammar of society. Tempting as it would be to identify the author with his protagonist, we generally recognize that the "voice" of James is constituted by both social conventions and the individual desire for expression. Daisy Miller and Isabel Archer are functional devices for exposing the linguistic regularities of the societies that threaten to exile or possess them. The writer defines himself through the presentation of these opposing functions, discovering his identity in his effort to reflect upon the differential process through which meaning is produced. The bringing to consciousness of what ordinarily takes place in any act of language is in itself an invention of consciousness. Narrative consciousness is produced by the mutual determination of social convention and the possibilities for innovation. Like the high modernist writer, James uses his characters as ironic personae in order to explore conventions within the culture. James's ironic characters, however, are not used to protect the author from the social determinants that generally triumph over even his most rebellious characters. James employs such a mode of characterization explicitly to investigate the nature of authority, in which his own narratives are so self-consciously involved.

The Sacred Fount is unique among James's works because it attempts a direct exploration of this question of artistic identity. The narrator's problem of social relation is from the beginning a problem of narration, of how to write himself into or out of the social scene. The dramatic action is restricted temporally and spatially in such a way that the constriction of social forms is given special prominence for both the narrator and the reader. These factors help James concentrate on the problem of aesthetic originality more explicitly than in the wider social dramas of *The American* or *The Ambassadors*. And the first-person narrative enables James to dramatize directly the inextricable relation between his characters' struggles for social identity and the author's desire for a distinctive voice. Thus, those critics who have viewed the novel as autobiographical are partially correct.[28] Fundamentally concerned with the ways in which authorial identity is made possible within the system of language, *The Sacred Fount* offers a paradigmatic demonstration of James's own aesthetic process. As such, it should provide us with an illustration of how the artist invents the possibility of his expression by means of an active reflection on the nature of signification.

The Sacred Fount at first appears to be a frivolous tale about a weekend party at a country house. The triviality of social life at Newmarch, however, is the primary motivation for the narrator's desire for individual significance and definition. The extreme conventionality of Newmarch compels the narrator to ask the epistemological and ontological questions that are behind his investigation of interpersonal relations at the party. As a country retreat, Newmarch offers an apparent release from the confinement of London society. Yet, this pastoral world is no more free and open than that of the exiled court in the Forest of Arden. This is a world of elaborate social contrivance, in which even nature is reduced to a mere stage set. Early in the novel we are reminded that Newmarch has its own particular style and tone, constituted by a history of similar weekend parties: "Newmarch had always, in our time, carried itself as the great asylum of the finer wit, more or less expressly giving out that, as invoking hospitality and other countenance, none of the stupid, none even of the votaries of the grossly obvious, need apply. . . ." [29] This social microcosm demands a complicated rite of passage by means of which the individual is subjected to the determinism of established conventions for behavior.

The host of this party appears to have selected the characters and setting to fit an artistic composition. Luncheon, afternoon tea, the formal dinner, and the piano recital have been designed to order social life and provide contexts for interpersonal relations. Yet, the host is unnamed and remains absent from the weekend drama, appearing only once at dinner, that "especial hour" for the narrator which "asked little of interpretation" (*SF*, 156). In his own effort to assert his centrality, the host appears to have been effaced by the conventions controlling his art. The subtle pervasiveness of social form is suggested by the grounds surrounding Newmarch. The walks, gardens, woods, and views reflect an eighteenth-century inclination to give the designed garden the illusion of sublime prospect and expansive form: "Distances were great at Newmarch and landscape-gardening on the grand scale" (85–86). In the development of the narrative, characters are frequently controlled by the labyrinthine order of the gardens.

The narrator's initial anxiety about his personal relation to this society is motivated to a great extent by his sense of its hermetic quality. Late in the novel, he watches the authoritative Mrs. Brissenden leave him and considers the possibility of escape: "If I was free, that was what I had been only so short a time before, what I had been as I drove, in London, to the station. Was this now a foreknowledge that, on the morrow, in driving away, I should feel myself restored to that blankness? The state lost was the state of exemption from intense obsessions, and the state recovered would therefore logically match it" (*SF*, 192–93). Throughout the novel, the narrator has a growing sense that he has no being outside the confines of a text, whether it be the arranged world of Newmarch or the record of his own story. From the beginning, he views his interpretative activity as an attempt to read himself into a system of relations in which he might find personal identity and significance. His basic problem is simply whether he is to be a character in the social art of Newmarch or the creator of his own independent world of meaning. The blankness of the outside world, however, offers only an illusory freedom, for implicit in the London world is a complicated system that would define and delimit the narrator. Newmarch merely makes explicit the boundaries restricting every effort at individual expression. The artificial closure of this little society is paradigmatic, suggesting the flaw in all of James's societies. The narrator's analysis of relations at this weekend party must be a means of returning him to a world in which values are more adaptable to his personal needs.

In his struggle to assert his own presence, the narrator develops a hypothesis concerning social relations at Newmarch. The theory of the "sacred fount" suggests the needs of these characters to discover some meaningful sense of existence in this unauthored world. Thus, the narrator's theorizing enables him not only to relate to the other characters, but also to analyze his own desire. On his train ride to Newmarch, he speculates that Grace Brissenden appears to have been physically rejuvenated by her marriage to the much younger Guy. At the party he reflects that their intimate relationship has led to a draining of Guy's vitality in order to feed the aging Grace's lust for youth:

> "One of the pair," I said, "has to pay for the other. What ensues is a miracle, and miracles are expensive. What's a greater one than to have your youth twice over? It's a second wind, another 'go' — which isn't the sort of thing life mostly treats us to. Mrs. Briss had to get her new blood, her new allowance of time and bloom, somewhere; and from whom could she so conveniently extract them as from Guy himself? She *has*, by an extraordinary feat of legerdemain, extracted them; and he, on his side, to supply her, has had to tap the sacred fount." [*SF*, 29]

The theory suggests a hierarchy of victimizer and victim, but the narrator is quick to clarify its dialectical function. Such a relation depends on the "love" expressed by the "author of the sacrifice." The apparent victim is completely conscious of what he is giving up for the sake of his love; whereas the other must be absolutely unconscious of the entire process. Guy Brissenden's sacrifice ironically becomes the foundation for his own sense of being in the world. For the narrator, Guy constantly lives this surrender; it is the meaning and purpose of his life. He becomes Grace's messenger, companion, and general servant. Grace Brissenden is the embodiment of social conventionality, with the possible exception of her marriage to a man much younger than herself. In this society, however, the relative values of usage are disguised as absolute laws of judgment. The supernatural adjustment in the physical appearance of Grace relative to Guy ought to be taken literally. Grace's breach of decorum is masked by a social order that preserves itself either by repressing differences or exiling alien elements. In this way, Guy's own rite of passage is enacted and his marriage provides him with a social role. Guy sees in Grace his own act of sacrifice, not her independent personality; she serves as an external validation of his social identity. Thus, the relation of master and servant works both ways, the victim controlling the unconscious recipient of such "time and bloom." For this reason the narrator refers to Guy as the "author of the sacrifice."

The narrator hopes to confirm his theory by finding a complementary couple at the party. Gilbert Long is usually fashionable but superficial: a "heavy Adonis" incapable of being more than merely a minor character in the social drama. On this occasion, however, he seems to have become a brilliant conversationalist. In contrast, the normally witty and charming Mrs. Server appears extraordinarily subdued and withdrawn. For the narrator, May serves up her wit to the greedy Long. His choice of her as the missing element in his equation seems further confirmed by her elaborate attempts to screen her lover from any public exposure. The narrator views this protective instinct as an act of self-preservation, insofar as the "author of the sacrifice" finds his or her identity constituted by that external other. To make such a relationship manifest would be to bring the other to consciousness of his or her role in such a process. Such an independence would call into question the entire circuit of sacrifice, threatening the peculiar form of love involved.

For the narrator, the sacrificial love involved in these relations follows an archetypal pattern. He associates Gilbert Long with a "mystic Egeria" — an unnamed lover whom the narrator believes to be May Server. In classical myth, Egeria is a water nymph in Diana's sacred grove at Nemi. She reputedly mated with Numa, second king of Rome, and gave him the laws he would deliver to his people. Just as the mating of Egeria and Numa is a ritual investiture of the king with a social authority guaranteed by natural law, so the ritual tapping of the sacred fount becomes a means of validating one's own sense of social being. For May Server and Guy Brissenden, it is a desperate quest for order and value in the very act of sacrifice. For Grace and Gilbert, the "miracle" itself is sufficient to provide them with a sense of personal vitality and well-being.

The narrator is terrified by the general implications of his theory, because the possibility of an independent consciousness seems to be threatened at every turn. All parties to such a process must end by living vicariously, whether or not they are aware of their involvement. For the narrator, any social relation involves a definite surrender of independence and free will, and one is forced to choose either sacrifice or unconsciousness. In their struggles to escape the ambiguity of life, these characters accept the security of social forms and the reliability of another's truth. May and Guy in particular seem to avoid the responsibilities of interpretation demanded by the ordinary functioning of language. Rejecting a discourse based on the arbitrariness of the sign, they submit themselves to the closed meaning of the social *logos*. In the course of the narrative, Mrs. Server and "poor Briss" both become more and more withdrawn and reticent, inclining toward that silence which would fulfill their surrenders.

In a very real sense, the narrator comes close to repeating in his own theorizing the submission of May and Guy. He begins with a scientific hypothesis which he attempts to validate on the basis of data drawn from his social observations. At first he speaks of a "law" motivating the actions of these characters and perhaps serving as a fundamental rule of social behavior: "I was just conscious, vaguely, of being on the track of a law, a law that would fit, that would strike me as governing the delicate phenomena — delicate though so marked — that my imagination found itself playing with" (*SF*, 23). His own existential desire appears to confirm his theory, for he too seeks to relate social appearances to an external law of determining force. Like the others, he is attracted by an authority that would secure his identity and guarantee him social significance. In this sense, his process of interpretation is merely a repetition of what he sees as the basic impulse of social man. Yet, the confirmation of his theory would only validate the power of the conventional to absorb difference and variety. Insofar as he believes that his investigation will uncover some hidden truth directly affecting the lives of the characters, the narrator identifies himself with May's and Guy's consciousness of submission.

The narrator appears to replicate the dialectic of master-servant relations in a more practical way as well. Although his theorizing is clearly a defense against the possessive society he encounters, he finds that his investigation implicates him vicariously in the lives of others at the expense of his own identity. Although his scientific investigation is designed to focus and sustain his own consciousness, it actually tends to subordinate him to the very social order he fears from the beginning.[30] Like May and Guy, the narrator appears to contribute to his own effacement: "It was absurd to have consented to such immersion, intellectually speaking, in the affairs of other people. One had always affairs of one's own, and I was positively neglecting mine. . . . A whole cluster of such connections, effectually displacing the center of interest, now surrounded me, and I was — though always but intellectually — drawn into their circle" (*SF*, 89).

This is all given further confirmation by Mrs. Brissenden's speculation that the narrator himself might be in love with May Server. The novel opens the possibility that he, not Gilbert Long, is the true recipient of May's wit, and that the narrative is made possible by her sacrifice. In the latter part of the novel, the narrator begins to protect and screen May from the curiosity of the other characters. Sensing the underlying fear and loneliness May's awareness of her situation must involve, the narrator even partially identifies himself with her imputed lover: "I had already shielded her — fought for her so far as I or as the case immediately required. . . . I was the only person save one who was in anything that could be called a relation to her. The other person's relation was concealed, and mine, so far as she herself was concerned, was unexpressed — so that I suppose what most, at the juncture in question, stirred within me was the wonder of how I might successfully express it" (*SF,* 95-96). The narrator empathizes with May as "the restless victim of fear and failure," insofar as her dilemma reflects his own aesthetic difficulties. He views himself as increasingly ensnared by social relations and tempted at every turn to surrender to the dialectic of this closed world.

In order to save himself from such effacement, the narrator appears to give up his scientific investigation for a more imaginative interpretation of social relations. His theory assumes an abstract purity in the form of a "palace of thought" aesthetically developed out of the social appearances of Newmarch. His "fine symmetry" appears to be a defense against the knowledge that "the mind of man doubtless didn't know from one minute to the other, under the appeal of phantasmagoric life, what it would profitably be at" (*SF,* 183). The struggle for artistic authority over the conflicting evidence of the actual betrays the ontological appeal of his creative enterprise. He begins to associate his theory with a Platonic "light of day," and thus his art seems to promise escape from the illusions of the "cave" of Newmarch. Poetic language appears to give special access to that being which remains hidden in ordinary discourse and behavior. At the center of this "castle of enchantment," the narrator discovers his own identity: "The very presence of the haunting principle, as it were, of my thought" (129). The privileged space of his art discloses a private authority, an identity apparently free from the ambiguous text of social relations. In this sense, the narrator's imaginative activity presents itself as a "fount" for being, an oracular voice that displaces the phantasmagoric world of Newmarch.

The narrator's artistry, however, remains hopelessly entangled in the world that has motivated it. Although he attempts to protect his private madness from public exposure (just as others attempt to screen their lovers), he still engages in the social dialogue which constitutes both the party and his text. May Server and Guy Brissenden have less and less to say in the course of the narrative. Their silence appears to reflect the degree to which they have been drained by their sacrificial efforts. In contrast, the narrator's theory is sustained by his interminable conversation, which appears to proliferate rather than reduce the conflicting evidence. He himself initiates the curiosity of Mrs. Brissenden and the portrait painter, Ford Obert, concerning May Server's behavior at the party. His imaginative act in its purest sense is a calling forth of interpretation, a motivation for the varied critiques that would question the social surface. Both Grace and Ford Obert finally refuse the freedom offered by such a critical stance and retreat into their accustomed roles. Insisting that May is "all right," Obert denies that her behavior is in any way extraordinary. Ford Obert, however, is a Royal Academy artist whose success depends upon his ability to represent the social surface; his "realism" is the studied repression of the "ugly" facts. The narrator's theory subverts the very illusion of social order that Obert's portraits help to sustain.

Recognizing that the quest for a law leads to inevitable self-surrender and that his "palace of thought" demands an impossible solipsism, the narrator moves toward yet another conception of his interpretative activity. As a critic of Newmarch society, the narrator deconstructs the apparently fixed conventions of this little world to reveal their arbitrary origins. In one of the central episodes in the novel, this critical activity is equated with one of the primary impulses of artistic creation. The portrait of "The Man with the Mask in His Hand" suggests an immediate contrast to the avowed realism of Obert's paintings:

> The figure represented is a young man in black — a quaint, tight black dress, fashioned in years long past; with a pale, lean, livid face and a stare, from eyes without eyebrows, like that of some whitened old-world clown. In his hand he holds an object that strikes the spectator at first simply as some obscure, some ambiguous work of art, but that on a second view becomes a representation of a human face, modelled and coloured, in wax, in enamelled metal, in some substance not human. The object thus appears a complete mask, such as might have been fantastically fitted and worn. [*SF*, 55]

The portrait is the center of interest for the narrator, May Server, Guy Brissenden, and Gilbert Long. In an attempt to test his theory of relations, the narrator insists: "'It's the picture of all pictures that most needs an interpreter. *Don't* we want,' I asked of Mrs. Server, 'to know what it means?'" The portrait abstracts the entire problem of social "masking" that is the subject of the narrator's inquiry, and May's anticipated answer could only be received by him as a commentary on the deceptive game she is playing.

In fact, May does offer a significant reading of the painting, entitling it "the Mask of Death" and thus hinting at the dehumanizing roles one is compelled to play in this society. The artificiality of the mask refers to the lies May must tell in order to screen her true lover. Despite the narrator's own conception of the deceptive appearances involved in the theory of the sacred fount, he refers to the "modelled and coloured" form in the young man's hand as the "mask of life." The masks worn by the characters at Newmarch certainly betoken a deathly ritual in which appearances are designed to repress basic needs and passions. The dynamics of the portrait, however, suggest an alternative mode of role-playing. For the narrator, the mask offers the possibility of creating meaning at the same time that it discloses the groundlessness of all meanings. The young man's face is "pale, lean, livid" without the artistry of the mask. Such a reading may suggest that reality can never be separated from appearance and that there is no objective ground for cognition at all. Yet, the mask achieves its form in relation to the young man's face, indicating the necessary disclosure effected by an art that would sustain its own dynamic qualities. Rather than hiding the blankness that motivates art and imagination, the painter and the narrator dramatize the tensive relation of meaning and meaninglessness in the act of composition itself. Deconstructing its own impulse toward determinate form, the painting preserves its artistry by refusing to complete its meaning. The mask remains the sign of interpretation itself, and thus prefigures the futility of the narrator's quest for any psychic or social law.

The subsequent responses of the characters to the painting seem to confirm the narrator's interpretation. It becomes a point of reference for understanding their own social relations. As Laurence Holland has written, "It embodies the multiplicity of its implications, in their tentative suspension, rather than establishing the certainty of some identifications while concealing them with the feigning appearance of others." [31] The painting dramatizes the crisis of artistic expression confronted by the narrator throughout his tale. The portrait achieves its "unique" form by subverting its own impulse to restrict its meanings. It is a critical commentary on the artistic activity, which must always depend upon its arbitrary origins and achieves its form through supplementary acts of interpretation. In a similar sense, the narrator anatomizes the conventions of Newmarch society in such a way that his own critical narrative becomes the object of his readers' critiques.

The narrator's art forces others to examine the values on which they have based their lives. Like James's narrative art, his theory brings others to consciousness of their social situation:

> The sharpest jostle to my thought, in this rush, might well have been, I confess, the reflection that as it was I who had arrested, who had spoiled their unconsciousness, so it was natural they should fight against me for a possible life in the state I had given them instead. I had spoiled their unconsciousness, I had destroyed it, and it was consciousness alone that could make them effectively cruel. Therefore, if they were cruel, it was I who had determined it, inasmuch as, consciously, they could only want, they could only intend, to live. [*SF*, 294–95]

This new awareness exposes the ontological terror that is the secret motivation for the submission of May and Guy as well as the unconsciousness of Grace and Gilbert. If the narrator offers them a partial reprieve from their imprisonment in social conventionality, he also understands the threat he poses to their security. He can only expect them to fight for their lives, and he thus prophesies his own expulsion from this closed world.

As the object of the other characters' fear and cruelty, the narrator achieves a fragile sense of his own identity. His aesthetic and ontological instability is a measure of his awareness of the individual's relation to an enveloping system of social signs. In view of James's other works, the theory of the sacred fount does offer a valid generalization about interpersonal relations. James's characters do tend to rely on outside authorities for self-definition. The closure of high society is the result of conventions for usage functioning as determining laws, which repress or expel alien elements. The narrator's weekend investigation serves to question the enclosing forms which constitute social authority. This subversion of the normative liberates the social signified, making it available as a new signifier for the interpreting mind.

In his final interview with Grace Brissenden, the narrator confronts her with his imaginative construction. Frightened by this threat to the quiet surface of social decorum, Grace fights to preserve the order that defines her. In her last word, she collapses his "house of cards" and expels him as a madman: "My poor dear, you are crazy, and I bid you good-night!" (*SF,* 318). Acting as a titular authority, Grace judges the narrator with a finality that insures the closure of Newmarch: "She had so had the last word that, to get out of its planted presence, I shook myself, as I had done before, from my thought" (318). Yet, if he is shattered by "the word that put me altogether nowhere," the narrator has prepared for his own expulsion and effacement from the social scene. In more than a mere technical sense, he does have the ultimate word in the act of retelling his story: "I *should* certainly never again, on the spot, quite hang together, even though it wasn't that I hadn't three times her method. What I too fatally lacked was her tone" (319). Escaping the confirmed "tone" of Grace's social conviction, the narrator recognizes the incompletion on which both meaning and identity depend.

The circularity of the social dance at Newmarch describes a mythology of endless repetition, in which the characters blindly act out the desire for individual significance. In his own quest, the narrator replicates the pattern, expressing a similar need in both his scientific and imaginative projects. The narrative of his adventure, however, offers a different kind of repetition. In the act of writing, he exposes to himself his involvement as a character in this society. *The Sacred Fount* has caused critics great difficulty because of its unreliable first-person perspective. It is just this bounded subjectivity, however, which the narrator has achieved in his text. Defining himself through the generative difference of established social signs and the play of his own invention, he recognizes the doubleness of his identity. Thus, the novel presents both the subject and its social other as incomplete and interdependent functions of the signifying process.

The Jamesian novel is anatomized in *The Sacred Fount* as a coming to consciousness not only of a central character, but also of the writer himself concerning the nature of language. The narrator longs to discover a sacred fount — an origin — for his social being. James's fount is a variant of the printer's font, from which the dissemination of writing issues. Rejecting the illusory completion of meaning reflected in the closed society of Newmarch, the narrator discloses an open language whose origin consists of the difference of impulses toward normalization and variation. The writer defines himself as an interpreter, whose fundamental object of interpretation is the social code. Refusing to know who he is, the narrator writes in order to discover how he functions in relation to such codes and how their boundaries might be measured. Asked about his apparent rejection of the idea of the subject in his essay "Structure, Sign, and Play in the Discourse of the Human Sciences," Jacques Derrida has answered: "The subject is absolutely indispensable. I don't destroy the subject; I situate it. That is to say, I believe that at a certain level both of experience and of philosophical and scientific discourse one cannot get along without the notion of the subject. It is a question of knowing where it comes from and how it functions."[32] Enclosed by the open system of language, the creative act serves to situate the function "man" within the history of that language. [Author] is forever bracketed, "art" inevitably qualified, and *interpretation* italicized as the shifting place of voice. The critical activity involves the continual reprieve of the subject from its loss in the totality of language. And yet, it is this very process that returns us to language by exposing and objectifying the varied ways in which meaning comes into being.

The narrator of *The Sacred Fount* rediscovers the arbitrariness of the sign, which is masked by the false authorities of the Newmarch world. He does not escape that world by means of his narrative, but enters more fully into social life by means of his continuing reflection on how to narrate his life. As a critic of this little world, the narrator approaches the vocation of the artist, whose imaginative palaces enable him to measure the conventional and determinate meanings that threaten him and thus prompt his renewed desire for freedom. Some will complain that the narrator creates his own germ of artistic instigation from the unreliable evidence available. His imaginative rendering of relations, however, has served to threaten the complacent proprieties of high society, allowing his reader to see what is ordinarily buried or repressed beneath a glittering facade. The code of Newmarch, as well as the larger society that sustains such weekend rituals, has not been abstracted from its necessary context, but *experienced* in the narrator's own efforts to write himself into the action. Unlike Ford Obert, R. A., who would naively portray things as they are, the narrator dramatizes the fundamental violence of the artistic act, which is only "more true to its character in proportion as it strains or tends to burst, with a latent extravagance, its mould."[33]

The narrator's story establishes a dialectical relation between social and imaginative structures, which performs more accurately the structuralist activity of transcoding. Barthes argued in an early essay that the analyst's "structure is therefore actually a *simulacrum* of the object, but a directed, *interested* simulacrum, since the imitated object makes something appear which remained invisible, or if one prefers, unintelligible in the natural object."[34] Recognizing that there is never a "natural object" under investigation but always a preinterpreted text, or event, we might agree with Barthes that the very idea of the paradigm in structuralist methodology depends upon a strategic, interested artifice. Yet, by virtue of its own interests or ideology, such a metalanguage can never be subjected to traditional criteria for "imitation." The structuralist method of transcoding succumbs too often to the naive belief that there is an accurate representation of a presumably unified object. Such a view involves by necessity some criteria for truth in the critical discourse that inevitably recurs to the "nature" of the object itself. Yet, if that object is reconceived as the differential system of language itself, whose essence has no meaning outside of its performance in a historical situation, then the mimetic assumptions of transcoding must give way to an idea of understanding as appropriation, as will to power. This view of linguistic analysis as active interpretation marks the boundary between scientific structuralism — a version of the formalism implicit in modern thought — and so-called poststructuralism, which is a hermeneutic possibility already inscribed within the structuralist and modernist problematic.[35]

Postscript:
Through the Custom-House

Some authors . . . indulge themselves in such confidential depths of revelation as could fittingly be addressed, only and exclusively, to the one heart and mind of perfect sympathy; as if the printed book, thrown at large upon the wide world, were certain to find out the divided segment of the writer's own nature, and complete his circle of existence by bringing him into communion with it. It is scarcely decorous, however, to speak all, even where we speak impersonally.
    — Hawthorne, "The Custom-House"

For all men who say *yes,* lie; and all men who say *no,* — why, they are in the happy condition of judicious, unincumbered travellers in Europe; they cross the frontiers into Eternity with nothing but a carpet-bag, — that is to say, the Ego. Whereas those *yes*-gentry, they travel with heaps of baggage, and, damn them! they will never get through the Custom-House.
    — Melville to Hawthorne, 1851

    These interpretations of nineteenth-century American fiction have employed some of the methods of those formalisms and literary histories that this study challenges. One of the central concerns in this work is what the New Critics termed *autotelicism* and the structuralists *metaliterature;* the very marginality of these texts depends in part on their attention to problems of narration and imaginative representation. This literary self-consciousness traditionally has depended upon a sharp distinction between literature and ordinary language. In recent years, antiformalist critics have devoted increased attention to the fragment, the transgeneric work, the "antibook," and the "self-consuming" text as alternatives to an idea of literature defined by structural coherence, realized characters, and organic action. Yet, to canonize indeterminacy or discontinuity as antithetical to a great tradition of acknowledged literary classics merely reinstates the privileged status of "literature." Literary indeterminacy, that divine stutter, is a concept that belongs among the various protective defenses of literary formalism. Indeterminacy and undecidability are merely linguistic possibilities, which every writer must confront and struggle to overcome in the desire for communication. The ways of this will-to-meaning are what should interest the antiformalist, and literature, which shares this *aporia* with all other discourses, offers itself as a reflection on this linguistic dialectic of repression and expression.

This study employs certain formalist methods in ways that are designed and inevitably unwitting. Such flirtation with formalism is designed in the effort to show that autotelicism results in aestheticism only when it is assumed that reflexivity marks off a distinctive literary style. Interpretation is the activity of demonstrating a text's possibility of existence, and that life of the text depends upon its complex interrelation with other forces. In the preceding chapters, my close textual attention has been strategically diverted from its central subjects to analogous issues in philosophy, psychology, and linguistics. If self-reflexivity is intended primarily as an ontological act — the determination of the author's or reader's self-consciousness — then it cannot escape literary formalism (even if it offers itself as analytic philosophy). In this sense, the metaliterary possibilities of a work transform abstractions (self, other, nature, consciousness) into objects in a poetic landscape in order to construct an alternative world in place of an unsatisfactory or illusory existence. Formalism, as the New Critics have demonstrated, usually relies on a romantic existentialism, which is only thinly disguised by the rigor of its critical practice. Yet, just as modernism imaginatively enacts this bid for an autonomous poetic realm, only to discover its poetry drawn ceaselessly back into "life," so the formalist's argument concerning the autonomy of poetic language discovers itself repeating the cultural values and norms it had hoped to escape. If literary freedom is measured in terms of self-consciousness, such self-consciousness must take as its ultimate object the language of which it is made — unless, of course, one argues for a consciousness that exceeds its representation, which is to say a consciousness achieved only *beyond* language. And if this is the case, then formalism must acknowledge that its aim is to shatter the literary text, to break its images for the sake of what lies beyond its form and style. What the text brings to consciousness or makes visible (to use two familiar hypotyposes) is what the language of the culture has produced. It is this hermeneutic circle that requires the formalist to insist upon an exclusive literary language, which denies ordinary language for the sake of something prior to representation of any sort: consciousness, being, spirit, nature. Henry James understands this dilemma, and he goes beyond it by accepting the fact that culture is the supreme artist, whose complexity and power generally master the poor efforts of the individual artist. His notable self-reflexivity, or metaliterary obsession, is less an effort to transcend the illusions of the social arts than to demonstrate their sociology in the psychology of his writing. Although James always hopes to avoid the corruptions and inhumanities of this social artistry, he knows well enough that he repeats those failings in his own imaginative will to power, which is exercised not only over his own characters (his "harmless" inventions) but over his reader, who is more than willing to be deceived. The ways of literary authority are always interested in the genealogy of social authorities: law, economy, philosophy, politics, and, of course, criticism and its theory. The governess in *The Turn of the Screw*, for example, is not merely an instance of a failed artist or self-deluded character; she is a version of the author's own desire for truth and the culture's need of law.

Literature may be a form of pleasure in both the popular sense and sophisticated Kantian idea; literature may occasionally offer us some transcendence of our willful and appetitive natures. But reading nineteenth-century American fiction, I am struck far more by the unsettling and disorienting qualities of these works. They are merciless in their refusal to allow us to forget how all representation is an effort to master, to control, and to repress what we ceaselessly reproduce as the "other" of our experience. Such uncanniness is not unique in this period or for this national literature; it is the consequence of a particular strategy of reading, which belongs neither to the literary text nor its critical commentary. This uncanniness is the result of those "crossings" that usually take place in interpretation, and which have been artificially exaggerated in the method of this work. Readers are tempted to think that the disorientation of their experience might have some therapeutic or restorative value, but we may conclude only that our response to the uncanny makes us what we are, inscribes our histories. Self-consciousness is in a sense the grand and noble illusion that we are tempted to greet in hopes that literature and knowledge might improve, edify, and heighten our experience of the world. There is a formalist blindness in this work that is inevitable and unwitting as well as designed; these readings cannot deny the illusion of self-consciousness that haunts all writing and reading. But it also suggests that self-consciousness is achieved only as a consequence of profound repressions — lies against time and language; the courses of such forgetting are at least as important for us to learn how to read as what we think to remember.

All of this argues that the text has no independent existence, but is instead always a complex of forces economized in formal and psychological ways that disguise its discord. What we thought we knew as the text is itself always an intertextual crossing, which has an energy that should neither be dissipated nor disguised; it should be *used* to do new and useful work. The artifice of intertextuality in this study is designed to expose its own falsification of what is the intertextuality — that is, the interpretative possibilities — of language itself. Certainly, reading one text with another misleads us into imagining intertextuality to be a literary game, a perverse bitextuality. This is one of the repressions operative in this study that we can never be done with, that continues to govern the readings and for this reason can only be announced as an artifice (even though sincerity is never a substitute for cure).

This artificiality, however, is designed to accomplish more than the demonstration of how the formal closure of a text can be worked through (that is, with a certain formal rigor) to open the text to other forces. The intertextuality of this study is also a comparatism that strives to establish a renewed commerce between American and European modes of interpretation. In this sense, it works against the apparent aim of the writers of the American Renaissance to create a national literature. The "idea" of American literature should be understood as the desire for an "Amerika," which in its broadest outlines describes the general poetic impulse for autonomy and originality.

In this regard, formalism and American literary history share certain theoretical assumptions that have been generally disregarded. Indeed, America as the New World may be studied historically in terms of its anti-historical, formalist yearnings. In contrast, Bloom has argued that Emerson's Americanness is not provincialism or literary isolationism, but a profound and anguished struggle to translate the past of Europe into the future of his America. Emerson's effort to read the past as if it were authored by him is equivalent to the regressive history of this study, which reads backwards from twentieth-century "influences" to nineteenth-century "followers." I suspect that this sort of retreat is what guides most of our histories, even if the final works correct the historical sequences to preserve some evolutionary ideal of "earlier" and "later." America, like Borges's Kafka, has invented its own precursors, even though we know that such invention, such freedom, is the result of an ineluctable historical necessity. Thus, the obsessive concern with literary nationalism in American studies disguises a fundamentally poetic and linguistic problem (such as the "anxiety of influence") as the particular issues of a unique culture, history, and literature. For these reasons, American literary study has remained notably untheoretical (despite a wealth of theories of American literature) and often stubbornly unphilosophical, despite a literature that insists upon its philosophical themes. Because the desire for "Amerika" is so pronounced among American writers, who are forever mindful of their belatedness, then American literature ought to prompt criticism that is demonstrably speculative and theoretical. And because American writers address the fundamental poetic problem of "Amerika" in terms of an ever-present mythology of "Europe," then American literary study ought to be essentially comparative.

The custom-house is the text, the space and time of the passage between past and future, tradition and originality, determinism and freedom, the unconscious and the conscious, the foreign and the familiar: "Europe" and "Amerika." We would like to think that the exchanges passing through the custom-house are quite simply those occurring between author and reader, producer and consumer. But the passage through the custom-house of language moves in both directions at once, each importation requiring an export, each acquisition a loss, which is why the architecture of this curious dwelling is always "unfinished to this day," perpetually requiring the "labor of the carpenter and mason," who would be better named "ship carpenters," keeping the vessel on its way by patching and repairing the wear and tear of the voyage.[1] Ishmael finds in the *Pequod*'s ship carpenter the sort of adaptability and *bricolage* that one might associate with the abstract power of language itself. "Unintelligent" and "literal" himself, the ship carpenter still carries "this same unaccountable, cunning life-principle in him; this it was, that kept him a great part of the time soliloquizing; but only like an unreasoning wheel, which also hummingly soliloquizes; or rather, his body was a sentry-box and this soliloquizer on guard there, and talking all the time to keep himself awake."[2] What this ship carpenter makes confirms his significance as an agent of language, because he is the one who crafts Ahab's new leg with "the little oval slate, smoothed ivory, where he figures up the latitude"; he is the one who builds Queequeg's coffin, from which Queequeg is reborn and on whose lid Queequeg copies "those hieroglyphic marks . . . written out on his body" that constitute "a mystical treatise on the art of attaining truth."[3] Language is kin to this ship carpenter, because it fashions those mobile spaces in which we might figure our own latitudes, write our own "mystical treatises" on truth, all the while reminding us that the medium of our inscriptions is, like Queequeg's coffin, a life buoyed up by death or, like Ahab's ivory leg, a surrogate of life, a supplement to our wounded beings.

Intertextuality may be made explicit in such mixed forms as the novel or criticism, both of which operate as shameless thieves, but intertextuality does not belong exclusively to literature. Language itself is the ceaseless activity of crossing, translating, transgressing that makes possible the passage between apparently exclusive realms or divided territories. Literature reflects upon itself only insofar as it enables us to reflect upon language, because literature calls attention to the complex of forces — historical, political, psychological, philosophical, linguistic — in every utterance, any mark. Literature achieves this reflection on language neither with consistent deliberation nor scientific rigor, even though the primary intention of literature is to free itself of language and to control its figures as if they were facts. In this sense, the literary will shares those impulses toward mastery that rely upon the commodification of the "other," in order to tame its threat. Literature can forget, repress, defer, and divert, but it cannot escape the knowledge that it is nothing but language, that its very inscription is a repetition of what it would flee. Literature finds itself in those uncanny moments in which an author's will is undone by the unconscious forces it has caused to appear. There are two stories in the custom-house of language, and although the commerce that passes through each is different, both are built on the same site. On the lower floor, the foreign is received and assessed, approved and accustomed to our tastes. On the upper floor, the foreign is met unexpectedly and recognized with an involuntary shudder as it brands us with "a sensation not altogether physical, yet almost so, as of burning heat."[4] With this brand, the letter marks the interpreter, both identifying and exiling him, but undeniably prompting an activity that is the proper commerce of language: that economy in which use guarantees further circulation.

Notes

Preface

1. Jacques Derrida, "Différance," *Speech and Phenomena and Other Essays on Husserl's Theory of Signs,* trans. David B. Allison (Evanston: Northwestern University Press, 1973), pp. 131–32. Derrida insists that *différance* cannot be understood in any pure or abstract sense, but this does not relegate *différance* to a transcendent category of unknowable being. The very generality of *différance* in its abstract exposition denies its functional nature. Like Hegelian negation (*Verneinung*), *différance* exists only in linguistic performances. There can be no theory or science of *différance,* unless our ideas of both "theory" and "science" are radically transformed. In a similar sense, Derrida cannot properly write an essay entitled, "Différance," as he himself indicates in the course of this attempt at such an essay.

Chapter 1

1. Martin Heidegger, "Der Spruch des Anaximander," *Holzwege* (Frankfort: Vittorio Klostermann, 1950), p. 303. Translation my own.

2. Gayatri Spivak, Translator's Preface, in Jacques Derrida, *Of Grammatology* (Baltimore: Johns Hopkins University Press, 1976), p. xliii.

3. Jacques Derrida, "Structure, Sign, and Play in the Discourse of the Human Sciences," in *The Structuralist Controversy: The Languages of Criticism and the Sciences of Man,* ed. Richard Macksey and Eugenio Donato (Baltimore: Johns Hopkins University Press, 1972), p. 272.

4. Friedrich Nietzsche, *The Will to Power,* trans. Walter Kaufmann and R. J. Hollingdale, ed. Walter Kaufmann (New York: Random House, 1967), p. 297.

5. I make no distinction in this study between *modernism* and *postmodernism* as distinct movements or terms descriptive of particular intellectual periods. What has been considered postmodern can always be located within the major works of modernism, even if the features of such postmodernism are distorted or disguised. The use of these two terms is misleading, because it tends to split the dialectic of modernity into two separate parts, and it tries to subordinate the forces of this integral dialectic to a naive conception of literary evolution and historical periodization. The confusion that has resulted from the casual use of these terms in historical studies is further evidence that traditional approaches to literary history tend to resolve anomalies or contradictions by assigning their predicates to separate periods or discrete movements.

6. Like Nietzsche's discovery of Dostoevsky's works, Twain's reading of Nietzsche served primarily to confirm and complement views that Twain himself had formulated much earlier in his career. As Twain wrote in 1907: "I knew I should not find in any philosophy a single thought which had not passed through my own head, nor a single thought which had not passed through the heads of millions and millions of men before I was born; I knew I should not find a single original thought in any philosophy, and I knew I could not furnish one to the world myself, if I had five centuries to invent it in. Nietzsche published his book, and was at once pronounced crazy by the world — by a world which included tens of thousands of bright, sane men who believed exactly as Nietzsche believed but concealed the fact and scoffed at Nietzsche. What a coward every man is! and how surely he will find it out if he will just let other people alone and sit down and examine himself. The human race is a race of cowards; and I am not only marching in that procession but carrying a banner." Quoted in *Mark Twain in Eruption,* ed. Bernard DeVoto (New York: Harper and Bros., 1940), p. xxix.

7. Much of what Thomas Kuhn writes in *The Structure of Scientific Revolutions,* 2d ed. (Chicago: University of Chicago Press, 1970) concerning the structure of scientific communities could be applied by analogy to scholarly communities in the humanities. See in particular chapter 2, "The Route to Normal Science," especially pp. 10–11. Literary critical paradigms are certainly less stable and, unlike scientific paradigms, may coexist with a variety of other paradigms. Yet, students of literature still do most of their preparation in fields, such as genre, literary history, and formal analysis, that reinforce the disciplinary boundaries of literary criticism and perpetuate the study of primarily literary influences and relations. Many interdisciplinary programs merely repeat such provincialism by treating philosophical concepts as literary themes and psychoanalytic methods as explicatory tools.

8. The idea of the marginal text is, of course, indebted to Derrida's concept of the margin as that "space" surrounding the text which is nonetheless the product of the text's own repressive power. The spatiality of the metaphor is somewhat misleading (although designed to question the presumed spatialization of time in texts) because Derrida wants to describe an activity that is both spatial and temporal. Derrida's "margin" derives from Nietzschean forgetting, Freudian repression, and Husserl's "horizon" or "marginal zone," which results from the delimiting process of perception itself. In his introduction to *Marges de la philosophie* (Paris: Editions de Minuit, 1972), p. xix, Derrida insists that the margin is not "white, virgin, vacant" but "another text, a tissue of differential forces without any center of present reference," which threatens the formal and disciplinary closure of the text. Such a margin, insofar as it is produced by the text, can be used to open the text, "crack its meaning," and undo its intentions. Deconstruction is just this effort to interpret the relation between text and margin, the mutuality of intention and its other. Translations from *Marges* are my own.

9. This study might have pursued some of the same problems concerning the development of certain critical mythologies by studying various conceptions of popular literature in relation to a classical tradition. One might write a history of American critical values and taste that concentrates on what has *not* been published in America, although the practical scholarly problems involved in such a project would be immense. I confess that I have chosen the easiest way to approach these issues, because what the critics *have* said about these minor nineteenth-century classics makes their silence on other matters all the more telling.

10. Fredric Jameson, *The Prison-House of Language: A Critical Account of Structuralism and Russian Formalism* (Princeton: Princeton University Press, 1972), p. 175.

11. Derrida, *Of Grammatology,* p. 13.

12. Ferdinand de Saussure, *Course in General Linguistics,* ed. Charles Bally and Albert Sechehaye, in collab. with Albert Reidlinger; trans. Wade Baskin (New York: McGraw-Hill Book Co., 1966), p. 120.

13. Jacques Derrida, "Différance," in *Speech and Phenomena and Other Essays on Husserl's*

Theory of Signs, trans. David B. Allison (Evanston, Ill.: Northwestern University Press, 1973), pp. 142–43.

14. Jacques Derrida, "Limited Inc a b c . . .," *Glyph 2: Johns Hopkins Textual Studies,* (Baltimore: Johns Hopkins University Press, 1977), p. 184.

15. Jacques Derrida, "Freud and the Scene of Writing," trans. Jeffrey Mehlman, *Yale French Studies* 48 (1972): 113.

16. The following passage from Derrida's "Structure, Sign, and Play," pp. 264–65, has frequently been used to illustrate the basic outlook of poststructuralism: "There are thus two interpretations of interpretation, of structure, of sign, of freeplay. The one seeks to decipher, dreams of deciphering, a truth or an origin which is free from freeplay and from the order of the sign, and lives like an exile the necessity of interpretation. The other, which is no longer turned toward the origin, affirms freeplay and tries to pass beyond man and humanism, the name man being the name of that being who, throughout the history of metaphysics or of ontotheology — in other words, through the history of all his history — has dreamed of full presence, the reassuring foundation, the origin and end of the game." Critics have generally read these "two interpretations of interpretation" to represent structuralist and poststructuralist views respectively. Although Derrida appears to maintain this distinction in a number of his other writings, I would argue that Derrida's own concept of the sign as *écriture, différance,* trace, etc., requires that *both* interpretations of interpretation operate together in every act of signification. One might say that one or the other hermeneutic tends to dominate in any given act, but no discourse ever escapes fully this fundamental difference: the desire for completed meaning and the destruction of established meaning. "Pure" deconstructive writing would run the same risks as a discourse in which the *différance* of the sign had been totally effaced.

17. Harold Bloom, *Kabbalah and Criticism* (New York: Seabury Press, 1975), p. 106.

18. E. D. Hirsch, Jr., *Validity in Interpretation* (New Haven: Yale University Press, 1967), p. 236.

19. Ibid., p. 242.

20. See Viktor Shklovsky, *Theorie der Prosa,* ed. and trans. Gisela Drohla (Frankfort: S. Fischer Verlag, 1966), esp. p. 14: "The aim of art is to give us a sensation of the thing, a sensation that is visual and not merely recollective. Thus art employs two devices: the estrangement of things and the complication of form, in order to prompt perception and lengthen its duration. In art the perceptual process is itself an aim and thus must be prolonged. Art is a means of experiencing the *becoming* of things; whatever already *has been* is unimportant for art." (Translation from Drohla's German is my own.)

21. Trotsky's criticism of the Formalists' limited linguistic model still has a good deal of relevance. See Trotsky, "The Formalist School of Poetry and Marxism," in *Critical Theory since Plato,* ed. Hazard Adams (New York: Harcourt Brace Jovanovich, 1971), p. 824: "Verbal form is not a passive reflection of a pre-conceived artistic idea, but an active element which influences the idea itself. But such an active mutual relationship — in which form influences and at times entirely transforms content — is known to us in all fields of social and even biological life. This is no reason at all for rejecting Darwinism and Marxism for the creation of a Formalist school either in biology or sociology."

22. Wolfgang Iser, *The Act of Reading: A Theory of Aesthetic Response* (Baltimore: Johns Hopkins University Press, 1978), p. 88.

23. Ibid.

24. Wesley Morris, *Toward a New Historicism* (Princeton: Princeton University Press, 1972), pp. 11–12.

25. Roland Barthes, "What Is Criticism?" in *Critical Essays,* trans. Richard Howard (Evanston, Ill.: Northwestern University Press, 1972), pp. 258–59.

26. Hayden White, *Tropics of Discourse* (Baltimore: Johns Hopkins University Press, 1978), p. 5.

27. Hayden White, *Metahistory: The Historical Imagination in Nineteenth-Century Europe*

(Baltimore: Johns Hopkins University Press, 1973), p. 431. See David Carroll's "On Tropology: The Forms of History," *Diacritics* 6 (Fall 1976): 64, for a cogent treatment of the "value systems" at work in *Metahistory*.

28. Barthes, "What Is Criticism?," p. 260.

29. Ibid.

30. Michel Foucault, *The Archaeology of Knowledge and the Discourse on Language*, trans. A. M. Sheridan Smith (New York: Harper and Row Publishers, 1972), p. 149.

31. Ibid., pp. 150-51.

32. Ibid., p. 151.

33. Ibid., pp. 155-56.

34. David Carroll, "The Subject of Archaeology or the Sovereignty of the Episteme," *MLN* 93 (1978): 720-21.

35. Michel Foucault, "Nietzsche, Genealogy, History," in *Language, Counter-Memory, Practice: Selected Essays and Interviews*, ed. and intro. Donald F. Bouchard; trans. Donald F. Bouchard and Sherry Simon (Ithaca, N.Y.: Cornell University Press, 1976), p. 142.

36. Edward Said, "The Problem of Textuality," *Critical Inquiry* 4 (Summer 1978): 676.

37. Eugenio Donato, "The Two Languages of Criticism," in Macksey and Donato, *The Structuralist Controversy*, p. 96.

38. Jacques Derrida, "Cogito and the History of Madness," in *Writing and Difference*, trans. Alan Bass (Chicago: University of Chicago Press, 1978), p. 36.

39. Walter Benjamin, "Theses on the Philosophy of History," *Illuminations*, ed. Hannah Arendt, trans. Harry Zohn (New York: Schocken Books, 1969), p. 255.

40. Paul de Man, "Literary History and Literary Modernity," *Blindness and Insight* (New York: Oxford University Press, 1971), p. 148.

41. Friedrich Nietzsche, *"The Birth of Tragedy" and "The Genealogy of Morals,"* trans. Francis Golffing (Garden City, N.Y.: Doubleday and Co., 1956), p. 299.

42. Ibid.

43. de Man, "Literary History and Literary Modernity," p. 149.

44. Ibid., p. 150.

45. Joseph N. Riddel, *The Inverted Bell: Modernism and the Counterpoetics of William Carlos Williams* (Baton Rouge: Louisiana State University Press, 1974), p. 226.

46. de Man, "Literary History and Literary Modernity," p. 161.

47. Ibid.

48. Ibid., p. 163.

49. Harold Bloom, *Poetry and Repression: Revisionism from Blake to Stevens* (New Haven: Yale University Press, 1976), p. 254.

50. Harold Bloom, *A Map of Misreading* (New York: Oxford University Press, 1975), p. 166.

51. Richard Chase, *The American Novel and Its Tradition* (1957; reprint ed., Baltimore: Johns Hopkins University Press, 1980), p. 1.

52. Bloom, *Map of Misreading*, p. 167.

53. Bloom, *Poetry and Repression*, p. 244.

54. Ibid., p. 287.

55. Bloom, *Map of Misreading*, p. 53.

56. Henry James, *The Art of the Novel: Critical Prefaces*, ed. R. P. Blackmur (New York: Charles Scribner's Sons, 1934), p. 341.

57. Ibid., p. 297.

58. Bloom, *Map of Misreading*, p. 52.

59. See Nicolaus Mills, *American and English Fiction in the Nineteenth-Century: An Antigenre Critique and Comparison* (Bloomington: Indiana University Press, 1973), p. 111: "I think that in a more sophisticated and often uncomplimentary way the genre critics and those whom they have influenced also reflect an exaggerated concern for the Americanness of American

literature. For in trying to describe the uniqueness of American fiction, genre criticism and its variants have found it necessary to postulate either a superform in which American fiction is depicted as a combination of qualities (which are not true for any one book and have no viable organizing principle) or a fragmented form in which single qualities are said to reveal the essence of American fiction (despite the fact that other qualities are often of equal or greater importance)."

60. Bloom, *Kabbalah and Criticism*, p. 63.

61. Friedrich Nietzsche, *Beyond Good and Evil*, trans. R. J. Hollingdale (Baltimore: Penguin Books, 1972), pp. 141–42.

Chapter 2

1. Henry David Thoreau, *A Week on the Concord and Merrimack Rivers*, vol. 1, *The Writings of Henry David Thoreau*, New Riverside Edition, 11 vols. (Boston: Houghton Mifflin Co., 1893), p. 477. Hereafter cited in the text as *Week*.

2. Henry David Thoreau, *Walden*, in *"Walden" and "Civil Disobedience,"* ed. Owen Thomas (New York: W. W. Norton and Co., 1966), p. 1. Hereafter cited in the text as *Walden*.

3. William Drake, "Walden," in *Thoreau: A Collection of Critical Essays*, ed. Sherman Paul (Englewood Cliffs, N.J.: Prentice-Hall, 1962), p. 81.

4. Ibid., p. 82; my italics.

5. Frank Lentricchia, "Coleridge and Emerson: Prophets of Silence, Prophets of Language," *Journal of Aesthetics and Art Criticism* 32 (Fall 1973): 43, succinctly summarizes this romantic attitude toward metaphor: "The romantic visionary must see metaphor ultimately destroying itself in order to function properly for the end of revealing a monistic universe which is hidden from us by our traditional sense of metaphor that insists we are never to understand the utter fusion of tenor and vehicle."

6. Ralph Waldo Emerson, *Nature*, in *The Works of Ralph Waldo Emerson*, Riverside Edition (Boston: Houghton Mifflin Co., 1876), 1: 31.

7. Stanley Cavell, *The Senses of "Walden"* (New York: Viking Press, 1972), p. 5.

8. Ibid., p. 104n.

9. Ibid., p. 105n.

10. Ibid., p. 106.

11. Emerson, *Nature*, p. 31. Emerson still insists on the priority of natural language, but the relation of the "original" to its "representation" persistently troubles his writings.

12. James McIntosh, *Thoreau as Romantic Naturalist: His Shifting Stance toward Nature* (Ithaca, N.Y.: Cornell University Press, 1974), p. 252.

13. Robert Evans, "Thoreau's Poetry and the Prose Works," *Emerson Society Quarterly* 56 (1969): 43.

14. Emerson, "The Poet," *Works*, 3: 35, 29.

15. Joyce Holland, "Pattern and Meaning in Thoreau's *A Week*," *Emerson Society Quarterly* 50, supplement (1968): 50.

16. Evans, "Thoreau's Poetry and Prose Works," p. 43.

17. See Carl Hovde, "Nature into Art: Thoreau's Use of His Journals in *A Week*," *American Literature* 30 (May 1958): 165–84.

18. Robert Stowell and William Howarth, eds., *A Thoreau Gazetteer* (Princeton: Princeton University Press, 1970), p. 3.

19. William Bysshe Stein, "Thoreau's *A Week* and *OM* Cosmography," *American Transcendentalist Quarterly* 11 (Summer 1971): 24.

20. Martin Heidegger, "'. . . Poetically Man Dwells . . .,'" *Poetry, Language, Thought*, trans. Albert Hofstadter (New York: Harper and Row Publishers, 1971), p. 222.

21. See Martin Heidegger, *Identity and Difference*, trans. Joan Stambaugh (New York: Harper and Row Publishers, 1969), p. 69: "Inasmuch as Being becomes present as the Being of beings, as the difference, as perduration, the separateness and mutual relatedness of grounding and of accounting for endures, Being grounds beings, and beings, as what *is* most of all, account for Being. One comes over the other, one arrives in the other."

22. Heidegger, "'. . . Poetically Man Dwells . . .,'" p. 223.

23. I prefer to use Thoreau's misquotation of Herbert in the first edition of *A Week* (Boston: James Munroe and Co., 1849). Thoreau's substitutions ought to tell us more about the use to which he puts his extracts than the "authorized" version, which reads: "Sweet day, so cool, so calm, so bright, / The bridall of the earth and skie: / The dew shall weep thy fall to night; / For thou must die."

24. An analogous case might be made for the three poems used by Thoreau as epigraphs to "Concord River," the opening section. The appeal "Be thou my Muse, my Brother" in the first poem announces John's absence and thus necessitates the lonely voyage of the second poem: "There it is, there it is, the treasure I seek, / On the barren sands of a desolate creek." The second line certainly prepares for the renewal promised by the goal of enduring brotherhood that concludes the third poem: "But when I remember where I have been, / And the fair landscapes that I have seen, / THOU seemest the only permanent shore, / The cape never rounded, nor wander'd o'er." The poems also prefigure the subsequent discussion of friendship in "Wednesday." This hasty explication suggests that the three epigraphs deserve to be considered as a single poem, even though Carl Bode's notes in *Collected Poems of Henry David Thoreau* (Baltimore: Johns Hopkins Press, 1970), p. 288, indicate that only the first two poems can be established as contemporary in composition (1839).

25. See Ethel Seybold, *Thoreau: The Quest and the Classics* (New Haven: Yale University Press, 1951), p. 11, for an example of how the scholar's assumptions about linear time simplify such complexes in Thoreau as ancient and modern, primitive and civilized.

26. The idea of strangeness as essential to one's being is, of course, fundamental to Heidegger's thinking in *Sein und Zeit*.

27. McIntosh, *Thoreau as Romantic Naturalist*, p. 165, calls this Thoreau's "creative tension."

28. Martin Heidegger, "Hölderlin and the Essence of Poetry," *Existence and Being*, trans., intro., analysis by Werner Brock (Chicago: Henry Regnery Co., 1949), pp. 288–89.

29. Heidegger repeatedly sounds a similar theme in his essays on poetic thinking, the essence of which is expressed in Hölderlin's question in "Bread and Wine" that Heidegger uses to open "What Are Poets For?" in *Poetry, Language, Thought*, p. 91: "And what are poets for in a destitute time?" Heidegger makes it clear in this essay that such destitution is a consequence of our own refusal to accept our temporal circumstances: "The time remains destitute not only because God is dead, but because mortals are hardly aware and capable of their own mortality. Mortals have not yet come into ownership of their own nature. Death withdraws into the enigmatic" (96).

30. Compare Thoreau's idea of poetic history with Heidegger's in "Hölderlin and the Essence of Poetry," pp. 289-90: "The essence of poetry, which Hölderlin establishes, is in the highest degree historical, because it anticipates historical time; but as a historical essence it is the sole essential essence."

31. Martin Heidegger, *An Introduction to Metaphysics*, trans. Ralph Mannheim (Garden City, N.Y.: Doubleday and Co., 1961), p. 12.

32. Ibid., pp. 108-9.

33. Ibid., p. 113.

34. See Joseph N. Riddel's analysis of *physis* and *logos* in *The Inverted Bell: Modernism and the Counterpoetics of William Carlos Williams* (Baton Rouge: Louisiana State University Press, 1974), pp. 56-60.

35. McIntosh, *Thoreau as Romantic Naturalist,* p. 174.

36. William Carlos Williams in *In the American Grain* (New York: New Directions, 1933) and in "Raleigh Was Right," *Selected Poems of William Carlos Williams* (New York: New Directions, 1969), p. 99, traces the American fall to a similar loss of the poetic power symbolized by Raleigh.

37. It seems timely here that I overtake the quotation governing my chapter title. Heidegger, "The Nature of Language," *On the Way to Language,* trans. Peter Hertz (New York: Harper and Row Publishers, 1971), p. 76, explains: "Language must, in its own way, avow to us itself — its nature. Language persists in this avowal. We hear it constantly, of course, but do not give it thought. If we did not hear it everywhere, we could not use one single word of language. Language is active as this promise. The essential nature of language makes itself known to us as what is spoken, the language of its nature. But we cannot quite hear this primal knowledge, let alone 'read' it. It runs: The being of language — the language of being [Das Wesen der Sprache: Die Sprache des Wesens]." It should be clear by now that my interpretation of Thoreau's *A Week* derives from this Heideggerian sense that language may never be "thought" outside of itself. The way to language is inevitably through language itself: poetic thinking. This appears to approximate the kind of "thinking" that Thoreau attempts in *A Week.*

38. Walter Harding, "Introduction," *A Week on the Concord and Merrimack Rivers* (New York: Holt, Rinehart and Winston, 1963), p. xiii.

39. Thoreau, *Summer: From the Journal of Henry D. Thoreau,* New Riverside Edition, 6: 261. Quoted in the "Introductory Note," *A Week,* 1: xvii.

40. Rosemary Whitaker, "*A Week* and *Walden:* The River vs. the Pond," *American Transcendentalist Quarterly* 17 (1973): 12.

41. Emerson, "Friendship," *Works,* 2: 190.

42. Ibid., p. 189.

43. Ibid., p. 203.

44. Ibid., pp. 204–5.

45. Ibid., p. 200.

46. Ibid., p. 195.

47. Ibid., p. 198.

48. Heidegger, "What Are Poets For?," p. 142.

Chapter 3

1. See in particular Frederick Crews, *The Sins of the Fathers: Hawthorne's Psychological Themes* (New York: Oxford University Press, 1966) and Jean Normand's psychopoetic biography, *Nathaniel Hawthorne: An Approach to an Analysis of Artistic Creation,* trans. Derek Coltman (Cleveland: Press of Case Western Reserve University, 1970).

2. Edgar Dryden, *Nathaniel Hawthorne: The Poetics of Enchantment* (Ithaca, N.Y.: Cornell University Press, 1977), p. 10. Dryden's emphasis on his own phenomenological experience of reading Hawthorne indicates an antiformalist intention, but it is difficult to see how his argument concerning the "centrality" of the "themes of enchantment" differs methodologically from such formalist studies as Richard Harter Fogle, *Hawthorne's Fiction: The Light and the Dark* (Norman: University of Oklahoma Press, 1952). Both works assume the unity of certain image-motifs as the key to Hawthorne's thought.

3. Kenneth Dauber, *Rediscovering Hawthorne* (Princeton: Princeton University Press, 1977), pp. 37, 21.

4. In the former case, Hyatt Waggoner, *Hawthorne: A Critical Study* (Cambridge, Mass.: Harvard University Press, 1955), offers some very lame explanations of *Blithedale's* failure. In the beginning of his chapter on this work he tries to redeem *Blithedale* by shifting the

generic ground: "I mean reading it with the closest attention to texture, as though it were not a novel but a poem" (175). The strategy actually enables Waggoner to disregard intellectual issues and concentrate on image-motifs and thematic consistencies.

5. Roy Male, *Hawthorne's Tragic Vision* (Austin: University of Texas Press, 1957), p. 155.

6. Richard Brodhead, *Hawthorne, Melville, and the Novel* (Chicago: University of Chicago Press, 1976), p. 91.

7. Nathaniel Hawthorne, *The Scarlet Letter*, ed. Sculley Bradley, Richmond Croom Beatty, and E. Hudson Long, Norton Critical Edition (New York: W. W. Norton and Co., 1962), p. 76. Hereafter cited in the text as *SL*.

8. See Immanuel Kant, *Critique of Pure Reason*, trans. Norman Kemp Smith (New York: St. Martin's Press, 1929), pp. 180–87.

9. For a more detailed discussion of the affinities between Hegel's romanticism and *The Scarlet Letter*, see John Carlos Rowe, "The Internal Conflict of Romantic Narrative: Hegel's *Phenomenology* and Hawthorne's *The Scarlet Letter*," *MLN* 95 (1980): 1203–31.

10. Alfred Marks, "Who Killed Judge Pyncheon? The Role of the Imagination in *The House of the Seven Gables*," *PMLA* 71 (June 1956): 355–69.

11. Nathaniel Hawthorne, *The House of the Seven Gables*, ed. Seymour Gross, Norton Critical Edition (New York: W. W. Norton and Co., 1967), p. 307.

12. Coverdale reinforces this association several times in his narration as in this passage of *The Blithedale Romance*, ed. Seymour Gross and Rosalie Murphy, Norton Critical Edition (New York: W. W. Norton and Co., 1978), p. 95: "I detested this kind of man, and all the more, because a great part of my own nature showed itself responsive to him." Hereafter cited in the text as *BR*.

13. Philip Rahv, "The Dark Lady of Salem," *Image and Idea: Twenty Essays on Literary Themes*, rev. ed. (Norfolk, Conn.: New Directions, 1957), p. 45.

14. See, for example, Waggoner, *Hawthorne: A Critical Study* p. 186, who suggests that "the veil imagery does not function in terms of an allegorical sort of symbolism. Like the laughter in 'My Kinsman' and the colors in *The Scarlet Letter*, it functions symbolically in terms of context."

15. Richard Harter Fogle, "Priscilla's Veil: A Study of Hawthorne's Use of the Veil-Imagery in *The Blithedale Romance*," in *The Nathaniel Hawthorne Journal 1972*, ed. C. E. Frazer Clark, Jr. (Washington, D.C.: NCR Microcard Editions, 1973), p. 63.

16. Brodhead, *Hawthorne, Melville, and the Novel*, p. 109.

17. Irving Howe, *Politics and the Novel* (New York: Fawcett World Library, 1967), p. 176.

18. This view of Westervelt's artistry should help complicate the traditional distinction that is drawn between Hawthorne's "artists" and "scientists." Taylor Stoehr, "'Young Goodman Brown' and Hawthorne's Theory of Mimesis," *Nineteenth-Century Fiction* 23 (March 1969): 409, provides a convenient summary of the traditional difference between Hawthorne's artists and his scientists.

19. The narrative is full of images related to feminine sexuality, virginity, and their violation by the male. The most notable are the purses that Priscilla makes, Zenobia's exotic flower and its jeweled surrogate, and the veil itself. The "night-cap" that Priscilla makes for the convalescing Coverdale has obvious sexual connotations, if only by association with the purses she customarily sews.

20. See, for example, Roy Male, "Hawthorne's Fancy, or the Medium of *The Blithedale Romance*," in Clark, *Nathaniel Hawthorne Journal 1972*, p. 69.

21. References to the following translations will be included in the text: *L'Imagination*, trans. Forrest Williams as *Imagination: A Psychological Critique* (Ann Arbor: University of Michigan Press, 1962) — *I*; *L'Imaginaire, psychologie phénoménologique de l'imagination*, trans. Bernard Frechtman as *The Psychology of the Imagination* (New York: Citadel Press, 1961) — *PI*.

22. See Edmund Husserl, *Ideas: General Introduction to Pure Phenomenology*, trans. W. R. Boyce Gibson (New York: Macmillan Publishing Co., 1962), p. 107.

23. See Edmund Husserl, "'Phenomenology,' Edmund Husserl's Article for the *Encyclopedia Britannica* (1927)," trans. Richard E. Palmer, in *Phenomenology and Existentialism*, ed. Richard Zaner and Don Ihde (New York: G. P. Putnam's Sons, 1973), p. 53.

24. Ibid., p. 55.

25. Husserlian phenomenology depends upon the individual taking his own intentional acts as the primary objects for philosophical investigation. See Dorion Cairns, "An Approach to Husserlian Phenomenology," in Zaner and Ihde, eds., *Phenomenology and Existentialism*, p. 41.

26. Edmund Husserl, *The Phenomenology of Internal Time-Consciousness*, ed. Martin Heidegger, trans. James Churchill (Bloomington: Indiana University Press, 1964), p. 60.

27. Fogle, "Priscilla's Veil," p. 64, argues that "Westervelt is Hawthorne's surrogate as the master of illusion, and conforms most closely to Coleridge's classic utterances on poetic faith and the supernatural." On this basis, Fogle makes a good deal out of the veil's freedom from spatio-temporal limitations: "It is interesting, too, that the Veil . . . is free of time and space, for this is an attribute of Coleridge's 'imagination,' which has 'an arbitrary control over both; and if only the poet have such power of exciting our internal emotions as to make us .present to the scene in imagination, he acquires the right and privilege of using time and space as they exist in the imagination, obedient only to the laws which the imagination acts by.'" Sartre's debts to romanticism may be clearly seen in this passage from Coleridge, which prefigures Sartre's insistence upon the imagination as an "unreal" realm that defines "a certain type of consciousness which is completely independent of the perceptual type, and correlatively, a type of existence *sui generis* for its objects" (*PI*, 134).

28. Jean-Paul Sartre, *Being and Nothingness: An Essay on Phenomenological Ontology*, trans. Hazel E. Barnes (New York: Philosophical Library, 1956), p. 44.

29. Ibid., p. 39.

30. Nathaniel Hawthorne, *Mosses from an Old Manse*, vol. 2, *The Complete Works of Nathaniel Hawthorne*, ed. George Parsons Lathrop, Riverside Edition, 13 vols. (Boston: Houghton Mifflin and Co., 1882), p. 13. Further references in the text as *OM*.

31. J. Hillis Miller, *Thomas Hardy: Distance and Desire* (Cambridge, Mass.: Harvard University Press, 1970), p. 3.

32. Sartre, *Being and Nothingness*, p. 28.

33. Hermann Broch as quoted in Theodor Ziolkowski, *Dimensions of the Modern Novel: German Texts and European Contexts* (Princeton: Princeton University Press, 1969), p. 241.

34. Coverdale's hermitage is curiously associated with Zenobia's eventual suicide. When Zenobia and Westervelt converse near his hiding-place, Coverdale considers "sending an unearthly groan out of my hiding-place, as if this were one of the trees of Dante's ghostly forest" (*BR*, 96–97). The editors of the Norton Critical Edition of *Blithedale* gloss this allusion: "The 'dark wood' in which Dante wanders at the opening of *The Inferno*" (97 n.). "The Dark Wood of Error" in Canto I would seem to fit this context, because it represents the pilgrim's wandering from the "True Way." But the most memorable "ghostly forest" in Dante appears in Canto XIII, which describes "The Wood of the Suicides." The introduction to Canto XIII in John Ciardi's translation of *The Inferno* (New York: New American Library, 1954), p. 118, provides a convenient summary: "The souls of the Suicides are encased in thorny trees whose leaves are eaten by the odious Harpies, the overseers of these damned. When the Harpies feed upon them, damaging their leaves and limbs, the wound bleeds."

35. Zenobia's grotesque death does seem to parody such romantic sentiments concerning the poetic transformation of death as Wordsworth expresses in *The Prelude*, ed. Ernest de Selincourt, new ed., Stephen Gill (London: Oxford University Press, 1970), book 5, ll. 466–81.

36. Hawthorne, "The Hall of Fantasy," *Mosses from an Old Manse*, p. 201. Properly understood, the Hall is the space of imaginative freedom: "Hither may come the prisoner, escaping from his dark and narrow cell and cankerous chain, to breathe free air in this enchanted atmosphere" (203).

37. See Jean Starobinski, "Truth in Masquerade," in *Stendhal: A Collection of Critical Essays*, ed. Victor Brombert (Englewood Cliffs, N.J.: Prentice-Hall, 1962), p. 119.

38. Philip Rahv, "Dark Lady of Salem," pp. 46–47, compares James's narrator with Coverdale, but primarily to suggest how both characters epitomize the man of imagination reduced to a neurotic voyeur.

39. D. H. Lawrence, *Studies in Classic American Literature* (New York: Viking Press, 1923), p. 57.

40. Jean-Paul Sartre, *What Is Literature?*, trans. Bernard Frechtman (New York: Harper and Row Publishers, 1965), p. 45.

41. Ibid., pp. 54–55.

42. Dryden, *Nathaniel Hawthorne*, p. 107.

43. Wallace Stevens, "The Comedian as the Letter C," in *The Palm at the End of the Mind: Selected Poems and a Play*, ed. Holly Stevens (New York: Random House, 1971), p. 75.

Chapter 4

1. Edward Davidson, *Poe: A Critical Study* (Cambridge, Mass.: Harvard University Press, 1957), pp. 160–61.

2. Joseph Ridgely, "Tragical-Mythical-Satirical-Hoaxical: Problems of Genre in *Pym*," *American Transcendental Quarterly* 24 (Fall 1974): 4–9.

3. Jean Ricardou, "The Singular Character of Water," trans. Frank Towne, *Poe Studies* 9 (June 1974): 4.

4. Maurice Mourier, "Le tombeau d'Edgar Poe," *Ésprit* 12 (1974): 924.

5. Jacques Lacan, "Seminar on 'The Purloined Letter,'" trans. Jeffrey Mehlman, *Yale French Studies* 48 (1972): 39–72; Jacques Derrida, "The Purveyor of Truth," trans. Willis Domingo et al., *Yale French Studies* 52 (1975): 31–113.

6. Derrida, "The Purveyor of Truth," pp. 45, 84.

7. Joseph N. Riddel, "The 'Crypt' of Edgar Poe," *Boundary 2* 7 (Spring 1979): 123.

8. Joseph N. Riddel, *The Inverted Bell: Modernism and the Counterpoetics of William Carlos Williams* (Baton Rouge: Louisiana State University Press, 1974), pp. 264–65.

9. Daniel Hoffman, *Poe Poe Poe Poe Poe Poe Poe* (Garden City, N.Y.: Doubleday and Co., 1972), p. 275.

10. Edgar Allan Poe, *The Narrative of Arthur Gordon Pym of Nantucket*, in *The Complete Poems and Stories of Edgar Allan Poe*, ed. Arthur Hobson Quinn and Edward H. O'Neill, 2 vols. (New York: Alfred A. Knopf, 1964), 2: 843.

11. Evelyn Hinz also considers *Pym* to be centrally concerned with the problem of narration rather than with Pym's questionable "adventures": "The subject of the work, as the curious phraseology [of the title] suggests, is not the adventures of Pym but his presentation of his adventures; not Pym as voyager but Pym as narrative." See "'Tekeli-li': *The Narrative of Arthur Gordon Pym* as Satire," *Genre* 3 (1970): 382.

12. Edgar Allan Poe, *Eureka: A Prose Poem*, ed. Richard P. Benton (1848; reprint ed., Hartford, Conn.: Transcendental Books, 1973), p. 139 [p. 75].

13. Davidson, *Poe: A Critical Study*, pp. 9–10.

14. Poe, *Eureka*, p. 139 [p. 75].

15. Ibid., p. 54 [p. 33].

16. Poe, "The Poetic Principle," *Complete Poems and Stories*, 2: 1039, 1037.

17. Jacques Derrida, "Freud and the Scene of Writing," trans. Jeffrey Mehlman, *Yale French Studies* 48 (1972): 75.

18. See Joseph N. Riddel, "From Heidegger to Derrida to Chance: Doubling and (Poetic) Language," *Boundary 2* 7 (Winter 1976): 589: "*Écriture* is not the name for the physical mark of writing, but the doubleness of which the physical mark is always a sign — a sign that has no signified except another sign."

19. Derrida, "The Purveyor of Truth," p. 101.

20. See John Irwin, *American Hieroglyphics: The Symbol of the Egyptian Hieroglyphics in the American Renaissance* (New Haven: Yale University Press, 1980), pp. 74–75.

21. Riddel, "The 'Crypt' of Edgar Poe," p. 128.

22. Ibid., p. 122: "The power of words is no more than a power to move other words. Words are already secondary, and they repeat only an original abysm that marks their distance from any 'first law.'"

23. Ibid., p. 121.

24. See Derrida, "Freud and the Scene of Writing," p. 110: "Writing supplements perception before the latter even appears to itself. 'Memory' or writing is the opening of that process of appearance to itself. The 'perceived' may be read only in the past, beneath perception and after it."

25. Hoffman, *Poe, Poe . . .*, p. 271.

26. Davidson, *Poe: A Critical Study*, p. 170.

27. The word echoes Daniel's interpretation of the writing on the wall warning Belshazzar and his kingdom of God's judgment: "Mene, Mene, Tekel, Upharsin" (*Daniel* 5:25). See Hinz, "'Tekeli-li,'" p. 381. In *American Hieroglyphics,* Irwin follows Poe's advice and tracks down the philological sources for both Tsalal and Tekeli-li in two Ethiopian roots, offering his own version of Freud's "The Antithetical Sense of Primal Words": "If the ultimate root of Tsalal is *ṣl* (shadow) and that of its polar opposite Tekeli-li is *tkl* (original, fixed spot), then together the origins of the two words are a hieroglyph of the final scene in *Pym* — the shadow at the pole — a pictograph of that shadowing or doubling that is the origin of the bipolar oppositions of the linguistic world" (pp. 232–33).

28. See Jonathan Culler's discussion of the icon in *Structuralist Poetics: Structuralism, Linguistics, and the Study of Literature* (Ithaca, N.Y.: Cornell University Press, 1975), p. 16.

29. Marie Bonaparte, *The Life and Works of Edgar Allan Poe: A Psycho-Analytic Interpretation*, trans. John Rodker (London: Hogarth Press, 1949), p. 332. Walter Bezanson, "The Troubled Sleep of Arthur Gordon Pym," in *Essays in Literary History Presented to J. Milton French,* ed. Rudolf Kirk and C. F. Main (New York: Russell and Russell, 1965), p. 169.

30. Ricardou, "The Singular Character of Water," p. 4.

31. Mourier, "Le Tombeau d'Edgar Poe," p. 905.

32. Irwin, in *American Hieroglyphics,* p. 235, reads the doubleness of the inscriptions on Tsalal and the white curtain at the Pole as the indeterminacy of Poe's textuality and as a specific alternative to the formalist and metaphysical longing for a unity that is never anything other than death.

33. Georges Poulet, *Studies in Human Time,* trans. Elliott Coleman (Baltimore: Johns Hopkins Press, 1956), p. 330. The influence of the *Symbolistes*'s poetics on Poulet's phenomenology is quite explicit in this passage.

34. *Eureka,* pp. 36–37 [p. 24].

35. Harry Levin, *The Power of Blackness: Hawthorne, Poe, Melville* (New York: Random House, 1958), p. 129.

36. Bonaparte, *Life and Works of Poe,* pp. 350–51.

37. *Eureka,* p. 44 [p. 28].

38. Irwin, *American Hieroglyphics,* pp. 232–35.

39. Derrida, "Freud and the Scene of Writing," pp. 93, 90.

40. Ibid., p. 109.

41. Hoffman, *Poe, Poe . . .,* p. 294.

42. Derrida, "Freud and the Scene of Writing," p. 93.

43. See Jacques Derrida, *Of Grammatology,* trans. Gayatri Spivak (Baltimore: Johns Hopkins University Press, 1976), p. 59, where Derrida clarifies his own conception of literary modernity as part of a commentary on Hjelmslev's glossematics: "That which, within the history of literature and in the structure of a literary text in general, escapes that framework, merits a type of description whose norms and conditions of possibility glossematics has perhaps better isolated. It has perhaps thus better prepared itself to study the purely graphic substratum within the structure of the literary text within the history of the becoming-literary of literality, notably in its 'modernity.'"

Chapter 5

1. Jacques Lacan, *The Language of the Self: The Function of Language in Psychoanalysis,* translated with notes and commentary by Anthony Wilden (Baltimore: Johns Hopkins Press, 1968), pp. 93-94.

2. David Minter, *The Interpreted Design as a Structural Principle in American Prose* (New Haven: Yale University Press, 1969), pp. 143-44.

3. Warwick Wadlington, *The Confidence Game in American Literature* (Princeton: Princeton University Press, 1975), p. 74.

4. Ishmael's effacement as a narrator at various points in *Moby-Dick* and his replacement in parts by dramatic monologue might be considered indications of Melville's loss of confidence in the possibility of such an exemplary narrative voice. Melville's tendency to question the ideas of "author" and "literary originality" is, of course, already functional in *Moby-Dick.*

5. Wadlington, *Confidence Game,* p. 99.

6. Ibid., p. 101.

7. I am thinking primarily of Norman Holland's "humanistic" model of reader dynamics in *The Dynamics of Literary Response* (New York: W. W. Norton and Co., 1975). Holland argues for a process of reading in which the gratification of our "puzzle-solving" instincts is a substitute for the more threatening and insoluble existential dilemmas we confront in daily life. Wolfgang Iser's conception of the reader's self-actualization in the process of giving the literary text a determinate form and meaning also suggests a fundamentally humanistic model. In *The Act of Reading: A Theory of Aesthetic Response* (Baltimore: Johns Hopkins University Press, 1978), however, Iser does argue that this process of self-recognition through reading is a function of the text's distortion and disruption of our complacent conceptions of ourselves and our social environment. Nevertheless, Iser's general model for communication compels him to maintain that the reader's response is ultimately a remedy for the experience of alienation.

8. Herman Melville, *The Confidence-Man: His Masquerade,* ed. Hershel Parker (New York: W. W. Norton and Co., 1971), p. 190. Hereafter cited in the text as *CM.*

9. John Irwin, *American Hieroglyphics: The Symbol of the Egyptian Hieroglyphics in the American Renaissance* (New Haven: Yale University Press, 1980), p. 321.

10. Friedrich Nietzsche, *The Birth of Tragedy,* in *"The Birth of Tragedy" and "The Genealogy of Morals,"* trans. Francis Golffing (Garden City, N.Y.: Doubleday and Co., 1956), p. 61.

11. Sigmund Freud, "Negation," *A General Selection from the Works of Sigmund Freud,* ed. John Rickman (Garden City, N.Y.: Anchor Books, Doubleday and Co., 1957), p. 55.

12. Herman Melville, "Bartleby," *The Piazza Tales,* ed. Egbert S. Oliver (New York: Hendricks House, Farrar Straus, 1948), p. 49. Hereafter cited in the text as *B.*

13. Wadlington, *Confidence Game,* pp. 102-3, 114. Wadlington plays on the etymology of "inert" — *"in ars,"* "without art" — to describe Bartleby as the "inert man [who] refuses to consent to the repetitive motion" of copying (114).

14. See, for example, Maurice Freedman, "Bartleby and the Modern Exile," in *Bartleby the Scrivener, Melville Annual 1965: A Symposium,* ed. Howard P. Vincent, Kent State Studies in English (Kent, Ohio: Kent State University Press, 1966), p. 75.

15. H. Bruce Franklin, *The Wake of the Gods: Melville's Mythology* (Palo Alto, Calif.: Stanford University Press, 1963), p. 136.

16. Leo Marx, "Melville's Parable of the Walls," *Sewanee Review* 61 (Autumn 1953): 603.

17. Ted Billy, "Eros and Thanatos in 'Bartleby,'" *Arizona Quarterly* 31 (Spring 1975): 23.

18. Marvin Fisher, "'Bartleby,' Melville's Circumscribed Scrivener," *Southern Review* 10 (January 1974): 79.

19. Scott Donaldson, "The Dark Truth of *The Piazza Tales*," *PMLA* 85 (1970): 1086n.

20. Mario D'Avanzo, "Melville's 'Bartleby' and Carlyle," in *Bartleby: A Symposium,* p. 138.

21. Herman Melville, *Pierre or The Ambiguities* (1971), in *The Writings of Herman Melville,* ed. Harrison Hayford, Hershel Parker, and G. Thomas Tanselle, 15 vols. (Evanston, Ill.: Northwestern University Press and the Newberry Library, 1968-), 7: 356. Hereafter cited in the text as *P.*

22. Plato, *Phaedrus,* trans. R. Hackford (Indianapolis: Bobbs-Merrill Co., 1952), p. 161 (277 D-E).

23. Ibid., p. 157 (275 A).

24. Jacques Derrida, "La Pharmacie de Platon," *La dissémination* (Paris: Éditions du Seuil, 1972), p. 155. The translation is my own.

25. The building in which the lawyer's offices are located closely resembles the "old Church of the Apostles" in *Pierre,* which has been renovated and "divided into stores; cut into offices; and given for a roost to gregarious lawyers." The upper offices are difficult to rent, so they are gradually filled with poor "artists of various sorts" (*P,* 266-67). Melville seems attracted to the idea of the law as a modernized and degraded metaphysics; see also "The Paradise of Bachelors."

26. G.W.F. Hegel, *The Phenomenology of Mind,* trans. J. B. Baillie (New York: Harper and Row Publishers, 1967), p. 706.

27. Irwin, *American Hieroglyphics,* p. 288, notes: "In *Pierre,* Melville represents this double ambiguity of physical nature and the self as that of reciprocal texts."

28. Derrida, "Freud and the Scene of Writing," trans. Jeffrey Mehlman, *Yale French Studies* 48 (1972): 113.

29. The second offer virtually paraphrases the first: "If, hereafter, in your new place of abode, I can be of any service to you, do not fail to advise me by letter" (*B,* 30).

30. Jacques Derrida, "The Purveyor of Truth," trans. Willis Domingo et al., *Yale French Studies* 52 (1975): 107.

31. Rodolphe Gasché, "The Scene of Writing: A Deferred Outset," *Glyph 1: Johns Hopkins Textual Studies* (Baltimore: Johns Hopkins University Press, 1977), pp. 155-56.

32. "Nippers" is a slang term for handcuffs or leg irons; but in view of the myriad significances that have been read out of this name, it would be folly to claim priority for this interpretation.

33. Sigmund Freud, "The 'Uncanny,'" in *On Creativity and the Unconscious: Papers on the Psychology of Art, Literature, Love, Religion,* ed. Benjamin Nelson, trans. under the supervision of Joan Riviere (New York: Harper and Row Publishers, 1958), p. 129.

34. Ibid., p. 141.

35. Freud, "The Antithetical Sense of Primal Words," in *On Creativity and the Unconscious,* pp. 55, 56.

36. Ibid., p. 60.

37. Freud, "The 'Uncanny,'" p. 148.

38. See John Irwin, *Doubling and Incest/Repetition and Revenge: A Speculative Reading of Faulkner* (Baltimore: Johns Hopkins University Press, 1975), p. 9, for a discussion of Freudian *Nachträglichkeit* in terms analogous to Derrida's trace-structure of the sign.

39. Emile Benveniste, "Remarks on the Function of Language in Freudian Theory," *Problems in General Linguistics,* trans. Mary Elizabeth Meek, Miami Linguistics Series No. 8 (Coral Cables, Fla.: University of Miami Press, 1971), 72.

40. Ibid., p. 67.

41. Ibid., p. 75.

42. Ibid., p. 72.

43. Ibid.

44. Fred See, "The Kinship of Metaphor: Incest and Language in Melville's *Pierre,*" *Structuralist Review* 1 (Winter 1979): 78.

45. Freud, "The 'Uncanny,'" p. 145.

46. Bartleby has traditionally been viewed as a double for the narrator, but most of the interpretations have been far too neat or literal. Mordecai Marcus, "Melville's Bartleby as a Psychological Double," *College English* 23 (February 1962): 366, offers a representative example: "The fact that Bartleby has no history . . . suggests that he emerges from the lawyer's mind."

47. One of the common complaints about the tale is that the narrator's appended note is an artistic flaw. Charles Hoffman, "The Shorter Fiction of Herman Melville," *South Atlantic Quarterly* 52 (July 1953): 421, complains: "It is a flaw because it takes the reader outside the confines of the story itself; it attempts to add biographical information about Bartleby after enough has been said." Hoffman's desire to edit the tale betrays a contextualist insistence upon literary order and coherence that may be related to the narrator's own conception of representation.

48. Dorothee Finkelstein, *Melville's Orienda* (New Haven: Yale University Press, 1961), p. 121; Irwin, *American Hieroglyphics,* esp. p. 325.

49. Herman Melville, *Journal of a Visit to Europe and the Levant, October 11, 1856–May 6, 1857,* ed. Howard C. Horsford (Princeton: Princeton University Press, 1955), p. 58.

50. Ibid., pp. 123–124; "The Great Pyramid," *Collected Poems of Herman Melville,* ed. Howard P. Vincent (Chicago: Packard and Co., Hendricks House, 1947), p. 255.

51. See G.W.F. Hegel, *Aesthetics: Lectures on Fine Art,* trans. T. M. Knox, 2 vols. (London: Oxford University Press, 1975), 1: 356.

52. Hegel, *Phenomenology,* p. 706.

53. Derrida, "La Pharmacie de Platon," p. 100.

54. E. A. Wallis Budge, *The Gods of the Egyptians, or Studies in Egyptian Mythology,* 2 vols. (1904; Reprint ed., New York: Dover Publications, 1969), 1: 408.

55. Ibid., p. 400.

56. Ibid., pp. 408, 415.

57. Derrida, "La Pharmacie de Platon," p. 106.

58. Ibid., p. 105.

59. See See, "Kinship of Metaphor," pp. 71–72, for a discussion of Pierre and Phaeton.

60. Herman Melville, *Redburn: His First Voyage* (1969), in *The Writings of Herman Melville,* ed. Harrison Hayford, Hershel Parker, and G. Thomas Tanselle, 15 vols. (Evanston, Ill.: Northwestern University Press and the Newberry Library, 1968-), 4: 162.

61. Ibid.

62. Jacques Derrida, "Fors," trans. Barbara Johnson, *Georgia Review* 41 (Spring 1977): 80.

63. Cicero, *The Offices,* in *Cicero's "Offices," Essays on Friendship and Old Age, and Select Letters,* trans. Thomas Cockman (London: M. M. Dent and Co., 1909), bk. 1, ch. 4, p. 10.

According to Merton Sealts, Jr., *Melville's Reading: A Check-List of Books Owned and Borrowed* (Madison: University of Wisconsin Press, 1966), p. 51, Melville owned the Cockman translation of *Cicero's Offices*.

64. Derrida, "La Pharmacie de Platon," pp. 105–6.

65. Gasché, "Scene of Writing," p. 155.

Chapter 6

1. *Mark Twain's Notebook,* ed. Albert Bigelow Paine (New York: Harper and Bros., 1935), p. 394. Hereafter cited in the text as *MTN.*

2. Henry Nash Smith, *Mark Twain: The Development of a Writer* (New York: Atheneum Publishers, 1967), pp. 113–37, develops the thesis that the conflict between a "sound heart" and "deformed conscience" governs Huck's education and thus the form of the river journey.

3. Albert Stone, Jr., *The Innocent Eye: Childhood in Mark Twain's Imagination* (New Haven: Yale University Press, 1961), p. 158.

4. See Roger Salomon, *Twain and the Image of History* (New Haven: Yale University Press, 1961), p. 210.

5. See Tony Tanner, "The Lost America: Despair of Henry Adams and Mark Twain," *Modern Age* 5 (1961): 299–310.

6. Bernard DeVoto, *The Portable Mark Twain* (New York: Viking Press, 1946), p. 20.

7. In the former case, see Robert Wiggins, *Mark Twain: Jackleg Novelist* (Seattle: University of Washington Press, 1964), p. 20: "His style of realism was a projection of an early shrewd, natively intelligent, primitive mind incapable of dealing significantly with a sophisticated problem. . . ."

8. Louis Budd, *Mark Twain: Social Philosopher* (Bloomington: Indiana University Press, 1962), p. 212.

9. William Spengemann, *Mark Twain and the Backwoods Angel: The Matter of Innocence in the Works of Samuel L. Clemens* (Kent, Ohio: Kent State University Press, 1966), p. 86.

10. Mark Twain, *Adventures of Huckleberry Finn,* ed. Sculley Bradley, Richmond Beatty, and E. Hudson Long (New York: W. W. Norton and Co., 1962), p. 42. Hereafter cited in the text as *HF.*

11. William Gibson, *The Art of Mark Twain* (New York: Oxford University Press, 1976), p. 159.

12. Richard Bridgman, *The Colloquial Style in America* (New York: Oxford University Press, 1966), p. 107.

13. Mark Twain, Notebook #32, 9 May 1892–24 January 1893, Humanities Research Center, The University of Texas at Austin. Copyright 1982 by The Mark Twain Foundation. This material, together with that in notes 23, 27, 30,and 40, is published with the permission of the University of California Press and the General Editor of the Mark Twain Project.

14. Friedrich Nietzsche, *"Twilight of the Idols" and "The Anti-Christ,"* trans. R. J. Hollingdale (Baltimore: Penguin Books, 1968), p. 38.

15. David Allison, Introduction to *The New Nietzsche,* ed. David Allison (New York: Dell Publishing Co., Delta Books, 1977), p. xiv. Nietzsche's insistence on the metaphorical character of all language and thought pervades his works, but it is most explicit in "Ueber Wahrheit und Lüge im Aussermoralischen Sinne," *Nachgelassene Schriften,* vol. 3, ii, *Nietzsche Werke,* ed. Giorgio Colli and Mazzino Montinari (Berlin: Walter de Gruyter, 1973), pp. 367–84.

16. Alexander Jones, "Mark Twain and the Determinism of *What Is Man?*" *American Literature* 29 (March 1957): 14, 16.

17. Friedrich Nietzsche, *The Will to Power,* trans. Walter Kaufmann and R. J. Hollingdale, ed. Walter Kaufmann (New York: Random House, 1967), pp. 268–69.

18. Mark Twain, *A Connecticut Yankee in King Arthur's Court* (New York: New American Library, 1963), p. 114. Hereafter cited in the text as *CY*.

19. The most infamous formalist misreading of *Pudd'nhead Wilson* is F. R. Leavis's glorification of Dawson's Landing as "a society that has kept its full heritage of civilization" and the aristocratic pretensions of the F.F.V. (Introduction to *Pudd'nhead Wilson* [New York: Grove Press, 1955], pp. 17-20.) Maxwell Geismar, *Mark Twain: An American Prophet* (Boston: Houghton Mifflin Co., 1970), pp. 135-36, traces Leavis's misreading of Twain to his formalist assumptions about artistic order.

20. Mark Twain, *Pudd'nhead Wilson and Those Extraordinary Twins*, vol. 5, *The Writings of Mark Twain*, Author's National Edition, 35 vols. (New York: P. F. Collier and Co., 1922), pp. 207-8. Hereafter cited in the text as *PW* or *ET*, respectively.

21. See Anne Wigger, "The Composition of Mark Twain's *Pudd'nhead Wilson and Those Extraordinary Twins:* Chronology and Development," *Modern Philology* 55 (November 1957): 93-102; Robert Wiggins, "*Pudd'nhead Wilson:* 'A Literary Caesarian Operation,'" *College English* 25 (December 1963): 182-86.

22. James Cox, *Mark Twain: The Fate of Humor* (Princeton: Princeton University Press, 1966), p. 246.

23. MS, The Mark Twain Papers, The Bancroft Library. Copyright 1982 by The Mark Twain Foundation.

24. Cox, *Twain: Fate of Humor*, p. 234.

25. The organic argument is made by Marvin Fisher and Michael Elliott in "*Pudd'nhead Wilson:* Half a Dog Is Worse than None," *Southern Review* 8 (Summer 1972): 533-47.

26. Stone, *Innocent Eye*, p. 193.

27. Notebook #32, Humanities Research Center, The University of Texas at Austin. Copyright 1982 by The Mark Twain Foundation.

28. Friedrich Nietzsche, *The Genealogy of Morals*, in *"The Birth of Tragedy" and "The Genealogy of Morals,"* trans. Francis Golffing (Garden City, N.Y.: Doubleday and Co., 1956), pp. 196-97: "An equivalence is provided by the creditor's receiving, in place of material compensation such as money, land, or other possessions, a kind of *pleasure*. . . . In 'punishing' the debtor, the creditor shares a seignorial right. For once he is given a chance to bask in the glorious feeling of treating another human being as lower than himself—or, in case the actual punitive power has passed on to a legal 'authority,' of seeing him despised and mistreated."

29. Robert Regan, *Unpromising Heroes: Mark Twain and His Characters* (Berkeley and Los Angeles: University of California Press, 1966), p. 210.

30. Notebook #32, Humanities Research Center, The University of Texas at Austin. Copyright 1982 by The Mark Twain Foundation.

31. *Webster's New World Dictionary of the American Language*, College Edition, s.v. "philopena."

32. See Jeffrey Mehlman's description of Freud's "fraying" in the translator's Introductory Note to Derrida, "Freud and the Scene of Writing," *Yale French Studies* 48 (1972): 73-74.

33. See Cox, *Twain: Fate of Humor*, p. 230.

34. John Irwin, *American Hieroglyphics: The Symbol of Egyptian Hieroglyphics in the American Renaissance* (New Haven: Yale University Press, 1980), p. 320.

35. Max Scheler, *Ressentiment*, trans. Lewis Coser (New York: Free Press, 1972), pp. 72-73, insists upon an "external *hierarchy of values* which are *fully as objective and clearly 'evident'* as mathematical truths" to the "noble" mind.

36. Alphonso Lingis, "The Will to Power," in Allison, *The New Nietzsche*, p. 52.

37. Nietzsche, *The Genealogy of Morals*, pp. 170-71.

38. Ibid., p. 173.

39. Martin Heidegger, "Who Is Nietzsche's Zarathustra?" selected from Heidegger, *Nietzsche* (2 vols.), in Allison, *The New Nietzsche*, p. 73.

40. MS, The Mark Twain Papers, The Bancroft Library. Copyright 1982 by The Mark Twain Foundation.

41. Nietzsche, *Twilight of the Idols,* p. 73.

42. Clark Griffith, *"Pudd'nhead Wilson* as Dark Comedy," *ELH* 42 (Summer 1976): 210.

43. Nietzsche, *Twilight of the Idols,* p. 92.

44. See Paine, *MTN,* pp. 374, 380–81.

45. Nietzsche, *The Will to Power,* p. 270.

46. John Irwin, *Doubling and Incest/Repetition and Revenge: A Speculative Reading of Faulkner* (Baltimore: Johns Hopkins University Press, 1975), p. 13.

47. Friedrich Nietzsche, *Beyond Good and Evil,* trans. R. J. Hollingdale (Baltimore: Penguin Books, 1972), p. 45.

48. Michel Foucault, "Nietzsche, Genealogy, History," in *Language, Counter-Memory, Practice: Selected Essays and Interviews,* ed. with an intro. Donald F. Bouchard; trans. Donald F. Bouchard and Sherry Simon (Ithaca, N.Y.: Cornell University Press, 1976), pp. 152–53.

49. Jacques Derrida, *Eperons: Les Styles de Nietzsche,* trans. Barbara Harlow as *Spurs: Nietzsche's Styles* (Venice: Corbo e Fiori Editori, 1976), p. 79.

Chapter 7

1. Naomi Lebowitz, *The Imagination of Loving: Henry James's Legacy to the Novel* (Detroit: Wayne State University Press, 1965), p. 78.

2. Joseph Warren Beach, *The Method of Henry James* (1918; reprint ed., Philadelphia: Albert Saifer: Publisher, 1954), p. 250.

3. James speaks of the "tenuity of idea" of *The Sacred Fount* in a letter to William Dean Howells, 11 December 1902, in *Letters of Henry James,* ed. Percy Lubbock, 2 vols. (New York: Charles Scribner's Sons, 1920), 1: 408–9. James refers to the novel as "the merest of *jeux d'esprit"* in an unpublished letter to Mrs. Humphry Ward, as quoted in Leon Edel, An Introductory Essay, in Henry James, *The Sacred Fount* (New York: Grove Press, 1953), p. xxx.

4. Ora Segal, *The Lucid Reflector: The Observer in Henry James's Fiction* (New Haven: Yale University Press, 1969), p. 169.

5. Ezra Pound, "Henry James," in *Literary Essays of Ezra Pound,* ed. T. S. Eliot (London: Faber and Faber, 1954), p. 327.

6. Ezra Pound to Felix Schelling, 8 July 1922, in *The Selected Letters of Ezra Pound: 1907–1941,* ed. D. D. Paige (New York: New Directions, 1950), p. 180.

7. Henry James, *The Art of the Novel: Critical Prefaces,* ed. R. P. Blackmur (New York: Charles Scribner's Sons, 1934), p. 256.

8. Cleanth Brooks, "The Heresy of Paraphrase," *The Well Wrought Urn: Studies in the Structure of Poetry* (New York: Harcourt, Brace, and World, 1947), pp. 213–14.

9. Cleanth Brooks, "Irony as a Principle of Structure," in *Literary Opinion in America,* 3rd ed. rev., ed. Morton Dauwen Zabel, 2 vols. (New York: Harper and Row Publishers, 1962), 2: 732–33.

10. T. E. Hulme, "Notes on Language and Style," *Further Speculations,* ed. Samuel Hynes (Minneapolis: University of Minnesota Press, 1955), p. 84.

11. Hulme, "Romanticism and Classicism," *Further Speculations,* p. 134.

12. Pound, *Literary Essays,* p. 4.

13. Roman Jakobson emphasizes the fundamental poeticality of language throughout his writings, as in this representative passage from "Linguistics and Poetics," in *The Structuralists: From Marx to Lévi-Strauss,* ed. Richard and Fernande DeGeorge (Garden City, N.Y.: Doubleday and Co., 1972), p. 117: "The poetic resources concealed in the morphological and syntactic structure of language, briefly the poetry of grammar, and its literary product, the grammar of poetry, have been seldom known to critics and most disregarded by linguists but skillfully mastered by creative writers."

14. Ferdinand de Saussure, *Course in General Linguistics,* ed. Charles Bally and Albert Sechehaye, in collab. with Albert Reidlinger, trans. Wade Baskin (New York: McGraw-Hill Book Co., 1966), p. 112.

15. Emile Benveniste, "Categories of Thought and Language," *Problems in General Linguistics,* trans. Mary Elizabeth Meek, Miami Linguistics Series No. 8 (Coral Gables, Fla.: University of Miami Press, 1971), p. 63.

16. Ibid.

17. Ibid., p. 64.

18. Ibid., p. 63.

19. Benveniste, "Language in Freudian Theory," *Problems in General Linguistics,* p. 73.

20. Fredric Jameson, *The Prison-House of Language: A Critical Account of Structuralism and Russian Formalism* (Princeton: Princeton University Press, 1972), p. 211.

21. See Jameson, *Prison-House of Language,* p. 214: "From the point of view of epistemological theory it has been suggested that it is rather to the dilemmas of Kantian critical philosophy that, consciously or unconsciously, Structuralism remains a prisoner."

22. Jacques Derrida, *Of Grammatology,* trans. Gayatri Spivak (Baltimore: Johns Hopkins University Press, 1976), p. 89.

23. See Samuel Weber, "Saussure and the Apparition of Language: The Critical Perspective," *MLN* 91 (October 1976): 928: "In using the category of difference to determine what is most proper to the innermost essence of language, Saussure has inadvertently but decisively called that 'essence' into question."

24. James, *The Art of the Novel,* p. 56.

25. Eugenio Donato, "The Two Languages of Criticism," in *The Structuralist Controversy: The Languages of Criticism and the Sciences of Man,* ed. Richard Macksey and Eugenio Donato (Baltimore: Johns Hopkins University Press, 1972), p. 96.

26. Ibid., pp. 95–96: "Literature can only be a denunciation of literature and is not therefore different in essence from criticism. Criticism, in as much as it is a denunciation of literature, is, itself, nothing but literature. Henceforth the distinction between two types of discourse is blurred, and instead what we have is language and the single problematic it imposes, namely that of interpretation."

27. Benveniste, "Subjectivity in Language," *Problems in General Linguistics,* p. 224.

28. See Wilson Follett's early attempt to argue the autobiographical thesis for the novel in "Henry James's Portrait of Henry James," *New York Times Book Review,* 23 August 1936, pp. 2, 16.

29. Henry James, *The Sacred Fount* (New York: Charles Scribner's Sons, 1901), p. 98. Hereafter cited in the text as *SF.*

30. The narrator employs a basically phenomenological method. In his early attempts to preserve his detachment, he approximates the method of Husserl's "transcendental reduction." The narrator's investigation, however, seems to be repeatedly frustrated by the inevitable distortions of his own acts of consciousness. The failure of the narrator to "confirm" his law indicates how impossible it is for any of James's characters to achieve that level of "pure subjectivity" that is necessary for a transcendental phenomenology.

31. Laurence Holland, *The Expense of Vision: Essays on the Craft of Henry James* (Princeton: Princeton University Press, 1964), p. 198.

32. Jacques Derrida, "Structure, Sign, and Play," in Macksey and Donato, eds., *The Structuralist Controversy,* p. 271.

33. James, *Art of the Novel,* p. 46.

34. Roland Barthes, "The Structuralist Activity," in *Critical Essays,* trans. Richard Howard (Evanston, Ill.: Northwestern University Press, 1972), pp. 214–15.

35. See Jameson's discussion of Greimas in the concluding paragraph of *The Prison-House of Language,* p. 216, in which Jameson imagines a transcoding beyond the formalist boundaries of structuralist analysis — a transcoding synonymous with the productive

signification of language: "Truth as transcoding, as translation from one code to another — I would myself have preferred to say (following an analogous expression of Greimas himself) that the truth-effect involves or results from just such a conceptual operation. This would be a perfectly exact formal definition of the process of arriving at truth, even though it would presuppose nothing about the content of that truth, nor would it necessarily imply that every such transcoding operation results in a truth-effect of equal strength or 'validity.' Yet such a formula would have the advantage — in Derrida's sense — of freeing structural analysis from the myth of structure itself, of some permanent and spatial-like organization of the object. It would place the 'object' between parentheses, and consider the analytic practice as 'nothing but' an operation in time."

Postscript

1. Nathaniel Hawthorne, *The Scarlet Letter,* ed. Sculley Bradley, Richmond Croom Beatty, and E. Hudson Long, Norton Critical Edition (New York: W. W. Norton and Co., 1962), p. 25.

2. Herman Melville, *Moby-Dick,* ed. Luther S. Mansfield and Howard P. Vincent (New York: Hendricks House, 1962), p. 465.

3. Ibid., pp. 469, 477.

4. Hawthorne, *The Scarlet Letter,* p. 28.

Index

Abel, Karl, 129–31
Adams, Henry, 141
Allison, David, 144
Augustine, Saint, 62

Bain, Alexander, 129
Barthes, Roland, 12–13, 17, 26, 189
Baudelaire, Charles, 5
Beach, Joseph Warren, 169–70
Benjamin, Walter, 17
Benveniste, Emile, 130–31, 173–75, 178
Bergson, Henri, 69, 172
Beylr, Henri. *See* Stendhal
Bezanson, Walter, 104
Billy, Ted, 120
Bloom, Harold, 9, 17–19, 27, 193; *Kabbalah and Criticism,* 9, 26; *A Map of Misreading,* 21–23; *Poetry and Repression,* 20–22
Bode, Carl, 201
Bonaparte, Marie, 104, 107
Borges, Jorge Luis, 168, 193
Brentano, Franz, 68
Breton, André, 131
Bridgman, Richard, 143
Broch, Hermann, 204
Brodhead, Richard, 53–54, 62
Brooks, Cleanth, 170–72
Budd, Louis, 141
Budge, E. A. Wallis, 134
Burke, Kenneth, 13

Cairns, Dorion, 204
Carroll, David, 15

Cavell, Stanley, 30–31
Chase, Richard, 20–21
Chaucer, Geoffrey, 47
Cicero, 136
Clemens, Olivia Langdon (Livy), 140
Clemens, Samuel Langhorne. *See* Twain, Mark
Clemens, Susy (Olivia Susan), 140
Coleridge, Samuel Taylor, 204
Cox, James, 148, 150, 154
Crews, Frederick, 202
Culler, Jonathan, 206

Dante, 204
Dauber, Kenneth, 53–54
D'Avanzo, Mario, 120
Davidson, Edward, 91, 97, 103
Deconstruction, 9, 16, 142. *See also* Derrida, Jacques
de Man, Paul, 17–22, 94
Derrida, Jacques, 5, 21–22, 26, 92, 142, 197, 209; "Cogito and the History of Madness," 15–18; critique of structuralism, 7, 11; "Différance," 8–9, 196; "Fors," 136; "Freud and the Scene of Writing," 9, 99, 108–9, 125, 206; "Limited Inc.," 9; *Of Grammatology,* 7, 175, 207; "La Pharmacie de Platon," 123–24, 134–36; "The Purveyor of Truth," 93, 99, 109, 126; *Spurs: Nietzsche's Styles,* 167; "Structure, Sign, and Play," 3, 188, 198
Descartes, René, 69

De Voto, Bernard, 141, 197
Diderot, Denis, 5
Donaldson, Scott, 120
Donato, Eugenio, 16, 177–78
Dostoevsky, Fyodor, 5, 197
Drake, William, 29
Dryden, Edgar, 52, 89

Edel, Leon, 212
Edwards, Jonathan, 21
Eliot, T. S., 94, 169
Elliott, Michael, 211. *See also* Fisher, Marvin
Ellison, Ralph, 5
Emerson, Ralph Waldo, 20–22, 24–25, 55, 174, 193; "Friendship," 48–50; influence of, on Nietzsche, 5; *Nature,* 30; objections of, to philanthropy, 83, 115, 117; "The Poet," 33–34
Evans, Robert, 33, 35
Existentialism, 5, 114, 132

Finklestein, Dorothee, 133
Fisher, Marvin, 120, 211
Flaccus, Aulus Persius, 47
Fogle, Richard Harter, 53, 61, 204
Follett, Wilson, 213
Ford, Ford Madox, 171
Foucault, Michel, 14–18, 167
Franklin, H. Bruce, 120
Freedman, Maurice, 208
Freud, Sigmund, 3, 5, 9, 12, 19, 22, 93, 108, 118, 131, 133–34, 153, 174, 197, 209; "The Anti-Thetical Sense of Primal Words," 129, 206; "Negation," 118; "The Uncanny," 129–30, 132

Gasché, Rodolphe, 126, 138
Geismar, Maxwell, 211
Geneva School, 10. *See also* Poulet, Georges
Gibson, William, 143
Goethe, Johann Wolfgang von, 47
Greimas, A. J., 213
Griffith, Clark, 160

Harding, Walter, 47–48
Hardy, Thomas, 78

Hawthorne, Nathaniel, 22, 24, 52–53, 119; *The Blithedale Romance,* 2, 24–25, 53–54, 57–90, 113, 119, 203, 204; *The House of the Seven Gables,* 25, 53–54, 56–58; "The Old Manse," 76–77, 79, 205; *The Scarlet Letter,* 24–25, 53–58, 67, 194–95
Hegel, Georg Wilhelm Friedrich, 2, 5, 55–56, 124, 133, 135, 146; *Aesthetics,* 134; *Phenomenology of Mind,* 124, 134
Heidegger, Martin, 2, 31, 40, 43, 45, 51, 134, 155, 176; *Introduction to Metaphysics,* 46; on Nietzsche, 155
Herbert, George, 41–42
Hinz, Evelyn, 205, 206
Hirsch, E. D., Jr., 10
Hoffman, Charles, 209
Hoffman, Daniel, 95, 103, 109
Hölderlin, Friedrich, 40, 51, 201
Holland, Joyce, 34
Holland, Laurence, 186
Holland, Norman, 207
Howe, Irving, 63
Hulme, T. E., 172
Husserl, Edmund, 2, 197, 204, 213; *Ideas,* 204; *Phenomenology of Internal Time-Consciousness,* 72; and Sartre, 68–71

Irwin, John, 108, 116, 133, 154, 166, 206, 209
Iser, Wolfgang, 10–11, 207

Jakobson, Roman, 10, 174, 212
James, Henry, 18, 22–23, 24, 141, 171, 178, 191–92; *The Ambassadors,* 179; *The American,* 179; *Daisy Miller,* 179; *The Golden Bowl,* 179; *Letters,* 212; *The Portrait of a Lady,* 176–77, 179; *Prefaces,* 22–23, 169–70, 176–77, 189; *The Sacred Fount,* 4, 25, 85, 168–69, 176, 179–89; *The Turn of the Screw,* 192; *The Wings of the Dove,* 61
Jameson, Fredric, 7, 175, 213
Jones, Alexander, 144
Joyce, James, 94, 169, 171–72

Kafka, Franz, 193
Kant, Immanuel, 31, 55, 174–75, 192, 203

Kaul, A. N., 20
Keats, John, 113
Kuhn, Thomas, 197

Lacan, Jacques, 93, 112, 126
Lawrence, D. H., 87
Leavis, F. R., 211
Lebowitz, Naomi, 169
Lentricchia, Frank, 200
Levin, Harry, 107
Lingis, Alphonso, 154

McIntosh, James, 33, 46, 201
Male, Roy, 53–54, 203
Mallarmé, Stéphane, 94, 113
Mann, Thomas, 169
Marcus, Mordecai, 209
Marginality, 6, 139
Marks, Alfred, 56
Marx, Leo, 20, 120
Mehlman, Jeffrey, 211
Melville, Herman, 5, 22, 24, 28, 133, 154;
   "Bartleby the Scrivener," 3, 5, 6, 25,
   113, 117–23, 126–38; *The Confidence-
   Man,* 24–25, 113–20; *Moby-Dick,*
   24–25, 61, 113–15, 126, 194, 207;
   Pierre, 113, 116, 117–20, 124–25,
   127, 131, 135, 138, 208; *Redburn,*
   135–36
Miller, J. Hillis, 78
Mills, Nicolaus, 199
Minter, David, 113
Modernism, 95, 169–73, 189; and post-
   modernism, 196
Morris, Wesley, 12
Mourier, Maurice, 92, 105
Mukařovský, Jan, 10. *See also* Prague School

New Criticism, 10, 170–71, 191
Nietzsche, Friedrich, 3, 5, 9, 15, 20, 197;
   Beyond Good and Evil, 26–27, 166; *The
   Birth of Tragedy,* 17, 18, 117; *The
   Genealogy of Morals,* 18, 152; *ressenti-
   ment,* 154, 164, 166; *Twilight of the
   Idols,* 143, 160–62; *The Use and Abuse
   of History,* 18; *The Will to Power,* 4,
   144, 165
Normand, Jean, 202

Olson, Charles, 5

Pearce, Roy Harvey, 20
Plato, 121, 123–24, 184
Poe, Edgar Allan, 119; *Eureka,* 25, 95–97,
   106–9; "Fall of the House of Usher,"
   95, 103; *Narrative of Arthur Gordon
   Pym,* 3, 25, 91–110, 112, 119; "The
   Poetic Principle," 97; "The Purloined
   Letter," 99
Poirier, Richard, 20
Poulet, Georges, 10, 106
Pound, Ezra, 60, 94, 169, 170–72; *Hugh
   Selwyn Mauberley,* 170–72; *Literary
   Essays,* 172
Prague School (linguists), 10
Proust, Marcel, 169, 172

Rahv, Philip, 60, 205
Raleigh, Sir Walter, 46–47
Rank, Otto, 129
Ranson, John Crowe, 171
Regan, Robert, 153
Ricardou, Jean, 92, 104
Riddel, Joseph, 19, 94–95, 99, 103, 201
Ridgely, Joseph, 92
Rogers, Henry Huttleston, and Mark
   Twain, 140
Russian Formalists, 10, 19

Said, Edward, 15, 17
Salomon, Roger, 210
Sartre, Jean-Paul, 2, 68; *Being and Nothing-
   ness,* 75, 79; on freedom, 79, 88–89;
   and Husserl, 68–71; *L'Imaginaire,*
   69–74, 77, 81, 88, 204; *L'Imagination,*
   69; *What Is Literature?,* 89
Saussure, Ferdinand de, *Course in General
   Linguistics,* 7–8, 172–73, 175, 213
Scheler, Max, 154
Schelling, Friedrich, 129
Sealts, Merton, Jr., 210
Searle, John, and Jacques Derrida, 9
See, Fred, 209
Segal, Ora, 169, 170
Seybold, Ethel, 201
Shklovsky, Viktor, 10, 198. *See also* Russian
   Formalists

Smith, Henry Nash, 210
Socrates, and *Phaedrus,* 121, 123, 135
Spengemann, William, 142
Spivak, Gayatri, 3
Starobinski, Jean, 205
Stein, William Bysshe, 39
Stendhal, *The Charterhouse of Parma,* 82
Stevens, Wallace, 18, 60, 90, 94, 169
Stoehr, Taylor, 203
Stone, Albert, 140, 151
Structuralism, 11, 173, 189
Symbolistes (French), 5, 94–95, 169–70

Tanner, Tony, 210
Thoreau, Henry David, 22, 24, 65, 115, 119, 201; "The Atlantides," 49; *Journals,* 35, 48; objections of, to philanthropy, 83; *Walden,* 25, 28–35, 38, 42, 49–51; *A Week on the Concord and Merrimack Rivers,* 2, 24, 31–51, 112–13, 201, 202
Thoreau, John (brother), 35, 47–48, 50, 201
Thoth, 123, 134–35. *See also* Melville, Herman, "Bartleby the Scrivener"
Transcoding, as structuralist idea, 12–13, 16, 189. *See also* Barthes, Roland; Jameson, Fredric; Structuralism
Trotsky, Leon, 198
Twain, Mark, 22, 24, 197; aphorisms, 142–45; *A Connecticut Yankee in King Arthur's Court,* 141–42, 145–47; *Following the Equator,* 142; *Huckleberry Finn,* 25, 140–43, 145, 151, 155–56, 160–65, 167; *Life on the Mississippi,*

144, 162; "The Man That Corrupted Hadleyburg," 146; *The Mysterious Stranger,* 146; *Notebook,* 139, 142, 148, 167, 211; *Personal Recollections of Joan of Arc,* 140; *The Prince and the Pauper,* 140; *Pudd'nhead Wilson,* 3, 25, 118, 140–42, 145–67; *Pudd'nhead Wilson and Those Extraordinary Twins* (as a single work), 148; *Those Extraordinary Twins,* 147–49, 152, 162, 165; *Tom Sawyer,* 161; *Tom Sawyer, Detective,* 140; *What Is Man?,* 140
Tynianov, Jurij, 10, 19. *See also* Russian Formalists

Wadlington, Warwick, 114–15, 119
Waggoner, Hyatt Howe, 53, 202, 203
Weber, Samuel, 213
Whitaker, Rosemary, 202
White, Hayden, 13–14, 17, 26
Whitman, Walt, 22, 24, 28
Wigger, Anne, 211
Wiggins, Robert, 210, 211
Williams, William Carlos, on Sir Walter Raleigh, 202. *See also* Raleigh, Sir Walter
Wittgenstein, Ludwig, 30–31. *See also* Cavell, Stanley
Wordsworth, William, 21, 55, 204; *The Prelude,* 79

Ziolkowski, Theodor, 204

The Johns Hopkins University Press

Through the Custom House

This book was composed in Baskerville text and
Souvenir display type by Capitol Communications from
a design by Cynthia Hotvedt. It was printed on
Glatfelter's 50-lb Offset paper and bound in Kivar-5 by
Thomson-Shore, Inc.